Contents

THE ART AND SCIENCE OF NURTURING DANCEMAKERS:
Papers from the Greenhouse Effect Conference

Edited by Jo Butterworth,

Assisted by Sita Popat

THE UNIVERSITY OF WINCHESTER

For my dear friend Pat Richards,

Who inspired the planning of this conference

1946-1998

ISBN 1 900857 25 1

First published in 1999 by the Centre for Dance and Theatre Studies at Bretton Hall

Designed, typeset and produced by SHOUT Communications 0113 203 0800

Preface & Acknowledgements

The Greenhouse Effect: the art and science of nurturing dancemakers has evolved from research instigated by the Centre for Dance and Theatre Studies at Bretton Hall. The result was a unique and stimulating programme divided into five projects. This publication records four days of an intensive and exciting international conference held in September 1998 encompassing lectures, performances, interviews and discussions organised by Bretton Hall and Yorkshire Dance.

The dearth of research into choreographic development has been recognised for some time. Academic inquiry into this complex discipline, however, has to be guided by practitioners in the field and by the evident diversity and range of praxis. The four days and nights in Yorkshire brought together a rare mix of people, attitudes, skills and alternate views to address concerns about the education, training and continuing support of creative dance artists, and the changing nature of existing formal and informal structures. Generously supported by the National Lottery through the Arts Council of England, and by ELIA Thematic Network, the programme gave opportunity to choreographers, dancers, promoters, educators and funders to debate and reflect from a number of perspectives.

I would like to thank the Conference Steering Group, which consisted of Simon Dove and subsequently Mairead Turner from Yorkshire Dance, Theresa Beattie, Director of The Place Dance Services, Dan Bates from West Yorkshire Playhouse, Sharon Donaldson, Alice Smith, Sue Doubell and Claire Nicholson. Elizabeth Anderson was a very able Conference Manager who brought to fruition all aspects of the complex planning and organisation. The support of my colleagues in the School of Dance and Theatre, and Dance Officers from the Arts Council has been much appreciated. In preparing and editing the transcripts for publication I am indebted to the enormous support of Sita Popat, who has undertaken Assistant Editor role with generosity and thoroughness. The three conference monitors, Fleur Darkin, Louise Katerega, and Claire Nicholson not only supported Gregory Nash in preparing notes for the plenary sessions, but have also contributed to the editing process. In addition, my thanks go to each and every presenter at the Conference, all of whom have either prepared papers or further edited transcripts. Little would have been achieved without the hard work and commitment of Anne Garbett, Val Oakes and a number of members of staff in the Business Centre at Bretton Hall who between them transcribed all the recordings. Tom Wildish deserves mention, not only for his magnificent organisation of 17 student assistants during the event, but also for his editing of the BPM session. The photographic material which documents aspects of the conference was produced by Dave Daggers.

Due to the length of the document we are not to be able to include the complete transcripts of all of the rich audience discussion sessions; the Points raised in Discussion sections hardly do justice to all of the valuable contributions by delegates. Equally, where recordings were void or unintelligible, sessions are published without reference to audience participation.

Jo Butterworth
Head of Centre

Welcome Address

The first session of the Greenhouse Effect conference welcomed the presenters and delegates, offered a context to the four day event, and outlined the aims and intentions of the conference steering group. Presenters were Jo Butterworth, Head of the Centre for Dance and Theatre Studies at Bretton Hall, and Conference Director; two other members of the Conference steering group, Mairead Turner, acting Director of Yorkshire Dance, Theresa Beattie Director of the Place Dance Services; and Hilary Carty, Dance Director of the Arts Council of England. The session was chaired by Sue Hoyle, General Manager of the Place.

Sue Hoyle welcomed everyone to the Greenhouse Effect. Having returned to England from some time working for the British Council in Paris, she felt able to comment upon the diversity and business of creativity of dance in Britain, including the need to reflect on what has been achieved and the ways in which we can work together to plan for the future. She introduced some of the key people who were involved in developing the concept of the Greenhouse Effect and in organising the event.

Jo Butterworth

Welcome to the West Yorkshire Playhouse and to the Greenhouse Effect from our partnership of Centre for Dance and Theatre Studies at Bretton Hall, with Yorkshire Dance. We are all here to concentrate our focus on the future of the art of dance making in all its aspects, and to recognise and appreciate the relationship between the different groups and facets that we all represent: education and training, funding, promotion and research.

The Greenhouse Effect programme in its entirety covers two years and involves five projects:

1. Making and Mentoring, the development of a project begun last year when my colleague Janet Smith taught a choreographic residency at Bretton Hall;

2. the Choreographic Audit, which plans to collect and collate information about various choreographic projects around the country through a series of questionnaires:

3. This International Conference.

4. Two publications which will disseminate our research. *The Dancemakers Portfolio*, which has been edited in partnership with the British Association of Choreographers, and the proceedings of this conference which will be published in the Spring of 1999.

5. Out Turn, the final project which should allow further development for two of the choreographers whose work you will see in process on Friday and Saturday evening.

The whole programme has received funding from the National Lottery A4E Main Scheme and from the Thematic Network project of the European League of Institutes of the Arts. It could not have been achieved without the effort and commitment of the Steering Group, and of many other groups and individuals who are all listed in your conference pack, to whom I owe heartfelt thanks. The Conference has been managed with capability and determination by Elizabeth Anderson, who has organised, cajoled and rallied us all. We have a formidable lineup of presenters for you, representing an immense amount of expertise. My thanks go to all of them and also to those who have willingly agreed to chair each session. I thank also our 17 student assistants from Bretton Hall, ably organised by Tom Wildish.

The meaning of the project title, Greenhouse Effect, is not simply an environmental or ecological reference but is used symbolically to signify the desire to feed, water and give light to our British choreographers. The aims of the Conference are

- to establish a picture of the range, diversity and scale of dancemaking nationally
- to examine and contextualise current practice, theory and infrastructures
- to create opportunities for presenting choreographic work in progress,
- to increase opportunities for interchange and critical debate between artists, producers, funders and the Academies, both the HE and vocational sector.

Mairead Turner

It seemed very appropriate that Bretton Hall and Yorkshire Dance formed this partnership, as we are two very different organisations who are united in our concern to develop strong and useful systems which nurture choreography, and I think that this may be a common concern for everybody here today. Our two organisations form a small part of the infrastructure which supports dance, and all of you form the other parts of that map, so I hope that together we can all share ideas and experiences about processes in the hope that we can all forward the debate and the practice.

Jo Butterworth

From an educational point of view we are interested in exploring the range, scale and diversity of courses in Higher Education and the vocational training sectors, the nature of current training in relation to future needs, and in particular what is taught under the aegis of choreography courses, and why. How should intending choreographers learn their craft? What are the best models for initial training and for the continuing education of the dance artist in the broadest sense?

Mairead Turner

Much of what a National Dance Agency does relates to nurturing choreography in the form of supporting established structures. Some of those known common structures are research and development, choreographic platforms, residences, commissions, extending training provision and so on. One thing I would like this Conference to do is to question and challenge these structures in a very honest way, identify how we can improve them, and possibly offer alternatives.

Jo Butterworth

Whilst recognising and celebrating the considerable achievements of the dance world over the last 20 to 30 years, we feel that it is time to take stock, to reflect on and evaluate the current status quo, and to agree collectively on a long term strategy which embraces all the current strengths, deals with the problems and ensures the future health of the art form.

Mairead Turner

So I hope that we can all use this time to stop, take a break from the mechanics of our everyday work, and try to discuss issues and look ahead to explore our visions for the future of dance.

Jo Butterworth

Let us all try to improve communications, to create strategies that are clear and transparent, and to share responsibilities.

Sue Hoyle

The next person I want to introduce is Theresa Beattie, Director of the Place Dance Services, who is going to tell us something of the context for developing this Conference.

Theresa Beattie

Hello. Jo approached John Ashford, the Director of the Place Theatre, and I almost three years ago now, whilst she was working at The Place doing research, to discuss the possibility of

gathering people together to explore issues around nurturing and developing choreographers. It was apparent from the beginning that to do justice to such a complex and multi-faceted subject, such a gathering would need to target a very broad group, a group of people who do not customarily meet together, choreographers, dancers, dance managers, funders, promoters, educators and students. From the outset the need for collaboration and close partnership was apparent in order for such a project to come to fruition.

Jo Butterworth

From the beginning we wanted to stress the UK- European link, and to develop our knowledge of practices in other European countries. For John, the methods and perspectives gleaned from meeting promoters and seeing work abroad were key; from my own experience with the ELIA Dance Section, the visits to a number of European vocational schools and university departments gave new insights; the networks instigated by such competitions and gatherings as Bagnolet... Then two years ago, discussions and seminars held at Yorkshire and Humberside Arts on the new lottery opportunities for Project rather than Capital funding became significant. There were growing opportunities presented by development in my own institution, Bretton Hall, together with the obligations and opportunities of the Research Assessment Exercise in the Higher Education sector, and all these factors contributed to our discussions. Eventually Yorkshire Dance and West Yorkshire Playhouse became key players in the plan.

Theresa Beattie

I want to finish on a very positive note about the work which has been undertaken so far on the Greenhouse Effect choreographic audit. It is not finished yet, but the data so far indicates really encouraging growth in a number of laboratory and research opportunities available to choreographers in England. These are provided by a wide range of organisations, including National Dance Agencies, festivals, venues, HE institutions, umbrella organisations and promoters, and supported by an equally wide range of funders. There is greater recognition of the necessity for investing time and money in a range of research opportunities for choreographers at all stages of experience, who are addressing a diverse range of choreographic concerns. Some choreographers who participated in research projects will be sharing work in progress tomorrow and Saturday. I hope you will support them by attending these events, and I think they are very brave to make this contribution. I hope that during the course of this Conference we can raise issues about nurturing choreographers very honestly, share our experience and ideas, and above all develop effective advocacy strategies for this important area.

Sue Hoyle

Next I want to introduce Hilary Carty, Director of Dance at the Arts Council, who will place the Conference in a national perspective.

Hilary Carty

On behalf of the Arts Council of England I would like to extend a very warm welcome to everyone here today at the *Greenhouse Effect, The Art and Science of Nurturing Dancemakers.* I say the full title because it really does give me quite a lot of pleasure to be participating in a debate of such a dynamic subject. I extend a particular welcome to the many visitors from outside of England, who have endorsed the importance of this conference with their presence.

I do remember quite a long time back speaking to the Principal of Bretton Hall, Professor Gordon Bell, and then Jo Butterworth and Simon Dove, and being really excited by the proposals that they were putting forward for choreographic development. This Conference was just one of the initiatives that they proposed to explore and expose the real artistic and cultural mechanisms that go into creating dance today. What excited me most was that the emphasis would continually be placed on getting practitioners to lead the debates and developments, something that we have not always been good at doing in this country. It is not unusual to find a group of keen and knowledgeable enthusiasts talking about aspects of dance development, whether that is the infrastructure, the funding or the creation of the form. But all too often, representation from the actual creators of the form (and that includes dancers as well as choreographers) is not the highest on the agenda. Indeed, there is a tacit acknowledgement that the past and some of the current training for dance actively encourages dancers to 'put up and shut up', - 'don't create waves, just let your body be the instrument'! Thankfully there are always artists who defy that tradition and air their views, and it is well nigh time that we look actively to encourage that airing of views, not just in an ad hoc manner, but as a really important aspect of dance training. For it will feed the issue of critical self -assessment and peer group assessment, as well as firmly placing the artist at the forefront of the dance debate rather than somewhere in the middle being talked about.

So I save my warmest welcome today for all the artists that are participating in this weekend because I think first and foremost, that this event should be a platform for you to think, speak, discuss, argue, listen and generally participate in this critical debate on the art and science of dance. I did ask Elizabeth Anderson to put me down as an artist but I see she resisted!

The Greenhouse Effect comes at a critical time in dance development. Contemporary dance, which started as a really powerful trickle from the States has now emerged, consolidated and matured. Events like the recent British Dance Edition:98 in Newcastle give testimony to the wealth of creative talent that we can now enjoy. But that is despite and not because of the arts environment in which we operate. In funding terms, it is no secret that the amount of funding spent on contemporary dance in particular, is too little for the task - the amounts, the systems and structures are trying desperately hard to meet tomorrow's needs on yesterday's finances and mechanisms. And the task can be demoralising for all.

The Arts Council Dance Department is in the middle of a process of review, looking at several aspects of its approaches to dance funding and support in order to try to create more dynamic and creative routes to nurturing and supporting the work of dance artists and supporters. But changing the systems will only partly deal with the problem, and hence we are also working to secure more hard cash for the art form as well, to really be able to encourage and respond to the current and future use of dance as we approach the Millennium.

I see this conference as making a very important contribution to that debate, and hence the Dance Department is keen not just to support the conference financially but to listen, participate and to take away the key messages from the various sessions throughout the four days, which will be fed into our own focus groups and debates happening this Autumn. Dance officers from the Regional Arts Board are also here to participate and listen as it is critically important that all individuals working in dance use this opportunity to share thoughts and solutions on ways forward.

Of course, there will be many and conflicting views as to what the best ways forward will be. There is a call for more funding direct to artists, but promoters and producers could also make important contributions if they had the funds and ability to make critical, artistic choices. We need, in fact, to ensure that the choice is neither one nor the other, but indeed both.

We need to look not just at the areas of dance training and the emerging artist, but importantly, at the artist who has already made significant contributions to the art form over a number of years and needs to be fed and stimulated as well as stimulating and encouraging others. So the issues of training, R & D and mentoring approaches need to address the mature artist as well as the emergent one. And that's no longer a small clique of named individuals but a significant band of important people in dance. It is important that we debate the provision of support for all artists as part of this conference, be they young or old, emergent or mature.

It is equally important that we use this opportunity to acknowledge and explore the full range of dance practice now evident. That is, dance influenced by a wide variety of cultures as well as a wide and growing range of arts media. A wide-angled lens is critically important as we tackle the art and science of dance making, as the art form is now at its most diverse — and that is to be celebrated.

I end by congratulating University College Bretton Hall and Yorkshire Dance Centre on organising this fantastic event and I very much look forward to the debates ahead.

Keynote Interview

*Robert Cohan in conversation
with Sue Hoyle*

Sue Hoyle:

In considering how to introduce Bob, I asked people beforehand if they had got any funny stories to tell about him as there are a lot of funny stories about Bob Cohan. I found out very quickly that Bob is probably everyone's favourite guru. The person who summed him up best is Robin Howard as written in the Preface to the programme when The Place opened:

"I challenge anyone to name one person in the world who is a better choreographer, performer, teacher, inspirer, explainer, leader, helper, bagcarrier, floor sweeper and friend - that's Bob."

Bob and I are going to have a conversation for about forty minutes, and then we will take questions from the floor. I thought I would begin by asking Bob how he learned to be a choreographer...

Robert Cohan:

The first time I heard the word 'choreographer' I was 8 years old in summer camp, and they were looking for a tap dance number to go in the closing revue. The music was already chosen so I didn't have any choice in that; it was 'Way Down Upon the Swannee River', and they asked me if I could choreograph a dance to the music. And I said 'I don't know what you mean', thinking I had to write something, and they said 'No, just make up a dance' and I said 'Sure, sure'. So I just did every step I knew, and, very smart at that age, I finished with the most complicated step I knew! It was a huge hit, and then people started yelling 'Encore', which I also didn't understand. Somebody started the music and I went out and did the whole thing again. This was my first choreographic experience...

Then, I was always a dancer. I had started dance when I was very young in a big old house in Brooklyn, and then went to the usual ballet, tap, and acrobatic school. When I reached the age when, I suppose, boys don't do it any more, that didn't stop me and I just kept going. In those early years, way back in the early thirties, we had these wonderful Hollywood musicals and we all went to the movies. My sister and I would run home and clear out the living room and just do every step we saw, from all the Fred Astaire dances and musicals. In a funny way, I think that this experience provided a kind of storehouse, a collection, the baggage, a closet of different dance experiences... I do think that a choreographer is only as good as his storehouse, and I certainly had that.

During the war I was stationed in California and fell in with a group of soldiers who were interested in the arts. We used to go to see American Ballet Theater, and there were special performances for the soldiers. This was the time that Anthony Tudor was creating all those great works, and I saw them with fantastic dancers - Hugh Laing, Maria Tallchief, Marjorie Tallchief, Andre Eglevsky, Igor Youskevich, Nora Kaye, - all the names that we now read about as history. They were all on the stage, sometimes in one night, so this was a fantastic experience.

Coming to England, I was stationed in Warminster. I used to go to London every weekend to see the Sadler's Wells Ballet. I saw Robert Helpmann's new choreography, de Valois' new choreography... all this building up, and wanting, at some point, to do it myself; it was all sort of churning around. When I got back to New York, just by accident I fell into the Graham Studio. I had never seen Martha Graham, though I had seen some modern dance with Jane Dudley. I went to the studio because the technique was so fantastic for me; it was physically exciting, it was new, and at that time it was the only technique like that. Another technique called Humphrey-Weidman had also come out of the Denishawn years (you have to have studied your history before this talk!) and the main techniques in New York at that time were just those two, Humphrey -Weidman and Graham, and Graham's was unique. It was very difficult; it was very hard and strong, and she was really forceful, and this suited me - it was what I wanted to do. It was just after the war, and Martha needed men! She passed me one day, hit me on the back after I had been in about five classes and said "Study hard boy, because I want you in the Company in the Fall"!

I still hadn't seen her work, and yet I was in the Company three months later. In 1946, one night in the small studio, I saw her dance for the first time; she did her solos from *Letter to the World*. It was just a series of solos, one after the other, but I was so excited by it that at that moment my life changed. I knew then that I was going to be a dancer as my profession through life, and that I was also going to be a choreographer. You see, it is not a new concept that art breeds art; I believe that you have to see art or you see something that is artistic, and suddenly a whole door opens in you and a flood of energy comes out, and that's what happened to me then. So I was set well on my way at that moment.

Sue Hoyle:

How did you become a choreographer though, did you study composition?

Bob Cohan:

OK, choreography was the next problem. One of the problems about working with Martha is that she was so good. Why choreograph when what she was choreographing was so challenging? It was so challenging to come up to the images that came from her, to perform her concepts, and it left very little time for that creative energy that you need within yourself to choreograph. But if you're a modern dancer (or now I should say if you're a contemporary dancer), all your friends choreograph and you think you should too. That's partly the way it starts; I mean, what defines one as a contemporary dancer is that you choreograph. So I start studying with Louis Horst who was also in the studio at that time.

Louis Horst was a remarkable man, a pianist and accompanist, but also a composer, incredibly smart and incredibly knowledgeable. He knew everything about the contemporary music scene at that time. He used to come to Europe often and come back to the States with knowledge of what was happening in Europe. He was Martha's teacher really; many times she would tell the story about Louis taking her to the zoo, making her stand in front of the lions' and tigers' cages and watch the way they walked, and then go back to the studio and try to move that way. He would sit there reading a newspaper and Martha used to be furious with him! But this was the way Louis worked; he was very much hands-on, and when I was there, he was, most of the time in the studio playing and accompanying when Martha choreographed. Everything she did had to pass his eye; I wasn't in on their personal conversation but I know from the way she fixed things afterwards that he was influential. Of course, that's what we mean when we talk about a mentor situation, and she had this incredible man Louis.

I read something recently that rather derided his method of teaching; he wrote two books, one called *Modern Forms* and the other *Pre-classic Forms*, and it's true that they sound old-fashioned now, like recipes, but that was just the means. Those were the projects that he gave to make you work. But the important thing was his criticism, whether you had used the material well. He could describe the movement you used accurately, and if he thought you were improvising he asked you to repeat it. He knew everything, so it was really important to reach his level when you did his work, because you are only in a real teaching situation you are really satisfying the teacher. Louis was a strong teacher, and he taught me the craft, the basics; we called it composition. Choreography was something else, a word in the dictionary!

Martha Graham was so good that she could be absolutely transparent when she was working. She trusted her own skills enough to actually create right in front of you and with you - most choreographers do, but Martha would go the whole way, and if you wanted to learn to choreograph then that was the best lesson in the world. You saw the process very clearly day by day by day. The way she used music for instance; all the music was written for her dances. Nowadays some music is written for the dance, but mostly we pick up a tape we like... Of course, Petipa had music written for him; Tchaikovsky wrote exactly the number of measures that Petipa required, so this was not unusual, but what Martha did was unusual. She gave the composer a script detailing the characters, the poetic images, the length of duets or solos, the transitions, the entrances - she worked out the whole thing in real time and gave it to the composer. She was commissioning very modern music, and when she received the music we had to work out how to use it. In those days before Martha Graham and Doris Humphrey, you danced on the music! In the first place, the music sometimes had no beat that you could find, but Martha was experimenting with things that are very common to us now: for example, how to dance off the beat on purpose, how to float through the music, (you know, X number of bars and X number time and you come together at the end), or how to use the melody as musical cues instead of meter. All of this she was discovering in front of us, with us, saying 'Is that better or is this better? Let me see, what do you think?' So this was a wonderful lesson in choreography.

In 1954, she and I taught together at the American Dance Festival summer course in Connecticut, and they had a programme where they wanted every teacher to do a short solo. In those days we all did solos; then there was no problem about getting dancers or studio space; you could wake up in the middle of the night and say 'Oh, now that's what I have to do next'. I think that's how everybody learned to choreograph, because we all did solo concerts! They were aerobically difficult, I can tell you, but we all were strong and we did them. They wanted a solo, so I asked Martha if she would choreograph it for me. She said 'Find some music, and then let's meet tomorrow'. The next day I was there with the music and she wasn't, and I called her up and she said 'Something came up. Just start, and I'll be over there soon'. She didn't come. And she didn't come the next day obviously, or the next, and pretty soon I was at the end of the piece, and then she looked at it. She made a few pertinent changes but basically, it was mostly there. That was my first solo. That was the start.

Sue Hoyle:

And was your work being shown in public at that stage? Did you have an audience?

Bob Cohan:

Oh yes. That was an evening up in Connecticut with a proper paying audience, and it went down very well. That started me off, then I didn't stop - I'm still going actually... I loved Hilary Carty's phrase "mature-choreographer nurturing". I think we need it desperately.

Sue Hoyle:

You must have come with the Company to London in the '50s and '60s?

Bob Cohan:

Yes, I was here with the Company in '54, my first time in London, and then '63, something like that...

Sue Hoyle:

When you came in the '60s, what impression did you have of the dance scene here?

Bob Cohan:

Well there wasn't much going on in contemporary dance. We were all overawed by the Royal Ballet when it came to the States; we had never seen such precise kind of controlled, withheld dancing, it was so understated. For Americans it was magic, amazing. I remember seeing *Cinderella* with Margot Fonteyn, it was simply stunning because in America - even the ballets were all brash! If you were a swan you were an American swan, so that was a huge change in the concept of ballet, and we didn't have very many full-length works at that time. You know, I didn't realise that *Swan Lake* had any other parts to it but the lake scene, that's the only thing we ever saw... and it was usually done as a triple bill with excerpts from *Les Sylphides*, *Swan Lake* and *Scheherazade*, as it toured round the country.

No, we didn't see any dance here in England. In fact, when the Graham Company went on the first tour to the Far East in 1956, the State Department insisted on us meeting local dancers, and we saw dance in every single country in the Far East. It took 6 months from Japan to Iran. We saw dance in every place except the British colony of Kuala Lumpur in which there was none, and we had a feeling that that's what was going on in London too. I think, at the time there was some "Modern Ballet", but we didn't see it. Mim (Marie) Rambert came backstage (when we were in

London) and she was very excited by what she had seen. That was when Robin Howard started to get involved in the Graham Organisation; Mim Rambert was pushing him on to do more...

Sue Hoyle:
So when you did come to Britain initially, it was to teach?

Bob Cohan:
Yes, yes. There are several versions of this beginning story, but it is Robin Howard that we have to thank for The Place and for the huge growth that has happened since he brought American modern dance to Britain. The point was not that he wanted to bring American contemporary dance here, but that this was the way he thought to stimulate dance excitement within Britain. He sponsored, or guaranteed the deficit, for the first performances of Paul Taylor, José Limon, Merce Cunningham and Twyla Tharp. Then he saw that there was a crowd of young people who wanted to study, so he brought teachers over from the US and they had a moving studio. Janet Eager used to wrap up the dance lino after every class and move it to another chapel or hall somewhere that would be rented for the night. Then Robin realised that he would need to get a studio together; he came to New York and negotiated teachers with Graham, and in 1967 he approached me and asked if would I come and stay in London...

I went running to Martha and said 'Do you believe he asked me that, why would I want to go to London?' and she said 'Darling, it would be good if you went'. We really have Martha to thank, because I was a co-director of the company at that time, and I had to say 'Do you really want me to go?' She said 'Well I think it's important and we really must do it for Robin'. So I came here, and immediately went home, and came back and forth about 10 times. And then in 1969 when we bought The Place, I realised that every time I left New York, New York went on fine without me, and every time I left London everything stopped until I came back. So I had to make a choice, and I chose London.

Sue Hoyle:
What did you start by doing to create choreographers, and to help yourself as a choreographer?

Bob Cohan:
Actually, the brief of this Conference was what Robin and I used to talk about all the time. How do we start? We weren't just talking about emerging choreographers, but we had the Company, the School and The Place theatre to form. We knew that it wouldn't work, unless we developed British teachers and British choreographers. So this aim was at the top of the list - how to achieve all this as quickly as possible.

In New York we had a wonderful theatre called the YMHA, - it's still there, up in 97th Street, - a small stage but nice theatre. For 100 dollars, which was a lot of money in those days, you could rent that theatre for one night, and that gave you the box office, the publicity and one technician; one day, several lights and one night to perform, and this was our showcase. Without that I have no idea what would have happened to modern dance in New York, because there was no other proper theatre, or even studio theatre, at the time. So we all used to perform at the YMHA, though we had no funding. As I understand it, to get a grant here you need to get a tour together, show the work is going to be performed somewhere and, of course, sell the work before you've created it! It is just weird - there's nothing artistic, there's no art involved, - well there is an art, it is called clever politics... In those days we used to create the work, then we would get the YHMA that was the only place we would do it, and through the reviews, the promoters, or by word of mouth we would get the bookings. We would actually sell the work we performed, and this of course makes much more sense. It is also a little more relaxing in that you can actually create the work! I know you should work to a deadline, but good choreographers make the deadline for themselves, they don't need a push from the outside. I think the whole idea (of funding) has to be looked at in another way. Certainly, when I was running the London Contemporary Dance Theatre, in order to book a tour and gain funding we had to put titles down that had nothing to do with the work, because theatres needed titles so that they could sell the tickets long before we even had started making the pieces. It was just a backwards way to work, and not very fruitful. If you're clever you rise to it, but why put that stress on top of all the others?

Sue Hoyle:

I think that is one of the issues that will be raised over the next few days. There are some grants available for experimenting for research and development, or for reworking, which there hasn't been enough support for in the past. So having the YMCA theatre where work could be shown and tried out was fortunate?

Bob Cohan:

Yes, but in London, once we had The Place theatre, we wanted to do the same thing but we just opened the doors and it was a nightmare, because everybody wanted to show whatever they did last night! It was a different scene then. There were people who wanted to choreograph but had no experience. Teresa Early was running workshops and that was going well, but there were other people who were just trying to express themselves with very little training, control, anything, supporting it. And we were inundated, and so much of the work that we were showing was not good. We decided that we had to pull back and focus on ourselves (in the School), and that's when we invited Nina Fonaroff to come to introduce the whole idea of teaching choreography. We were still, in those early days, struggling against the old ballet idea that choreographers have to be born, not trained. Well, it's true that some people are able to mske good work easily, so that actually there is much they don't need to learn as they seem to have it naturally. But certainly there is a huge amount to teach about choreography, and that's what we did in the school and in company workshops. I taught composition classes to the company whenever we had a week or two in between things, simple things just teaching the basic rules of composition. I tried very much to be like Martha by including the dancers in the choreography, so that they would learn what the process was.

And then we made two fateful decisions. After two years of running The Place we agreed that we would only take dancers into London Contemporary Dance Theatre from the school at The Place. It is true that during the twenty-five years that I ran the company we never had an audition, we always took students from the school. Our decision had a double purpose; it wasn't to exclude everyone else, but to make the school function so well that in the three years it could genuinely produce a professional student or someone who could at least become an apprentice to a professional company. There is a great deal to be said about how to hone down teaching methods so that you can get better students in a shorter time.

A couple of years later Robin and I decided that from this point on we needed to concentrate on developing choreographers. In the beginning we had most of the company repertoire from myself, Graham herself, Paul Taylor, Talley Beatty, Anna Sokolow, all Americans, and we decided that if we couldn't produce enough choreography from within the organisation we were failing. We agreed to take no more work from outside and that meant the teachers, the school, anyone at The Place could choreograph, and if the work was worthwhile I would get it on the stage in a national tour. And this made a big difference because suddenly it opened up several possibilities. It meant that the work wasn't just going to be seen in The Place theatre but it was actually going to go out on tour where it would be criticised professionally. Most important, it opened up the idea of being a choreographer as a profession - you too can be a choreographer, if you have the skills, if you have the talent, if you can do it.

Sue Hoyle:

And did you find that when you went on tour there was an audience for that new choreography? Is there an audience for new work?

Bob Cohan:

Ah well, we used to do the famous sandwich! There would be a proven work to start with to get the audience to relax, the new work in the middle, and something happy to close, so that the audience decide to come back next time. I'm negative about that famous sandwich but I am also positive about it because it worked. There is nothing wrong with dance being entertaining; the problem is what entertains who.

Avant-garde music does not entertain a lot of people. I was shocked when the company did a collaboration with London Sinfonietta; they invited me to a performance at Queen Elizabeth Hall and there were 40 people there, and they said 'Well yes, this is a normal audience'. We had been planning to run 5 nights with the show and then they were shocked because they couldn't afford the orchestra for 5 nights. There seemed to be a huge difference between avant-garde music on its own and avant-garde music with dance. With well made choreography you can make an audience listen to new music. We were at the Bradford Alhambra theatre once and an usher commented, 'I'm not sure I'm going to enjoy this week; I don't like this new music and new dance it's just not my cup of tea'. So I said 'Don't worry about it, don't try to look for any meaning in it, don't do anything else but look at the dancers. They are beautiful, they have beautiful bodies and they really dance well'. Later she said, 'You know, you were right, the dancers are beautiful, and it's easy to look at them, but the music, it's not like the ballet where you can close your eyes and listen'. That is absolutely true.

So is there an audience for contemporary dance? We tried very hard by starting here in Yorkshire in 1976 to do residencies and to build an audience. And it does work, of course it works to a degree but you just never get the overwhelming response that you want. Once we did a huge residency in Glasgow with three or four thousand young people in the week, but when we did the performances at the end not one of them showed up at the theatre. But they didn't want to come because they had the closest possible contact with the dancers in the workshop. What did they need to come to the theatre for? It was a whole foreign place. They knew the studios, the gyms where they made friends with the dancers. There's no solution there...

A more successful event was initiated by Margaret Dunn at Bretton Hall, with the idea that I should choreograph a dance for real in front of an audience. I finally agreed I would do it, but what I didn't know was that she had 250 young kids sitting on the stage on these bleacher benches. After an hour and a half or so the company would have a 15 minute break, and she would take all 250 out and bring 250 new ones in, so I as a choreographer felt this urge to have a climax to the event every minute and a half! It was a wild weird thing, but it worked, because everybody who saw a part of the dance done came back to see us. They wanted to see the little bit that was choreographed when they were there. We sold out when we came back to Leeds, because all these kids came back!

So, yes, education works if there's a hook. If we talk seriously about developing an audience for new dance, I think there is a real problem. There isn't an audience for new art or new writing; There is a small group of people in every urban centre that do understand and do appreciate it, but for the general public it has no meaning to their lives and I don't know how we bridge that gap. The UK is not an huge country, it's 60 million population. A few years ago The European weekly newspaper did a study to show how important culture was in people's lives in the EEC countries, and Britain came in 11th out of the 14. If that's the level, if it's true, then the Government appropriation for the arts is about right, even though we don't like it. Culture is simply not an important part of the British diet, now I may be wrong, but unfortunately we need an audience when we dance.

The artist Howard Hodgkins, who has just had a big show at the Hayward Gallery, is quoted in the exhibition catalogue as saying, "To be an artist in England is perhaps, even certainly, special, more difficult, more traumatic, and probably more fraught with the absolute certainty of failure than in any other country". Now, of course that's very negative. David Storey in the Guardian has said "The British have always been deferential about their art, that is, those who have a taste for it. The rest have been, if not indifferent, antagonistic". I think both these things are true and some-how we have to address it. Either that, or we have to be content with a specific group and we have to do art for art's sake. Now that's very hard to convince a funder, but essentially an artist does create art for art's sake. You become an artist to create art, not as a career move. You don't think, I'm going to make a lot of money, making dances. I only made money selling my London house!

Introductory Session
Conference Outcomes

Prior to his current position at the British Council, Gregory Nash was a professional dancer and choreographer working in the independent sector. He is thus knowledgeable about a range of issues raised by the Conference, and each day he led plenary sessions designed to ensure that all delegates had the opportunity to contribute to any decision-making about future outcomes.

Gregory Nash

I have been sitting here in the audience, listening to Bob Cohan's wonderful stories and recollections, becoming increasingly nervous about the prospect of following him on to this stage. The sensation takes me back 20 years to my first term as a sixteen-year-old student at The Place. Bob taught a one-off class for all the boys in the school and I was so nervous and so awestruck that he had to come over and put his hand just here on my chest to point out that if I held my breath I wouldn't actually be able to move. That moment has always stayed with me and the recollection of it now makes me think that however much, in the next few days, we talk about strategy, methodology, policy, it is really important to remember that it is visionary individuals like Bob who have inspired and will continue to shape the work that artists do, that we all do, and whose vision is so integral to the overall picture.

My role here at the Greenhouse Effect Conference is to draw together all the ideas. Every day there will be an opportunity to feed back and at the end of the conference I will collate it. I have been through the initial proposal written for the conference and also some of the papers that have been produced since. I have picked out some of the issues that leapt to my mind as being very important. I used the train journey from London this morning as an opportunity to canvas some definitions of the words 'art' and 'science'. For Richard Eyre, art 'ravishes the senses' and my colleagues on the train suggested that it was intuitive, mysterious, inexplicable, ambiguous, transformative; an expression of the intangible; a spiritual action to provide what life does not; that art is about open questions. Meanwhile science is perhaps more precise, its results are quantifiable, it is traditionally a closed question. People didn't have as many definitions of science as they did of art and it led me to think that – as an outcome of this conference – is an amalgamation of these two approaches, the artistic and the scientific, either possible or desirable?

Mentioned in the conference proposal is our responsibility to look at the past, the present and the future. Earlier Jo alluded to a focus on the future; Bob has reminded us that a focus on the past is also relevant because that is how we move forward. By surveying the past and the present and speculating about or projecting the future we may come up with some kind of map, and landmark events or key people will really colour that map.

There are three actions implicit in the document concerning this conference: enriching enquiry, exploring possibilities and determining action. I have been thinking about how we are all stakeholders in this process, in the process of choreographic exploration, of nurturing choreographers and dance artists, and of working out the best way to proceed to make sure that both the tradition and the future of the art form is preserved. Artists, funders, promoters, educators and students are all joint stakeholders. It is a joint contribution, a collaboration, and somewhere along the line there is either individual or joint ownership. And if we are all stakeholders then there will be a positive and negative impact on each of us. What, for example, happens to the young dancer in a company whose colleague is chosen as a potential choreographer and whose development then becomes a focus for company resources? Or to the local dancing school teacher and amateur choreographer whose local NDA adopts a London-based Associate Artist who then begins to interact with the same community? I think it is worth exploring the two sides.

And to finish, we will hopefully come up with some new structures, some new methodologies. Overall it will be the result of collaboration and it may not suit us all.

Session 1
Can Choreography be Taught?
An artist's response

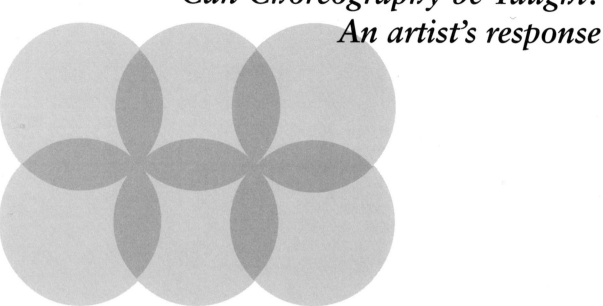

Key Words:

choreography   *training*   *Higher Education*

creative process   *role of the artist*   *mentors*

role of the teacher

Is choreography best learned through observation and osmosis in a professional dance context, or is it possible to teach it? And if so, what should be taught and how? Kate Flatt, Janet Smith and Rosemary Butcher are established professional choreographers who have experienced teaching in the Higher Education sector, and they are well aware of the tensions between the demands of the art form and the requirements and constraints of degree courses in Dance. Each offers her own personal experiences of teaching in the Higher Education context. The session was chaired by Christopher Bannerman.

Kate Flatt:

In response to the question, I asked myself how did I learn to choreograph? I realised that I had acquired fundamental insight from three particular teachers. My first experience of choreographic study was in a series of intensive courses from 1968-70 taught by Leonide Massine. His classes were a joyous liberation from the constraints of orthodox classical ballet training and offered riches in terms of choreographic possibility. Solo, ensemble and particularly rhythmic work was developed, in a demanding, rigorous and yet stimulating environment of concentrated study. Much of this foundation continues to influence my work today. I went on to study Contemporary dance and met Nina Fonaroff, a great teacher. She has a superb critical ability and made me look realistically at my work. She taught me to trust my own eye and to cut away what was not essential to my work; to make the dance more true to itself. The insights of her teaching came at the right moment and have had a lasting effect on my work.

During the era of British New Dance in the late 1970's, I was not only exploring new forms and influences from America, but received a travel grant to visit Eastern Europe and see traditional dance where it survived in its ritual and village context. This other teacher then, was the simplicity and earthy purity of the traditional circle and improvised pair dances, done by those for whom they still had a purpose and meaning. This experience not only influenced the work I made on my return, but continues to inform my thinking.

My career since then has involved working in a collaborative environment, in opera and theatre, and whilst it is an expansive field it is also full of deadlines and complex restrictions. Choreographic commissions present themselves as problems to be researched and solved and I utilise a range of methods and approaches which draw on my eclectic training ground and constant need for fresh enquiry. Moving to teach in Higher Education and not least in a modular degree structure was without doubt the fastest learning curve in fifteen years. It has generated a great many questions about the field of study. I believe that the study of choreography can develop intuitive perception, imaginative invention, and flexible thinking. Balanced subtly alongside that is the need for reflection and conscious insight into process. The problem lies in how to achieve that balance most effectively. In Higher Education, the study of choreography forms only part of a dance degree, and not all students become choreographers. It is important to realise what the craft of making dances can teach, and how that can benefit all dance students.

Choreographers in reality make themselves. They develop through ongoing enquiry, their discovery, research and need to communicate. They do this by thinking on their feet, being able to swiftly analyse and negotiate, by manipulating and ordering material they have generated and being able to take a realistic and objective view of their work. The most beneficial way of developing these skills is through the process of discovery, of experiencing by doing. How else can insight into the art form by achieved?

Janet Smith:

In preparation for this discussion, I found myself thinking about my role as a choreographer. What do I feel is worthwhile sharing? What can I try to teach about choreography? One of my first revelations about choreography was when I was a student and I suddenly realised that I had all these choices. Choreography is all about making choices. As teachers of choreography we need to find ways of introducing students to the notion of choices, to look at those concerns without fear and to embrace them. I want to make a situation that really allows students to look playfully at choice. Experimentation can lead to innovation and self-discovery. Teaching choreography should be an education of feeling, sensing and intuition and it is my understanding of this that I want to share. When you start to create work it is possible to identify a working pattern, your own individual creative process. I learned very early on that when I am making work I always need to have a notepad and pen at the side of my bed to write any sudden ideas. The whole creative process is very individual and it is useful to be aware of it. I want to help students to be able to get in touch with their own authentic voice. Students can learn from the work of others, but also should try to discover their own developing style and what excites and inspires them about choreography. I found it difficult when working in Higher Education to fit my experiences and understanding into the academic framework. I did not want to teach students set formulas for choreography as I know as an artist that whenever you start to make a piece of work there do not seem to be any rules. Desire is a very important factor in the choreographic process, the passion to create work. This cannot be taught; we can only try to help and support students in their creative development. There are many difficulties in teaching choreography in Higher Education. Class sizes tend to be very large. Each student needs the space and time to try out ideas and yet it is impossible with maybe thirty other people having to share the same space and resources. I feel that a prerequisite for studying at this level should be that students should have already reached a certain level of skill and understanding about craft and technique. These skills should then continue to be challenged and developed throughout the dance course. Within the University system there is always the pressure of limited time, teaching hours and funding. Consequently, technique classes are not considered a priority and are sometimes forfeited in order to provide theory and choreography lessons. I feel there needs to be a balance of all these classes, as the skills developed in technique class greatly inform and enhance choreography. In contrast to the University system, the vocational dance colleges are only just beginning to place greater emphasis on developing choreography skills. There are methods of learning about choreography, other than conventional dance courses at colleges and Universities, that should also be considered. Apprenticeships in dance companies where there can be the opportunity to observe and be part of the creative process are surely an excellent means of learning first-hand about choreography. Perhaps bursaries need to be made available to allow people the opportunity to do this. There are a myriad different ways that people can learn and develop choreographic skills and we now need to find the means to support this happening.

Rosemary Butcher:

I do not want to talk about how I came to choreography or about my past. My concerns are about the future. That does not negate my past it is just that I would like to incorporate the past into the present. I feel there is a radical need for update and modernisation of how we look at the nature of creativity. We are absolutely stymied by structures that are a stranglehold on how we work in terms of choreography and education. I never set out to choreograph. I was in America at a very exciting time during the development of the Judson Church. It was this period of discovery that led me to realise that for me dance was not sufficient. My personal direction has always been towards linking movement with visual art. That does not mean that there is not a need for dance and choreography; it is just that I believe the model has to be reviewed.

These are my suggestions:

> **Yes to the sense that the environment in which creativity is developed is very important**
>
> **No to expectancy**
>
> **No to predetermined language**
>
> **No to old-fashioned compositional forms.**

It is the future of the people we are teaching that holds the balance of how we go forward.

Points raised in discussion:

- Concern was raised about having to judge and grade students' choreography. This contradicts the notion of developing creative skills through experimentation. Grading systems can restrict students' creativity. They feel compelled to please the teacher rather than follow their own creative impulses.

- Do students need to learn about composition? By providing rules and formulas, students then have something to challenge.

- The role of artist-in-residence within educational establishments is considered to be extremely beneficial to the creative development of students. It was felt that more Colleges and Universities should offer these positions in Dance faculties.

Session 2

Dance Festivals: Can they nurture the emerging choreographer?

Keywords:

festivals   *new choreographies*   *experimental work*   *venues*

Estrella Casero Garcia from Spain and Victoria Marangopoulou from Greece give examples of specific European dance festivals and describe how and why they create opportunities for choreographers to make new work.

Estrella Casero García

The Situation in Spain

My intention here is to give a brief description of the situation of choreography in Spain, paying special attention to the places and possibilities offered to those choreographers who work and present their choreographies in Spain. With the intention of giving as much information as possible, I will make reference to all the important data about Dance Festivals in Spain.

As it is well-known, Spain was under dictatorship for almost 40 years and this kind of political regime implied the existence of a censorship from which choreography did not escape. However, due to that censorship, Spain is nowadays a country with a very important creative potential. This situation has provoked the late appearance of Spanish choreographers on the scene, but their appearance is strong and overall it has a great richness in the language of movements, on the one hand the movements coming from Spanish Dance, and on the other the movements taken from Modern Dance.

After this short historic explanation and placing ourselves back in current times, it is important to focus on the following questions: Where can choreographers present their choreographies? And which are their 'real' possibilities in the choreographic field?

There are quite a few festivals where choreographers have the opportunity to present their work. The most important ones are, from north to south,

· The Grec Festival (Barcelona)
· Dansa Valencia
· Madrid en Danza
· Festival Alternativo de Madrid
· Festival de Otono (Madrid)

The most important of these is Dansa Valencia, basically due to its internal structure: it was initially thought of as a Dance Market where professional choreographers could present their new creations, and at the same time where theatre programmers from all over Spain could establish contact with creators to hire them or their companies. The other festivals and fairs are quite varied in general terms and, with the exception of Madrid en Danza, most of them work directly or indirectly under governmental budgeting, which in a way means the dependence of choreography upon public institutions for its survival. Is this good? Is this bad? It would be difficult to say, and I think it also falls outside of the real subject of this presentation.

Another important subject in this case is how to participate in choreographic festivals in Spain. This participation varies from one festival to another; it depends on the organiser of the event, his/her preferences, likes and dislikes, and on many occasions, it depends on the money available to be invested. Among the festivals with a bigger budget is the Festival de Otono which takes place in Madrid, however this is one that shows a smaller number of dance performances. We shall also refer to a festival that is making its own way in the scene, the Festival Alternativo in Madrid. We could say it intends to be the leading voice of the new choreographers and, above all, of the innovative choreographers.

Regarding new choreographies, one of the best places to present new choreographies is the National Contests which are increasing their importance year after year. It is in these contests where we can acquire an idea of the situation of choreography in Spain. The National Spanish Contest and the Spanish Dance National Contest are the main ones at present. The best and most innovative choreographies have emerged from them. These two festivals originated in a private way with the aim of giving aid to new choreographers, those with very few possibilities to present their pieces of work in theatres and dance spaces. They are actually partly-financed by the Ministry of Culture and the Autonomous Regional Government of Madrid, and offer the possibility to apply for annual scholarships to train in foreign countries, particularly the UK and the USA. The first

National Contest to appear was the Choreographic Contest of Madrid (1986), dedicated to modern dance and ballet. Some years later and due to its success, the Spanish Dance Contest emerged (1991). Both events were originally thought up and directed by two North American women; Margaret Jova and Laura Kumin.

Another different and very important factor that has an influence on the situation of choreography in Spain is the economical support given to companies in order to present new performances and tour them around Spain and abroad. This scarce help comes from the Ministry of Culture (INAEM) and the Autonomous Regional Governments. Unfortunately there has been a considerable delay in this year's call for support to the Ministry of Culture, and expectations are not good for access to it in coming years. Regarding the Autonomous Regional Governments, there is an offer of support in Catalonia, Andalusia and Madrid to mention some of them. However, the support is only for companies and choreographers that live and work in the region where the offer comes from; that is, in Catalonia. Only Catalonian companies and choreographers can apply for and benefit from this support, a fact that limits the rest of regions and provinces which lack these offers.

One more problem to be added to these two kinds of support is the problem of time. Generally speaking, the offer of support, application, concession and dead-lines to carry out and present the work has to be done in the same year. Due to bureaucracy and paperwork the money is usually delayed (sometimes even by two years). Choreographers have to invest their own personal money in the project, which implies on many occasions a bank loan and a loss of money in interest to the bank.

To end to this presentation, I will say a few words about an important and worrying subject for Spanish choreographers. I am referring to copyright. The situation of copyright laws in choreography is improving day by day in Spain; I'd dare to say that Spain is one of the countries with better governmental agreements (with the exception of the U.K) to defend the rights of choreographic creators. This is due to the established agreement between the Spanish General Society of Creators, the several Dance Associations and the Spanish Dance Professionals Federation. By this agreement the Spanish General Society of Creators, which was previously dedicated to defend music composers and play writers, now also defends the rights of choreographers. It sounds a good agreement, but there is a long way to go yet so that choreographers can be equally considered in terms of rights, and can receive the amounts established. For example, one of the major problems is how to register a choreography and be able to prove one's authorship. Up to now this process consists of a video tape and a short description of the choreography; but we all know that this is certainly not enough in most cases.

I have a table of contents with the names of Festivals, addresses and name of contact person. (See end of Section.) I invite people to contact us at the Dance Division if they need more information.

Victoria Marangopoulou

The Situation in Greece

I have often visited your country, and I have lived here, and I confess that when I began studying at the Royal Ballet School, I could never have imagined that, thirty years later, dance would have evolved the way it did, or that my personal development would have taken the path it did.

I cannot believe that the people and circumstances that led me to the present were concerned about 'how to nurture a young artist' the way we are now concerned. As far as I can recall, my teachers and colleagues, by virtue of their love for this wonderful form of art, were always there to reinforce and encourage young artists to achieve their goals.

The fact that I found myself five years ago in the position of envisioning a new institution in a town where I had already been working as a teacher and director of the municipal dance school for 11 years, seemed like a natural development, but, if I bring to mind the immense obstacles and difficulties that I encountered along the way, I felt the spontaneous need to act in a way that would improve the way things are done for coming generations.

While we were planning the festival concept along with representatives of the Ministry of Culture and the Municipality of Kalamata, what was foremost in my mind was the need to redefine the concept of 'festival'. Instinctively I felt that innovation as a feature of the only international dance festival in Greece should not be exhausted in the choice or style of the companies invited to appear, but should rather focus on a reformulation of the possibilities and dynamics offered by a festival. I felt that we would be more effective if we made the Kalamata Festival a part of a greater conception – the International Dance Centre – whose activities would develop in the three areas of research, education and artistic activity throughout the year, and which would reach a peak with the Festival.

In Spring 1995, the International Dance Centre was established in Kalamata, a town where dance enjoyed prominence and had gained substantial support, as part of a project set up by the Ministry of Culture that went by the name of National Cultural Network of Cities.

An idea which seemed to emerge right from the start was that we should aim not at selecting each dance performance solely on the basis of style, but that our principle selection criteria should address authenticity, originality and high quality of performance, regardless of style. We wanted to present great choreographers in the history of dance, major figures in our century, whose work had not been shown in Greece, as well as revivals of historic Greek works and their documentation, works which would otherwise remain lost to us, since the limited subsidies available for dance cannot maintain them in regular repertoire. We wanted to act as a window of reciprocal communication bringing to Greece significant creations of the present, as well as showing the work of contemporary Greek choreographers, whose work is still unknown outside Greece – and we definitely wanted to provide a venue for the new emerging choreographers.

Our first festival was a homage to the Greek choreographer Zouzou Nikoloudi, so it opened with a performance of the revival of the work *Chorika*. The possibility given to the present generation of dance makers to become acquainted with and to re-evaluate the work of an important Greek artist created an enormous stir among students and artists who could never have imagined the artistic value of the work of their colleague from the past. The entire performance was recorded on video and sent to the Grand-Prix International Vidéo-Danse where it won the special jury prize with the rationale "a remarkable and honest work, aiming to give future generations an important heritage". While the festival began with an historic figure, it closed with a choreographer who had graduated from the Greek State School of Dance just two years earlier. He produced his own version of Stravinsky's *Les Noces* with OKTANA, the company which he had formed.

In its following year the Kalamata Festival presented *Medea* by Dimitris Papaioannou's EDAFOS company, a performance which two years later would be favoured in finding itself on the calendars of international events outside Greece; in Lisbon's 1998 Expo, London's Riverside Studios, Biennale de la Danse de Lyon, Tel-Aviv and on tour in the United States.

Further to presenting existing work, and in fulfilling its aim of encouraging new choreographers, the International Dance Centre also commissioned three new pieces by three young choreographers (Konstantinos Mihos and his company, Lathos Kinissi, and Kiki Baka and Dimitri Sotiriou, both founding members of the company Sine Qua Non). These works formed the programme of one of the performances in the 2nd Kalamata International Dance Festival. The choreographers were granted the sum of approximately ECU 35,190 (12,000,000 GRD) between them, to produce their works. In addition, they were given the use of the theatre and all its technical equipment (sound, light, etc) for their rehearsals and performance. The Festival also ensured advertising, promotion and media coverage to highlight the significance of this event, a practice followed in all cases. Both choreographers and dancers were offered accommodation in Kalamata for two weeks, throughout the festival.

We shouldn't fail to mention that they also all had the right to participate in the annual seminar organised by the Festival which invites renowned teachers to hold classes over a fortnight. Throughout the Festival they were also given the opportunity to attend performances and to participate in the lecture-demonstrations, workshops and masterclasses given by the artists invited. An interesting aspect of the entire venue was the participation in the performance of the students of the Kalamata Municipal School of Dance.

So, the outcome of this approach was that:

1. Three new choreographies were produced.

2. Distinguished artists coexisted with new creators within the same theatre, in the course of their work (Sara Rudner, for instance, in Konstantinos Mihos' performance).

3. Local young people came into contact with the creative process of dance, as they were invited to attend open rehearsals.

4. Dance critics, producers, organisers, artistic directors of other festivals attending the Festival at our invitation became acquainted with the work of new choreographers.

5. It allowed us to evaluate the process, thus identifying the outcomes, these being elements which emerge only through experience.

It goes without saying that problems arose as well. Some of them, mainly the practical ones, were of the sort that can be easily dealt with, while others provided us with material for reflection and further, in depth, investigation.

I mentioned seminars. That was the first year we held such classes and we have been organising something every year since. I consider this educational dimension in the course of the Festival to be of the utmost importance. Classes with teachers such as Shelley Senter, Irene Hultman and Gill Clarke, as well as the masterclasses, workshops and lecture-demonstrations held by the artists invited to the Festival and participating in it, contribute to the moulding and evolution of a new generation of dancers.

In the 3rd year, the experience we had gained made us seek a second, more intimate stage for experimental production for a smaller audience. In this way young creators are protected, as they do not have to compete with their more experienced and renowned colleagues, and can address a public more willing and prepared to accept experimental work. Four young women choreographers, also graduates of the State School of Dance, which shows how significant a part it plays in nurturing young choreographers, were selected to present four solos choreographed by themselves.

I should mention a crucial point here. The venues, and the way in which the artistic director of a festival can come into contact with new creators poses difficulties. Providing a platform at national and international level should be a priority. In my country such opportunities are very few and limited almost exclusively to Athens. Let me just say indicatively that so far as I know there are only three theatres hosting experimental work, a new choreographers' competition held by the Municipality of Athens each year for the past ten years, and the choreography workshops ofthe Greek State School of Dance which are open to the public.

And now, I will refer to one of the events which marked the third festival and which I regard as one of the happiest moments for the institution and for me personally. We began a collaboration with one of the most important and noteworthy museums in Greece – the Benaki Museum. In its archives there is a collection of photographs by Nelly's, an extraordinary figure in our century, who was the first and unique – at least for the first half of the century a photographer of dance in our country. A great part of her work was devoted to dancers, mainly female, of the era when Nelly's was at her peak, around the 20s and 30s, including many pictures of dancers of the Mary Wigman school.

Setting up an exhibition of such appeal, with dance photographs of historical and aesthetic interest was a great challenge to me. I visualised this exhibition outside the conventional surroundings of a gallery, where the photographs would seem to me like isolated museum pieces. I had the strong feeling that this material might be presented in a more contemporary and atmospheric setting and could inspire various creators and talented artists to gather and work together.

An old warehouse on the docks, situated in one of the most frequented areas of town, became a challenge for the architect designer, Antonis Daglidis, who transformed the huge warehouse into a camera obscura with bellows. This also served as the setting for our 'alternative' stage. The selection of the photographs was undertaken by researchers at the Benaki Museum in collaboration with the International Dance Centre (Irini Boudouri, Clementini Vounelaki) who worked together with the young painter Andreas Voussouras who mounted the exhibition. The choreographer Dimitris Papaioannou was invited to create a solo inspired by Nelly's for a young talented dancer. For his music he chose Anton Webern's Opus 1.

The fact that so many young talented artists from various areas joined together, generated an impact and reinforced the belief that dance reaches a unique dimension when it collaborates at a high level with the other arts. All this work in various disciplines was documented by photographs and video recordings. An art-book with the exhibition's photographs was also produced in collaboration with one of Greece's quality publishers. This was the first real publishing undertaking by the International Dance Centre.

It is a great pity that the warehouse could not become a more permanent venue for the Festival. We had to look elsewhere for the alternative space in the 4th Festival which took place in the summer of 1998. Kalamata's municipal theatre was used to host the Festival's new commissions, Konstantinos Rigos' *La Dame Aux Camelias* – 150 years later and Mary Tsouti's *Sunday Afternoon* which was a video dance and live performance.

I feel the need to mention that from my experience and throughout my course, I have always been very conscious of the fact that our own attitude towards people, situations and in our world today, plays a decisive role on the art and science of nurturing dance makers. At a time when time and space become less and less sufficient for all of us, and the possibility to maintain our uniqueness is more and more limited, the need to give new creators time and space to do so has been a constant motivation for me. The need to be personal, persistent and faithful to what one firmly believes, even at the risk of failing, was often the only, the imperative choice.

SPANISH FESTIVALS

NOMBRE	FECHAS	LUGAR	ORGANIZA	NOTAS
Festival de Otoño	Octubre - Diciembre	Madrid	C.M. Mercedes Calvo tlf.91 580 2533 91 580 2630 fax.91580 2680	Festival cultural en el que se incluyen espectáculos de danza
Desviaciones	Noviembre	Madrid. Cuarta Pared tlf.91 517 23 17	UVI. La Inesperada	Ciclo Nueva Danza. Espectáculos, mesas redondas y confesiones de autor.
Certamen coreogr·fico de Madrid	Diciembre	Madrid Sala Olimpia	Centro Dramático Nacional. MAGA Prod. Margaret Jova Tel/Fax. 91 547 69 79	Certamen de danza contemporánea.
Danza en Diciembre	Diciembre	Madrid. Sala Olimpia.	Centro Dramático Nacional. MAGA Prod. Margaret Jova Tel/Fax. 91 547 69 79	Espectáculos de grupos de danza estables y consagrados
Dansa València.	Enero Febrero	Valencia	Teatres dc la Generalitat Valenciana Manel Chaqués tlf.96 351 0051 fax.963520287	Panorama de la danza contemporánea espanola. Espectáculos, mercado, mesas redondas.
Miradas Atlánticas	Febrero	Madrid. Sala Cuarta Pared tlf.91 517 23 17	UVI. La Inesperada Forum Dança EIRA	Espectáculos nueva danza portuguesa, mesas redondas
Festival Alternativo	Febrero Marzo	Madrid. Salas alternativas	C.M. Mercedes Calvo tlf.91 580 2533 91 580 2630 fax.91580 2680	Teatro, música y danza
Madrid en Danza	Mayo Junio	Teatros de Madrid	C.M. Mercedes Calvo tlf.91 580 2533 91 580 2630 fax.91580 2680	Danza para todos los espacios
Muestra de videodanza	Mayo	Madrid	MNCARS Canal Dansa Nuria Font tlf.93 296 8146 fax.93 4317195	Muestra incluida en Madrid en Danza
Festival de Musica y Danza	Mayo-Junio	Granada		Música y danza.
Certamen coreográfico de Madrid	Junio	Madrid	C.M. MAGA Prod. MAGA Prod. Margaret Jova Tel/Fax. 91 547 69 79	Certamen de danza espanola y flamenco.
Festival del Grec	Julio-Septiembre	Barcelona	Ajuntament de Barcelona	Festival de verano de música y danza que ofrece también sus propias producciones
Festival de Perelada	Julio-Agosto	Perelada. Castell de Perelada	Ajuntament de Perelada	Música, danza y teatro.

Points raised in discussion:

No discussion points were available due to a recording error.

Session 3

National Dance Agencies: Their Role in the Infrastructure of Choreographic Development in Britain

Keywords:

National Dance Agencies *dance artists*
choreography *commissioning facilities*

Janet Archer, John Ashford and Jane Greenfield are Directors of three of the existing National Dance Agencies, which were formally recognised in response to 'Stepping Out', the Arts Council of Great Britain report authored by Graham Devlin in 1989. The discussion documents how individually and severally, these Agencies contribute to the development needs of regional and national choreographers. How as directors do they balance the aims of the Agency with the requirements of their respective funding bodies? To what extent do their individual preferences as directors influence strategy and affect change? Veronica Lewis chairs this discussion.

Veronica Lewis

The National Dance Agencies are an ongoing, evolving topic. They are animals that you either love or you hate, and sometimes you do both at the same time. I know from my own experience, which was very painful, writing five applications before we were allowed to be an NDA, that they can be things that you aspire to and then when you are successful you think 'oh God, was it worth it?'

I would like to introduce Janet Archer who directs Dance City in Newcastle; Jane Greenfield who directs Dance Four which has its main base in Nottingham; and John Ashford who is the director at The Place in London. Until this summer I was one of the directors of the North West National Dance Agency. I'm now working in London with London Contemporary Dance School.

There has been a lot of work done recently on evaluating the work of the NDAs so far. There are eight NDAs in England at the moment, and then there are other models similar to NDAs around the world. I was recently in New Zealand and came across one. The idea of having an agency which has responsibility for developing dance is actually quite new, so everybody's been looking at core expectations of NDAs recently. The very nature of NDAs is that you have different biases in different parts of the country. However all NDAs are expected to deliver a mixed programme of the following core activities:

- An associate artist programme; – this might be a bursary, an artist in residence, or a programming commission. Length of time and selection process is determined by the individual NDA, but should aim to be developmental for the artists and companies.

- The commissioning of new work; - a professional performance programme. There should be a liaison point with other organisations, local, national and international, for commissioning, residency work, performance and teaching opportunities as well as general advocacy and development.

- A professional training programme for dance artists including professional classes, access to studio space, access to computer and office space for dance artists and managers, management advice and support. There should be networking opportunities for local and regional artists, links between dance artists and the local community, a developmental community programme, marketing, professional and community programmes tackling aspects of cultural diversity, and finally they should maintain a national overview to inform local practice.

This is an overall view of what NDAs should provide. Now we will hear about individual cases.

Jane Greenfield

I am going to speak both wearing my official hat as the Director of Dance 4, but also, more importantly, give my own personal perspective on how I see National Dance Agencies and their role in choreographic development. Very briefly I will give a bit of background to Dance 4 because that will give you a clear sense of why it is we do what we do.

Dance 4 is one of the youngest National Dance Agencies with the exception of the North West Dance Agency. It began life based in Leicester in 1993 and almost immediately achieved NDA status and also took on the 1993 Year of Dance. For various reasons, The Year of Dance faced many difficulties and was not as successful as it could have been. Dance 4 had only just been created and there were no structures in place to support artists, companies or development. So in 1994 there was a major review and the Agency shifted base to Nottingham. That's when I came on board as a Director. We started life without a building and with a brand new remit. I decided that the remit needed to be artist-focused rather than community or education-focused. So it was an early decision to become an artist-based organisation.

Not having to run a building was in many respects, fantastic. Because we didn't have a building we didn't have the massive overheads that virtually all the National Dance Agencies have. This literally meant that Dance 4 was able to channel virtually all of its finances and resources, except for a very small staff of two, into supporting artists and supporting the development of work. This is something which we still do and it's the main focus for our work. It drives the Agency even though we now have a building. Our money was concentrated into commissioning, presenting, research and development, professional training and development, particularly for local artists.

We now have a space, called PreSet, but we only got it about eighteen months ago. PreSet is quite a small, intimate space and it's a working space with one main studio. We share the whole space with a theatre company based in Nottingham. The idea is that PreSet is a home to lots of different artists; not just dancers but theatre people, live artists, installation artists, a whole range of people. This means there is a very interesting and exciting mix and movement of ideas and people there. Even though we have a building, Dance 4's aim and focus is still the artist and creating work, so virtually all of our projects and initiatives are focused towards that. We run the usual mix of projects that I suppose most people will be familiar with now, mentoring schemes and choreographic platforms, training events for young dancers, choreographic residences, associate artist schemes. These are the kind of projects that all the NDAs undertake, its just that we do them to slightly different levels.

The other thing that I want to say about Dance 4 is that it is very much influenced by what's happening in Nottingham. Nottingham's arts activities are very rooted in collaborative projects, experimental and live art, and performance art based work. Obviously Dance 4's artistic development has been influenced by that and complements that tradition. I think that now, after four or five years, Dance 4 have begun to develop quite a clear artistic identity which supports dance work that, if you like, sits on the boundaries between dance and other art forms. Dance 4 is very interested in work that by its nature is going to challenge expectations and perceptions of what dance is. An example of this is a recent piece of work by Frank Bock and Simon Vincenzi which we co-commissioned. There has been some very interesting discussion about that piece. Some people have absolutely loved it, some people have hated it and are made very angry by it. I think this is very exciting because even though the work at this early stage might not be quite there yet, it already challenges our perceptions of what choreography is.

Going on to the specific question about choreographic development and National Dance Agencies, I think National Dance Agencies and independent agencies, regional dance agencies, dance houses, all play a role in choreographic development; it's just that we do it in our own way. I think the phrase 'safe house' is now fairly well used and fairly well understood and as I say, we all have our own ways of interpreting that, whether it's mentoring programmes, research and development, or commissioning. My personal feeling is that we should never aim to have one kind of grand blue print or template for what makes or determines good choreographic development because I don't think that allows for diversity or individuality. I think in the same way that artists have different needs, National Dance Agencies and their artistic directors have their own needs, likes and artistic preferences. I actually think that's a positive thing and something to be encouraged. I think however there are common reference points that we can all use which then guide us when we are looking at choreographic development.

I want to finish by going through those guiding principles which mean something to me, or which I apply to my work particularly when it comes to supporting artistic and choreographic development. I think it's important for an NDA Director to have a discerning eye, to have the freedom to follow his own artistic nose rather than fulfil other agendas, to not be ashamed of making certain artistic choices. It's important to be selective and to treat artists as individuals. We should be encouraged to do things out of the ordinary, and put our money and resources where our mouth is and by doing so, commit to and invest in choreographic exploration.

Janet Archer

I went to work in the north in 1991 and I found a terrain which was completely unique and a little bit alien to me, with some very particular needs and attitudes and a hunger for some very specific things. There had been a history of dance development in Newcastle prior to my time there - English Dance Theatre was there creating and commissioning work, and I think Michael Clark made one of his first works for English Dance Theatre.

When I arrived in Newcastle, English Dance Theatre had long gone and there was a blank canvas awaiting me, apart from the very first Newcastle International Dance Festival which had been established and set up by Val Bourne as one of her satellite programmes. It was run twice in Newcastle in 1990 and 1992 and then handed over to the National Dance Agency as yet another thing to take on board and be responsible for. Thankfully we've managed to run it twice too and we're about to embark upon our third programme.

What do National Dance Agencies do as far as choreographic development goes? I think the most fundamental thing that we do is that we simply provide more opportunity for choreographers to work. It's quite difficult in our region, because although we're based in Newcastle we have a region wide remit. We have a Regional Arts Board that is very adamant that any regionally funded agency should not have an impact on any one particular location. We are based in Newcastle, with a population of about two hundred and fifty thousand. The greater region has about a million people living in it, and we're supposed to provide for them. We're also responsible for work in the north west, as far away as Barrow-in-Furness which takes three hours to get to (which is exactly the same time it takes to get to London), and Teeside down to North Yorkshire and up as far as the borders of Scotland. It is quite a challenge to find ways of encouraging people to become involved in dance and to find ways of supporting artists, some of whom choose to live in the rather remoter parts of the region. At times I feel very anxious and guilty that we are not able to provide those artists with as much support as perhaps we can for others.

Over the last seven years we have seen the amount of choreographic activity in Tyne and Wear develop hugely. We have sixteen dance companies, or dance project companies based in Newcastle alone, and very quickly I believe we will start to see dance projects establish themselves in other parts of the region through initiatives that are being taken up by local authorities and individuals. It's a much healthier canvas than when I arrived a few years ago. But you can't do it by yourself. I think one of the fundamental things about National Dance Agencies is that we have to create a vision and a direction and a leadership, but we have also to admit that one of the biggest roles that we can play in terms of supporting initiatives is to work in partnership with a whole range of other people who are interested in working with us.

We do all the things that Veronica and Jane have listed in terms of providing space. We provide free space to artists at Dance City and the artists can access free space on a 'first come first served' basis. Maybe that's not going to be the most appropriate policy for ever but at the moment it works for us. We provide office space for seven dance artists a year, after which we will in future be moving them on to another place.

Some of the specific new initiatives that we are starting to work with have been funded through Arts For Everyone. We are also lucky enough to have received a substantial award from the Lottery which has meant that we have been able to appoint an artist to be a part of Dance City's team. David Massingham is our Project Manager and he works very closely with regionally based artists to explore ways of helping them develop their work and of providing new opportunities for them to work within. David's work also includes nationally based artists at the moment - Ted Stoffer is in residence and has been for six weeks. We have given him a tiny grant in real terms but nevertheless there's enough money to enable him to have a studio for six weeks away from his home, away from London, away from all the harassment possibly, which is what some people say when they come to us of their day-to-day lives. We are supporting another artist, Jane Mason, who was a dancer and has just started to show some very tangible choreographic skills. She happened to be on a training programme at Dance City and literally whispered to somebody in the organisation that she might be interested in making work. She was encouraged to bring in some video work. I saw it, liked it, and we gave her again a small grant and encouraged her to take some time and space. She has made a relationship with a local theatre company and she is actually working with actors not dancers which is interesting. We have just seen her first piece which again I think is a very exciting piece of work. David is working in partnership with those artists to find ways of creating long term relationships with promoters in the region who have shown an interest in dance. We know that we are not going to be able to provide for every dance artist who wants to make work at Dance City. We have to find other people who are prepared to offer those dance artists space to work in. So through the arts we are managing to find ways of acting as matchmaker, brokering relationships with artists and venues that we hope will have an impact on the day-to-day lives of the artists, the venues and the localities.

We run a choreographic training programme. For a long time I've believed that not enough questions are asked about the art of making dances, why we do it and who it is for. Not enough practical support is given to independent artists and companies in terms of simply equipping young choreographers and indeed administrators with relevant tools to be able to go out and run their businesses. So we started a space programme which this year is interesting because it works in London and in Newcastle. Very keen artists based in the region tend to be locked into a bubble, without the opportunity to integrate and fertilise their ideas with artists from other parts of the country. So we established this space course which runs at Greenwich Dance Agency and at Dance City in Newcastle. There are thirty choreographers on that programme, and every month artists go from Newcastle to London and vice versa. At the end of that programme, all of those artists will have created works, and we have made a pledge this year to present their works at a consortium of venues in the north and Scotland. The choreographers on the space course will present their work in Glasgow, Edinburgh, Newcastle, at The Arc in Stockton and Darlington Arts Centre. Each will go to one venue and a team of promoters will follow them to all the venues to give them immediate feedback, act as the interface between them and their audience, and give the opportunity to debate their work.

I think it is very important in a region like ours not to operate behind closed doors but to let the audience into the creative process of the work itself. The idea of allowing people to watch a piece in creation is a very exciting one. We try all the time to find new ways of creating better platforms; with people who understand exactly what dance is all about, people who don't want a short, sharp fix simply to be entertained, people who are prepared to go and be curious about work and ask questions about work and talk about it afterwards. I think in terms of a regional choreographic development it is almost impossible to focus on the art form without focusing on the context that the art form is going to be set in. So we have a course called a Preliminary Access Course to Dance which is a statutory course from a Further Education College. It runs for sixty hours and for groups of twenty adults over the age of sixteen. We work in partnership with all kinds of people to find the adults for us and we go out and we open their minds about dance and dance making. We give them information about different choreographers and the kinds of work that they achieve, and at the end of the course they all have to go and see a performance and write a critique on the performance. We hope that by keeping them and supporting them through that process that at the end of the day they will have a more open and enquiring mind about dance.

On Monday I had a phone call from an organisation called The Newcastle Initiative who said 'we would like you to be half of our application to the millennium commission, and what we would like you to do is to carry out dance activity all over the city and offer different people the opportunity to find out about dance.' They thought that was a fundamental message to the city of Newcastle. Just before Christmas, Gary Top who is the Arts Officer there asked us do some dance in Hartlepool. We commissioned Amanda Tufnell to create a special piece of work which was very successful. A knock on effect from that is the possible launch of a new group of creative artists working from Hartlepool. Sunderland Football Club rang us this week and asked us to commission a piece of work which will be shown to an audience of football attenders. We even had a call from our local sports centre who rang and said they've got empty squash courts, would they be of use to us in terms of offering artists somewhere to rehearse? So people are starting to ask how they can get involved in dance We are continuing to support dance artists and the work that they are doing and, potentially I hope that there will be more people in our region who will want to engage with dance and will have a greater depth of understanding of what dance actually means.

John Ashford

The crucial thing about The Place as a National Dance Agency is that there's a theatre there and in a sense it defines many of the things we do. The Place uniquely brings together the vocational training of London Contemporary Dance School, and resident dance companies including that of Richard Alston Dance Company which is produced by The Place. The Place Theatre runs a season of thirty two weeks of dance a year. Anything else which isn't dance is there to pay the rent and a number of services which have now accumulated organically around that vortex of dance activity.

In the twelve years since I was appointed by Robin Howard as Director/Manager of The Place Theatre, we have developed a lot of choreographic initiatives which have emanated from the practical needs of developing the theatre programme. Many of the things which are now regarded as common practice within NDAs are to a certain extent based upon practice which has developed at The Place as a result of responding to the needs of artists. When Bob Cohan talked about replicating the programme of the YMWA of New York when Robin Howard first bought The Place, I think what he said was that it was an open house and then they found they were putting on a lot of rubbish, so they closed it down and concentrated on their own work. So instead of putting on a lot of other people's rubbish, they put on a lot of their own rubbish and that was a problem. When I got there twelve years ago I thought it would be a good idea to open it up again and so various practices were put into process in order to do that and one of them was called Resolution. A hundred people can present their work in this season and out of that developed various initiatives in order to help the choreographic development of those people who applied to be in Resolution. People who have applied to be in Resolution are Wayne McGregor, Mark Murphy - there is a big list. It is a point where many people started, and I think there is a great responsibility if you are presenting work at that point in people's careers to look after those that you believe are a talent. We do that in a number of ways. The most obvious way I think is simply to provide the opportunity and to provide an audience to give feedback. There is formal feedback offered through a scheme called Talkback, whereby an administrator and a more mature artist offer feedback to the choreographer if they wish it one week after the event. That is to me very important, because what happens in the bar in the interval after somebody has just done a show on no money, and put their heart and soul into it, is that all their friends say it's great. It's very important one week later, with the effervescence of the event dying slightly, to have two people come along and give a much more stable impression of what happened that evening.

Out of Resolution we have identified people who we have invited to be Associate Artists. Emily Burns is one of those who was offered the position of Associate Artist and in Emily's time all you got was a desk - now you get a bit of administration as well. There are five Associate Artists. We also have a Choreographer in Residence who is kind of head boy or girl of the Associate Artists and likely to be there for a bit longer. The current one is Charles Linehan, the next is Carol Brown, previous ones have included Aletta Collins and Victoria Marks. Also out of Resolution we identify those people to whom we are able to offer small commissions. It is certainly the case that having a bit of money at that stage of one's career, which perhaps hasn't come from the Regional Arts Board yet, is very important in the development of somebody's choreographic process. It allows them to hire a studio, maybe to pay travel expenses for the dancers or even give the dancers a little bit of money, and so the relationship between a dancer and a choreographer is fundamentally changed. No longer is it somebody doing it for you for free because you were at college with them and you have to provide interesting things for them to do. There is a contract between the choreographer and the dancer, and the choreographer can ask that dancer to do things perhaps they don't want to do and that is absolutely crucial. Finally, for some of those people who appear in Resolution, we are able to offer studio space when the Contemporary Dance School is not using it over Christmas.

So there is a pattern of things there which as I say have become relatively common practice in the development of choreography, which all result from the bringing together of an audience in a three hundred seat theatre to watch dance performances. This year we made a further advance I think in the way in which we are able to help people make dance by providing an alternative to our Choreodrome device. Choreodrome is a nine week period over the summer where the eight studios of The Place, its Theatre and everything in it is made available to upwards of thirty artists. It's called Choreodrome because 'drome' means 'a big place' where things come together like an aerodrome, and 'choreo' because that's for movement. The important thing about Choreodrome is that firstly the goals of each individual piece of research and development are identified by the artist and elaborated and judged in interview - that's how we make a selection - and secondly, that the work has no performance outcome, it is research and development. So the work which happens in our studios over the summer for which anybody can make an application, is directed by the artists themselves. That's a very important principle which is codified in our practice at The Place by the phrase 'we are led by the artist we choose'. We thought this year that perhaps there should be a counterbalance in terms of choreographic development, and so we invited Victoria Marks, who was formerly a teacher of choreography at London Contemporary School, and in her own right a important choreographer and film maker, to run a workshop over ten days entitled The Hot House. Three choreographers were selected through application to take part in that process. I don't know what the process was, but I did see the results and I think what I saw was everything that was made during the course of those ten days from those three choreographers. It was quite astonishing in the way in which there was a release of individual creativity and yet a clear singularity of purpose in the way in which both the choreographers and the dancers were approaching the tasks that they had been given. I think the balance between the self-directed activity of Choreodrome which is a huge opportunity, and the direct opportunities offered within Hot House are right in terms of that kind of provision.

When I first started developing a programme at The Place, I recollect that for three years my name appeared on DV8 Physical Theatre programmes as Producer. I had no formal role in fact and I think I only raised eight hundred pounds for the company before anyone else did - maybe it was only four hundred actually. I had no training as a dancer, but I nevertheless found a role for myself which was to talk to Lloyd outside the studio. Lloyd Newson was dancing then, and it was when he stopped dancing that basically my role fell away. But during that period I got enormous insights into the choreographic process, and I guess Lloyd got some help as well otherwise he wouldn't have gone on discussing at the end of each day what he had been doing in the studio. I think that's an important role in terms of what NDAs can offer the choreographic process, making a personal and enduring relationship with an artist whom you choose over a period of time until such time as its right to let it go. It's that personal choice and that personal interest and commitment to an artist, not just in the studio if you've had the dance training, but also outside the studio in terms of engaging in debate with an artist who might need an outside eye. It is also about going around and saying 'hey, you should look at this, this work's good,' which I had to do for three years before anybody took any notice. I think in the end, that's what we all do but we hide behind all of these things because we have to provide opportunities for many, and the fact is we're providing particular opportunities for a few. We have to own up to that and we can't justify those choices. It's just what we like and if it's wrong then we have got to be sacked.

Points raised in discussion:

- Although the Arts Council may automatically assume that it is the largest and most important partner, the NDAs are jointly funded by a wide variety of activities and bodies.

- Accountability is a problem because of the number of joint funders, but final choices have to be made by the Directors of the NDAs.

- The problem of accountability to both the regional and the national funding bodies was raised. These bodies have different criteria involving different levels of outreach which can be in conflict.

- Hothousing choreographers by providing them with everything they need to make dance (including food) is a very positive experience for them.

- It is important not to forget the different levels of artistry. The community level style of artistry must not be pushed aside in the pursuit of professional artistry.

- One of the questions which always arises for National Dance Agencies is what right do they have to make artistic choices. However, there are not enough resources and money to be shared out for everyone, so it is necessary to make choices as to where and on whom it will be spent.

- The NDAs are still relatively new and are under great and very public pressure to be seen to perform.

Session 4

The Creative Voice: Reflections on the Independent Dance Review Consultation

Key words:

choreography	training	creativity
importance of the artist	creative process	funding

Gill Clarke and Rachel Gibson discuss some of the issues which emerged through their consultancy work on Independent Dance for the Arts Council of England, focusing particularly on those aspects of the review which effect the development of choreography in the UK: research, training, creativity, working conditions, the need for dialogue and the importance of the artist. The session was chaired by Sue Hoyle.

Sue Hoyle

As you can imagine, when a report is written and published, that's not the end of the dialogue. Rachel and Gill continue to reflect on the issues, and today we begin by explaining the process of the Independent Dance Review and talking through some of the issues that came out of their research. They would also like to talk about relevant issues that came up yesterday and how that has informed their thinking.

Rachel Gibson

We were commissioned at the very end of '97 by the Arts Council to carry out a review of the Independent Dance sector. We carried out our research between January and March of this year and tried to consult as widely as possible. What this entailed was a kind of road show around the country where we undertook at least one consultative meeting in each of the Regional Arts Board regions. We also did a series of consultations in London which included open sessions before performances where people could come and talk to us informally, and we participated in a range of existing meetings such as the Management Liaison Group meeting and the Thursday Group meetings. During the process as a whole we had inputs from about 600 people through Britain, responses, and the meetings and long telephone conversations with people, so it was as wide a consultation as we could possibly make it. We spent the month of April trying to collate, coordinate, reflect on and write up the findings.

Gill Clarke:

Other ideas that influenced our thinking came from discussions with artists and funders from other art forms and from other countries.

Rachel Gibson:

During our reflections we looked back on the report that Graham Devlin produced 10 years ago *(Stepping Forward: some suggestions for the development of dance in England during the 1990s)* about dance. There he stated that dance was primarily a form of theatre and predicted that in 10 years it would be difficult to see it as something distinct and different, that it would become part of the greater understanding of theatre. However, in terms of the creative process, in terms of the way in which the work is made, it is not true. There is something very distinct and unique in the way that dance is made, and it doesn't conform very happily to the theatre model in which we traditionally fund and tour and view it.

Gill Clarke:

In some senses much theatre has become more like dance, particularly in the use of devised work. Two years ago the Music Department at the Arts Council did a consultation process, recognising that some of the communal creative processes currently utilised in Dance were also relevant to Music, and to the way in which it might be funded.

Sue Hoyle:

Reflecting back on the presentations by Bob Cohan, the Keynote speaker, and Janet Smith, Kate Flatt and Rosemary Butcher in Session 1, how did they effect your thinking?

Gill Clarke:

I found it was so inspiring to have four wonderful artists setting the tone yesterday. Their talks made clear a way forward for dance; what we need to set up are, simply, conditions which enable dance artists to be able to have more freedom within their creative process without the restrictions imposed by the funding process. Some wonderful phrases were used in yesterday's sessions - 'charting the unknown', 'being able to get into the heat and excitement of the moment without fear', 'to be playful with choice', and although fostering such activity might not be structurally or systematically easy, maybe it should be an aim.

Rachel Gibson:

Many dance artists that we spoke to during the research for the Independent Dance Review felt that the ongoing nature of their creative process had to be constrained or compromised in order to comply with the inflexible structures of funding and touring commitments.

Gill Clarke:

A feeling of isolation and fragmentation was apparent from many of those we spoke to throughout the country. Dance is the most human art form and we need to support and trust the people involved in it, yet for some periods of their professional lives, those now respected artists who spoke yesterday - Robert Cohan, Janet Smith, Kate Flatt and Rosemary Butcher have all felt rejected. Was that necessary? Can we have a broader vision that will avoid this in the future? I became increasingly aware during the research for the Independent Dance Review of how so many artists felt that their creativity was limited by the stranglehold of structures. Yet these artists are not complacent, they continue working despite little or no funding, and their drive and passion to make work is so clear. Perhaps we need to look to the past in order to move forward? Artists such as Robert Cohan were given the opportunity, trust and support to be able to experiment with creative ideas rather than be pressurised to create a 'finished product.' I recently acted as a mentor on a project with three young choreographers, and it was a totally unpressurised situation, without the preconceived notion that they had to make a finished choreography. The choreographers were able to experiment with ideas and had the time to watch movement and discover, for the first time, what really interested them about it as a medium. Perhaps more opportunities which allow young choreographers to spend time in the studio with dancers would be a good investment in the development of dance artists?

Sue Hoyle:

I have just read an interesting report on a task force in the USA on the development of dance audiences and the two slogans in that were 'care' and 'curiosity'. It defines care as to do with valuing people at all stages in their development, and curiosity as what has just been mentioned, the drive, energy, almost anxiety, eagerness to try things. But the other factor is about giving people a chance and opportunities to play, and in the course of your research you must have thought a lot about the raw materials that are needed to enable people to play and to try things out. I wondered, Rachel, in your research, what you thought about in terms of raw materials to provide this chance?

Rachel Gibson:

Quite simply, the raw materials are space and time and people, and yet we have such difficulty because we are so constrained by the money, strategies and structures that provide those raw materials. In a sense the things that should be simple become infinitely complex to deliver to the people that need them at the right moment. One of the ongoing frustrations is, why, if it is so simple (a) have we not got there yet, and (b) can we not see clearly the way that we should be able to get there? Structures and systems need to become more flexible. We need to find ways to cater for individual needs rather than trying to feed everybody into the same mould.

Gill Clarke:

Certainly the importance of the individual has become increasingly more apparent. It can be very easy to overlook the individual journey each artist makes during the creative process. Each dance is a unique reflection of the artist's own experiences, approaches, history and expression, but unfortunately the systems that are in place at present are not good at recognising individuals. It all results in artists feeling the need to conform.

Sue Hoyle:

Do you have any further reflections on how we can support the development of the creative artist?

Rachel Gibson:

To be able to work alongside or even just observe established choreographers can be a fantastic learning ground for students or young artists. Not enough people have the chance to do this, so perhaps bursaries need to be more widely available to fund that kind of opportunity.

In watching the performance last night, partly because it was small numbers of people, solos and duets, and also because in some cases choreographers were performing their own work, it brought home to me yet again the importance of the individual. The quality that makes them individual, the uniqueness of each piece and each expression is so important. And yet because it's transient, because we only ever see it when we are sitting in a theatre watching a performance, it's very easy to overlook (a) the importance of it, and (b) the individual journey each artist has had to take to get to that point. Hearing Janet, Kate and Rosemarie talk about their very individual approaches to teaching choreography, it is evident that their power as teachers comes from their own individual experiences as artists and their own very different approaches, and histories and forms of expression. Unfortunately, systems are not good at recognising individuals, and I think we need to shift the culture in order to respond to that more fully.

Gill Clarke:

I think there is a certain unstated pressure now to make the decision to choreograph very early, rather than follow your curiosity and find where it might take you. Of course, the process can be very different for different people. Hearing Bob mention his training with different choreographers, and with one choreographer over a period of time made me feel that not enough people have that chance these days. Janet (Smith) spoke about that learning in the real world and we could use that model more, we could let students or people on bursaries, go and be the fly on the wall, find the individual they really want to learn from. I think there is a real training ground out there that is a structure that already exists.

David Massingham (from the floor):

I don't think young people try to be choreographers, they try to be companies! They come straight from College, and see the way the funding system is presented to them... I think that is so damaging, they are not going to the studio, they are going to the computer.

Jane Scott Barrett (from the floor):

As one who graduated in 1985, in the middle of the independent dance explosion, we found ourselves in an area of innovation. There was a recognition of the temptation, almost a collusion among the dancers and funders, to identify themselves as innovators. Artists defined themselves against the agenda of the funding; as a dancer, I spent all my time innovating for my friends!

Sue Hoyle:

It seems that there is a need to develop more flexible systems to allow individuals the kind of support that will allow creativity to flourish.

Gill Clarke:

Flexibility could be facilitated through bursaries and stipends. For example, choreographers might want to be supported at one time for an extended period of experimentation, and at another for production. Again, fluidity is the important message; there are too many glass ceilings at the moment, and it would be much more creative to allow movement up, down and across structures and boundaries. I also think that the onus to change can also rest with the artist. If artists change their activity then support systems will change as well.

Rachel Gibson:

There is an issue of judgement here. The Independent Dance Review has been read by some as suggesting that we should be supporting everybody all the time, regardless of the quality of what they do. This is not what we were saying. Because of the sector's heavy dependence on the funding system, judgements about quality have become equated with success in raising funds from the public arts funding system. We need to unpick this and to strive both for rigour in assessing the work that we make and the way that we view it, and clarity in the decision-making processes that effect the sector. These two things are inter-related but they are not the same, but they have become damagingly confused.

Gill Clarke:

Another issue is about the current role of dancers. The creative contribution that dancers make to the choreographic process is generally greater than it was in the past, and we need to support dancers as creative artists rather than just as technical dancers. We also have to help artists be less dependent, and one of the ways in which we can do this is by developing different attitudes during training.

Stuart Hopps (from the floor):

We should also consider the opportunities available to emerging choreographers through film, television and theatre. A more flexible attitude towards gaining experience and moving from one context to another can be a real learning curve. Last night's performances all demonstrated directorial skills as well as choreographic skills. We tend to make an early decision between the serious or commercial sector in dance which is unprecedented in theatre or music. Perhaps we need to stop pigeonholing in the UK, but open the doors and provide ourselves with flexible choices. For instance, we don't have to give up being an artist because we take up management jobs...

Gill Clarke:

The profession has tended to be too reliant on funders as the catalyst and dancer/choreographer as fixer, an unhealthy hierarchy. We tend to value promoting directing individuals, and not facilitating, enabling ones. My wish list would be for funding flexibility, a recognition of dancers' needs, fresh ways of supporting individual working processes, and new ways of providing seeding money.

Rachel Gibson:

We must also remain aware of the need to support our mature dance artists in this country, rather than placing them in a position where they feel constantly pressured to create new works. Focus should be placed on continuity of funding for well-established artists as well as on supporting emerging artists.

Gill Clarke:

I would like to finish with a favourite and, I feel, relevant quote from Morton Feldman – 'If you settle for a system, you cannot go further than this system allows. So don't talk to me about systems, don't talk to me about aesthetics, it all has to do with nerve'.

Points raised in discussion:

- Current funding policies were generally considered to have a negative effect on creative development.

- Artists felt that they have to place more time and emphasis on administrative tasks rather than on the development of choreography.

- Need to develop more flexible systems that whilst satisfying beaurocracy still allow creativity to flourish.

- Concern was expressed that funding often fails to support well-established choreographers. Focus should be placed on the continuity of funding as well as on supporting emerging artists.

- The role of artist-in-residence within Higher Education institutions was considered a very important factor in the development of emerging creative artists.

- It was suggested that perhaps artists are too reliant on Arts Council funding. Perhaps other areas of financial support could be sought in education, community, administration and the commercial sector.

Session 5

Your Brain is a Muscle: Flex It!

Keywords:

| language | communication, | Neuro-Linguistic Programme |
| choreographers | audience | |

This forum introduced participants to the dance training work initiated and developed by the Manchester based arts development and training organisation, Kaizen Arts. By concentrating on the centrality of language to convey how the individual thinks and moves through the world and how we communicate with each other, this seminar workshop invited participants to explore the idea that if language expresses our thoughts and desires then how is this to be translated into creative action? The speakers were Rivca Rubin and Steve Purcell.

This is the first section of a longer workshop presented as part of The Green House Effect Conference. The workshop concluded with Rivca Rubin taking audience members present at the workshop through a practical exercise exploring the notion of perceptual positions. This exercise can enable an individual to gain valuable experiential information about any situation from 'visiting' and reviewing and potentially modifying one's responses to that situation to improving it from three different positions: Self - Other - Observer. It was an exercise that was undertaken by the participants on The Changing Room programme.

Steve Purcell

Hello, my name is Steve Purcell. I'm a lecturer in performance at the University of Derby in the School of Art and Design. I graduated from Dartington Hall in 1980 with a background in theatre and dance making. I also work as a co-director at Kaizen, which is an arts organisation based in Manchester but we work in different locations throughout Europe. I'm working with professional artists, principally dance makers and choreographers to date, but there are projects on line to work with film makers and with theatre artist devisers. So the model that we are going to talk about this morning is not just a model for training dance makers. We hope it will be a model that will apply to working with other artists creating in different forms.

Rivca Rubin

My name is Rivca Rubin and I'm also a co-director of Kaizen, which I set up with Steve just over a year ago. At the moment I'm a Research Fellow in the Department of Contemporary Arts at the Manchester Metropolitan University. Previously, which might be a more familiar reference for many people here, I was the Artistic Director of Physical State International which ran for about eight years, setting up a variety of summer schools, live art projects, choreographic developments and workshops from about 1987 until 1994. I have provided training opportunities through workshops outside the educational establishment on generally postgraduate levels since about 1981.

Steve Purcell

What we hope to do in this session is to give you an outline of a training programme we ran earlier in the year as a pilot project, to describe how it came into being and to receive some feedback from you in response to it. *The Changing Room* was a residential choreographic project which involved the choreographer and teacher Victoria Marks, myself and Peter McNab, a professional trainer in personal development employing Neuro-Linguistic Programming techniques, or NLP for short. The project had three distinct yet inter-related areas of concern. The first was to develop strategies to facilitate choreographic artists to understand through practical experience the ways they are currently working as communicators in the world, and how they choose to communicate from the specific position of choreographer, with the possibility of offering additional ways of enhancing their communication skills. The second was to experience and develop specific new choreographic methodologies, and finally to investigate and consider how the 'languages' of choreography are manipulated and offered as acts of communication.

Rivca Rubin

Prior to this course, Physical State International had organised a number of training projects which were anything between one day and six weeks in length for a number of years. We had worked with people from this country who were operating in choreography and the performance of dance as well as live art, theatre and performance making. We generally worked with people who we felt were good pedagogues, as well as being good artists, so as much as possible we looked to see them in action and look at their teaching abilities, not just at what they could do on stage in performance. Part of the drive for PSI was to introduce artists to this country who were touring and teaching elsewhere, or whom we thought had something interesting to offer.

After a number of years of hearing responses from participants and teachers, not through formal research but during workshops, and specifically in various conferences and debates, and also by observing some discomfort with the current training situation at that time, we began to question our work. Were what we were providing in the form that we were providing it, and the methodologies being applied in the different courses, the most appropriate for dance development for professionals in the mid to late nineties in the UK? Now we couldn't answer that question because we didn't have any specific information to do that with, just a sense of a growing inadequacy of plentiful but ad hoc workshop training opportunities. So we decided that in the absence of that we would stop and take a step out, and gather information from a variety of very different sources in order to begin to deal with the training issue.

I think one of the important factors was that it felt to people that a lot of little laboratory situations or workshops were not enough to develop the whole person. It may be enough to gain a new skill, or at least to begin to gain a new skill and then maybe take the decision to go onto another training school if that was possible. But it certainly didn't stretch people's maps of the world to become 'larger' as artists rather than just becoming more skilled as technicians; it didn't challenge people to learn about learning. In hindsight this is what we noticed. So we stopped and I did what I felt would be the most appropriate, and went to study in two different areas. I did an MSc in Applied Behavioural Sciences which meant I could read philosophy, psychology and sociology and at least get involved with reading, thinking and learning about creativity and learning about learning, and I also trained in Neuro Linguistic Programming. It was not my intention to do this in order to bring it back into the arts context. But when I started doing this work or when I got more experience of it, I thought maybe this is one stepping stone, maybe this is one possibility, one route that will actually help us to develop both ourselves as individuals and the systems that we are part of.

Steve Purcell.

I was actually on the Board of Directors at PSI at the time so I watched from the position of participant observer. I didn't do any of the PSI courses as such but was aware that many of the participants coming onto the courses didn't seem ready to do the Summer School with Nigel Charnock or to spend a week with Russell Maliphant. Many participants enrolled on the courses I think out of a genuine interest to work with these artists, to find out something about the working methods of those artists. But there was also a lot of 'CV stuffing' going on and if I can say I've worked with 'X', then I might get employed with this or that company or get money from the Arts Council to do this project. Rivca and I just became more and more interested in what the specifics for the training of a professional dance artist might be, and where and how might it begin.

So the work that we became involved with wasn't specifically focused on specific body disciplines. We are not replacing anything that exists in the world in terms of dance training, but we see clearly that the work we are involved with runs parallel or has a relationship to the teaching of current and emerging body disciplines. Our focus is very much on the quality of the delivery and the materials, so people like Victoria Marks or Simone Forti who we have both worked with mainly in France are good examples of individuals in whose dance praxis we are very interested. We wanted to explore the possibilities of structuring a training programme that firstly dealt with the issue of how we learn about learning, and secondly to recognise that this, for us, implied that we dealt with 'the person in the world' first, and the 'person as artist' second. In practice of course, these positions have the potential to be constantly shifting in focus.

Rivca Rubin

Yes, and I would also like to add for clarification one very key point - we don't tell people what to do and we don't at the moment engage in any training about what it is they need, but we engage in how to do something well. So how to develop a particular aspect of the self, how to access the imagination and develop a strategy by becoming aware of that particular strategy's strength for that particular individual. Also how to develop communication with other people. So it's not 'Be like this!' or 'Be more productive!' or 'Communicate' but rather 'How do I do that?' 'How did I do that?' and how does each person do/achieve 'that' differently? The notion of working with difference productively is of key concern to us because it implicitly demands flexibility of thought and action.

Steve Purcell

I would like to add just one more thing to that, and then we will describe *The Changing Room* as a model. What feels like the most radical potential in the training programmes that we are creating, is the notion that we are not training the choreographer or the dancer or the video artist, we are actually working with the person. Part of the debate that we initiate is the whole difficulty of what happens when you say 'I am a choreographer' or 'I am a dancer'. By stating that singular position, albeit as an affirmative and creative position, it automatically excludes "I' or 'Me' from adopting other multiple positions. So if you are 'this person' or 'this kind of maker', you're not B, C, D, E, F or G kind of person or maker. Identity politics from the seventies onwards has struggled with the problematic of making a single statement saying 'I am this'. The dancers and the choreographers were principally on the training programme starting with 'I want to be a better choreographer or dancer at the end of it', and we say, we think you will be but let's start by exploring and exposing some notions of the self.

Some of you will have heard Janet Smith yesterday saying that there was a really important moment for her when her life and her work as a choreographer took on a very meaningful relationship. She didn't stop being Janet Smith when she went into the studio, but things about her life and how she was living actually became impacted together. There was no way you could disentangle those two moments. We feel that many artists at the beginning of their training are not ready or not able to make that close fusion of identities in the plural that is really necessary for good and interesting art to emerge. So the notion of working on the self and how you operate, the quality of your perceptions about yourself and others is also key. The American philosopher Wyatt Woodsmall argues that the most productive way to survive into the 21st Century will be through the development of the quality of our perceptions (plural) of that world. There is something about training people's perceptual positions or abilities to understand 'me' as subject in relation to 'it' as object or other subject out there. Information is doubling every twenty months, the latest statistics suggest, so there is a lot of potential information to transpose into material for an artist. But what you choose and how you choose is really central, and what we do is initiate that process and the debates around that. So there is a practical investment in an intellectual/philosophical 'liasing' in the studio space.

Rivca Rubin

I would like to pick up on the word 'talent' that was mentioned yesterday in one of the sessions. Although I've not really specifically used or looked into the word 'talent', there was a quotation that Robert Cohen accredited to Martha Graham, that we all have our moments of genius. I think the second half of the statement was about knowing when to use it. It reminded me of the question 'how do some people do certain things really well?' It is not necessarily something that is particularly God given or in the genes or something. We can investigate how certain individuals/groups have these moments of 'genius', and if they can produce it and have it once, then there is held in this belief that it can also happen again. So there exists the possibility to scrutinise, recall or re-create and access our moments of 'genius' if we know how they come about in the first place.

If a *parent* is aware and notices something that is going on and can consciously nurture it, surely we must be able to add strategies, techniques, ideas for ourselves? If we actually begin to put ourselves, let's call it, in the position of agent, so we are able to make changes to our life, we are able to change our perceptions of what is going on. If I can have one view of the world and you have a different one then I must be able to change my view because essentially we are made of the same basic materials, although culturally we are inscribed differently. So I would throw open this whole thing about 'genius' and 'talent'. I would also say that there is always a key concern or focus on notions of intention, and it is very important to ask the question what do we really want? I think if we really want something, then we can get it and we can do something about it. It might be a lot of work - and it is not just about hard work on the outside; at the level of the body, it is internal hard work - at the level of internal resources and connectedness to match the two.

The Changing Room has only happened once. I think it is still in its embryonic stage. It happened with the help of Dance NorthWest. Twenty-five choreographers attended and they were together for four days and four nights and we worked with them from nine in the morning to about ten at night, which was far too long! In the morning we introduced or let's say exposed people or even threw people into training exercises drawn from NLP. So we brought in a very good trainer, Peter McNab, who had worked with us before, and who had also worked with choreographers before. This work was practically based, but taught in a seminar-styled space. Then in the afternoon we let them go into the studio because that's where a lot of the choreographers really wanted to be.

They were scheduled to go into the dance studio and work with Victoria Marks and she really brought what she wanted to do, as we had asked her to do the thing that she was most interested in at the moment. However, Victoria didn't have any previous exposure to the NLP work, which I think again in hindsight is not ideal. Under the circumstances what she provided, and I knew it would be extremely appropriate, worked very well with the work from Peter's session. Then in the evening we took the choreographers out of the studio and asked them to talk and debate with each other, and I think you should explain that because you led the evening sessions, Steve.

Steve Purcell

I ran all the evening sessions which were fairly complex heavy theoretical discussions introducing the question - how might choreography and choreographers create meaning? We looked at examples of choreographic work on video. I introduced in the most accessible way possible, selected elements from semiotics and some main frame ideas about post-modernity, post-structuralism from the point of view of raising questions about the body, meaning, authorship and role of the spectator in the performance event. The material in part is difficult but really essential and worth struggling with. I wanted to encourage the dance makers to be aware that there were other disciplines, other vocabularies, other issues in circulation, other than the immediacy of their own bodies and the body disciplines they wished to choreograph with. I wanted them to understand that opening up or re-contextualising their current concerns by placing them in a very different light might allow them to move their performance praxis on. As Honi Haber remarks in her book *Beyond Postmodern Politics* (1994):

> "creation is only possible given the tools of our vocabulary, and since vocabularies are always already social, cultural and historical products, they always speak for an interested viewpoint - though we may not always be conscious of this interested dimension."

I'm interested in each individual addressing the questions of what's pushing them through the world to make this piece at this moment in time, and also how is that piece going to be received and 'read' by the audience. So, there were the NLP skills training - learning about learning in the morning; working with Victoria in the studio - learning about choreography; and then working with me in a seminar/analysis format in the afternoon - learning about how choreographic work as a cultural activity carries meaning.

Rivca Rubin

We hoped that what people would find out in the morning about how to communicate, how to develop various strategies, be that communicational, creative strategies, would be applied in the other sessions. That certainly did take place so there was a big shift that could be seen in people. Individuals actually consciously began dealing with the way they had always done things in the past, and seeing, hearing, thinking and feeling the possibilities of doing things in a different way. By different in this context I mean that if it's a better way for you, your dancers or your audience than how you've operated before then it is useful to do it differently. There is no need to change something if it is already actually working well and achieving your aim or outcome.

Steve Purcell

For me a principle observation from *The Changing Room* was that the main drive in the dance studio seemed to be that the making process was principally for the benefit of the dancers themselves. The question of 'how do you as the creator have some control over how your material/experiences might be received or read in a performance?' seemed to have very little significance. It might be that in a choreographic exploration, you begin to address that much later in the process. But I did not get any hint in quite extensive discussion that that would be a concern anywhere in the process, but rather it was up to the audience to do with the material whatever the audience wanted! This is an extreme example of course, but one I've encountered in a wide range of teaching contexts.

Rivca Rubin

We noticed was that there was a perceived lack of ability to deal with the audience's position. What some of the participants found in the work that we did with them in a morning NLP sessions, meant that for the first time they could take the position of the 'other' i.e. choreographer to dancer, choreographer to audience position, and make certain reflections about their work that they had not done before. So there was a great amount of discovery in that sense.

Another possibility is to take the audience out of the equation. So if some choreographers or dance makers or other makers within the arts actually want to explore and make discoveries that aren't really anything to do with an audience, then maybe we should just take the audience out of the equation and have a few invited people. I think there are different ways of dealing with this question.

Steve Purcell

I would put it into a broader context, by saying that there seems to be an increased anxiety amongst artists working in very different fields, generated perhaps by the difficulties encountered when trying to answer the questions of who we are, how we are, why we are, and where are we heading? Perhaps even approaching the questions generates the anxiety. We struggle to answer those difficult and complex questions, which were being answered much more clearly at the beginning of this century because the Modernist artists on the whole believed these were valuable questions that had a potential answer. It was just a question of finding it. Perhaps our dilemma at the other end of the century is that the question/answer part is no longer so clear cut and easy or even so valid.

Rivca Rubin

I would say that none of this work is new. It is not that suddenly something new has come along and here we have our answer. It's a means, and it is only as good as the user. It is what you do with it, so I think we have to be very, very careful of any systems or any kind of new tools and learning. They are not the answer to problems we had, but they might be a tool or process that we haven't engaged with before which gives us an ability, an opportunity to deal with things differently. This is based on pre-positions - if you always do what you always did, you will always get what you always got. If it does not work - do something else! What we tend to do in the society that I experience, is that if something doesn't work we do more of the same. At this conference, everybody, all of us here are involved in dance. I don't see any scientists, philosophers, mathematicians or physicians. Now that is fine in itself, but I think that our tendencies are more likely to be looking in rather than outside our current spheres of knowledge and expertise. Another part of the work we are doing is to try and provide forums in which people from different disciplines, thinkers from different disciplines, philosophers from different disciplines can begin to talk together, and for us to develop or progress because we are part of these other systems of thought. We are not separate from these other systems but we might feel isolated from them for a whole variety of reasons.

Let me explain a little about Neuro-Linguistic Programming. I start with a quote that I think relates to some of these questions. 'Twenty-five hundred years ago it might have been said that man understood himself as well as any other part of his world, today he is the thing that he understands least'. Sorry for the gendered statement! I think that for me is still pretty accurate. Neuro-Linguistic Programming is about understanding how our programming works or how we come to 'be'. If anything, it allows us to de-programme certain things that are not useful, whether that's behaviours or emotional responses that we find are hindering our development, or particular obstacles that we seem to recreate from some point when we were young or older, and we turn them into individuated responses. So that's what programming means in this context. I will just read from my definition here: 'Neuro-Linguistic Programming comes from the three areas it brings together: the mind and how we think, not what we think but how we think; how we use language and how we are affected by it, both our internal language as we are speaking to ourselves, as we are telling ourselves, as we are preparing our dialogues for when we are about to speak, but of course also the languages that we hear and interpret and the external language that we use. So how are we affected by language and how do we use it and how does each person use language somewhat differently and choose different words to say the same thing and what may be pre-supposed in that for it to be true for me? The third one is what we do, i.e. our sequence of actions and thinking patterns to achieve our goals. What strategies do we use and continue to use to achieve our goals?

So this is what it's really about. NLP provides the 'how to' to gain results. It is more than just a collection of techniques and exercises. It has its roots in the early 1970's so it has been around for quite some time and probably parallel to some of the developments in the New Dance area. Richard Bandler, a student of psychology began working with a man called John Grinder at the university where he was a Professor and they modelled three people who were very good at what they were doing. One of them was Gestalt Therapist Fritz Perls, the second was Virginia Sateer, the prime force of family therapy who moved things from dealing with the individual to dealing with the whole system. The third one was Milton Erickson, a world famous hypnotherapist who used language and storytelling with great results. So Bandler and Grinder collected this information in order to model the created patterns of excellence in the work of the three individuals studied. They set up some processes and tools that were teachable and started with 8 or 10 processes and over the last 15 years, that grew to become a 20-day training programme. It is now still being developed. In the arts we haven't heard much about it until recently. It was brought into the areas of therapy, so therapists started learning those tools because they found they could help people make changes that were effective.

One area in which NLP is used is in business. Of course business will pick up what works and use it quite quickly, and has very different objectives. It is one thing to work efficiently and effectively and to make money but also to be able to do that creatively, because in business they have to be pretty creative to do it in such a way that they can make their new products have an incredible speedy effect. In the sports world a number of Olympic team coaches have been using NLP for years to help people who are already very good at something to be just that bit faster or clearer; to develop their own particular strategy, to be free of any interference that might happen in that moment of concentration or for that game or bout. In education it has been used more and more, but mainly through individuals so teachers who know this work will begin to feel quite differently about the kids in the classroom. They actually understand that the kids might use very different languages, some much more visual, others more auditory, and by reflecting that in their language the teachers don't change the content of what they say but how they say it. I understand after speaking to people yesterday that there are individual artists around the world who have some NLP training as part of their background and are now using it. I know Phelim McDermott, the theatre practitioner who has had enormous success with his junk opera *Shock Headed Peter*, is using it in his work with his actors in this country, and so are a number of other people. But it is still very unknown to us in the dance world.

At the end of *The Changing Room*, one of the main things that I noticed was that the performers and the choreographers seemed much more capable of articulating what they wanted and also how they chose to work. There were levels of clarity in the rehearsal space that had previously not really been there and which meant that there was less fumbling about for statements, descriptions, objectives. Preparation before you went into the studio to meet your dancers was something that we worked a lot on in terms of setting outcomes - what do you want the outcome for this 4 day rehearsal period to be? Rather than just to turn up and go in and hope that something would happen, but to be more intent on achieving specific outcomes. So there was a lot more clarity. An interesting point from one of the dancers was that in the making process when the work seemed to get stuck or it wasn't energised in the way that was productive for the choreographer or for the dancers, there was a tendency for the dancer to say 'why don't we do this' and to throw more ideas in, and perhaps that is not the most useful thing for the choreographer to do at that moment in time. We found that the dancers were much clearer about what position - self, other or observer - to go into in order to help the choreographer to achieve what s/he wanted to achieve. I think that we are very good at doing that most of the time but to be able to be really clear about doing it all the time when you choose to do so was a really important learning curve for the dancers and the choreographers. *(The remainder of the session consisted of the workshop.)*

Session 6
Promoting Choreographers:
What does the Promoter bring to the Table?

Key Words:

promote   producer   presenter   artist   audience

This session was chaired by Clare Stewart, Touring Officer at the Arts Council; the speakers were John Ashford, The Place Theatre Director, London; Ron McAllister, Artistic Director of the Lawrence Batley Theatre in Huddersfield; and Nigel Hinds, Artistic Producer of Sadler's Wells in London. The session gave an opportunity to look at some of the individual skills and organisational structures that lead to an individuals' ability in this field, as each of them have each developed a particular interest and focus in developing artistic opportunities for choreographers. The session also looked at some of the issues to do with the nature of this relationship for choreographers and promoters, the scale and influence of the regional versus London focus, and also the commercial imperatives that a promoter may well bring to this relationship.

Nigel Hinds

Not surprisingly, for those of you who've read the little biographies, I'm going to draw on my experiences at both the Phoenix Arts Centre in Leicester, a 270 seat performing arts centre presenting live and film work, and at Sadlers Wells in London. We three representatives are not from producing venues; we are presenting venues, so we are not concerned with making our own work. We are concerned absolutely, in my words, to engineer meetings between artists and audiences; the artists and audiences do not live or work in our buildings, but come in and use the buildings as meeting places. That means that all the time I am looking both ways at artists and audiences as the essence of my work. What has driven me to work in theatre in the first place is the excitement I get when I sit in an auditorium and experience something new, which I find exciting, delightful and revealing. My motivation is the energy that I get from achieving a 'full house', sharing the excitement and the buzz that comes from a successful meeting that I have helped bring about.

Perhaps part of the reason that I am quite a good person to do this kind of work is that I have no specialist training. I am entirely uneducated in the performing arts. I have a law degree, though the only aspect of my training used on a daily basis is to do with contracts. The starting point of each of the jobs I did at the Phoenix and Sadlers Wells was developing policy and shaping, clarifying, focusing and prioritizing a role for the venue. To give a small example, when I arrived at Sadlers Wells Theatre it had already started a process of reinventing and refocusing itself. Its aims were formally expressed by the organisation and its supporters as the national middle-scale dance house, the national middle-scale dance agency, Britain's leading contemporary lyric theatre and a model for the large scale national dance house. Now we aim, in twenty years' time or so, to be Britain's leading theatre for the promotion of adventure in dance, opera and musical theatre. This objective enabled us to get £36m from the National Lottery so it had some use.

My next role is to gain and apply knowledge of the two areas which I am interested in, artists and audiences. I have to develop an understanding of the audiences I work for and of the artists who might be interested in working with me. I need an overview of the field and a knowledge of my options; the more options I know about and am in touch with, the better I will be able to do my job. The Phoenix is a smaller theatre in a much smaller catchment area and it was easier to gain an understanding there of the range of potential communities and levels of interest in the contemporary arts. We had a very specific brief from the City Council, who were (and still are) the Phoenix's chief funders, that our audiences should reflect the demographic profile of the people of Leicester. It is fairly easy to tease that out and to see what the ethnic and interest divides are, to do a matrix and to think of ways of working with audiences. Having done those two things, the next part of my job as a manager is to find ways of helping the people I work with to release their energy, to get excited about what they're doing, and to work to a high standard to support other people in their work.

Another required skill is the ability to fundraise from public bodies who are dedicated to supporting the area of work, which is where my experience lies, and increasingly at Sadler's Wells, particularly in the new theatre, fundraising from sponsors and private sources and donors. This is not a skill I profess to have, but it is one clearly crucial to Sadler's Wells' future existence. I also say 'no' when I have to; it is sometimes necessary to say 'actually we should stop doing this for a bit' or 'that is a wrong idea'. When you have had a relationship with an artist for three years, it is the most difficult thing to say no to the fourth year. Perhaps the work is no longer good enough or the work has moved away from the audience, or the audience needs a break... I believe that part of my role as a programmer is to create surprise, and the idea that an audience could say 'gosh it's the last two weeks in November it must be so-and-so' is an anathema. Clearly I need fixed points in my calendar for the year, but equally I need to be a circus ringmaster and bring on the changes and surprises. Similarly I like designs which inspire in me the thought 'what an interesting space to play in', and then I look for shows which play with the design in ways which I never could have imagined. To be controversial, I do think that a good programmer should have something in the programme once a year for everybody to hate … it's essential that there be at least one in that programme! My final point, which is evident in everything I have been saying, is that I see my role as serving other people and their creativity. Not being a producer or a creative artist myself, I do not have to take care of my own creativity and I can be entirely focused on the creativity of others. I try to keep a balance between the organization's own producing and resident artists, and other artists who are brought in. Other skills required include marketing, general coordination, administration and how to appeal to audiences. We also need to know about technical presentation in our spaces and in any other spaces we present work in; we need to look after sponsors and funders, making certain that people who are supporting the work feel happy and rewarded.

As regards the relationship with artists and companies, beyond the skills that my organization professes to have, the most important benefit that I can offer is space. The space for an event is a very important part of the experience, and artists and audiences respond to it. I refer too to the way the relationship between stage and auditorium works visually and orally, supporting the work and adding something positive to the experience. This is an issue entirely divorced from money. In fact, the only time I actually had a marriage of space and money was when I was at the Phoenix for the first four years, when we were very well funded by most people's standards. The Phoenix is a wonderful space for performance; in terms of plays the acoustics are good, but it also has very good visual contact and a good physical contact. Equally I am very excited about the potential of the new Sadler's Wells. The second thing I can offer artists is acceptable working conditions, and the third thing is obviously an audience for their work. If I fail to do that, then I am either doing my job badly, trying to sell it to the wrong audience or I am trying to bring the wrong artist in front of those audiences. The one thing that I don't very often offer artists is any chance of making money!

What I look for from artists first of all, is work which I can advocate, and the second thing is an understanding from them of what I am trying to achieve in the space, venue or festival, and a willingness to buy into that an understanding in partnership. In Leicester, for example, I was an effective advocate for Kathak dance. At Sadler's Wells, however, I am a much more effective advocate for Flamenco. It's partly what audiences are potentially there for, and which directions I can take them in. I don't need to advocate work where audiences are already attending, but I do need to be able to argue for and promote work that is new. We try to do this in partnership with audience representatives, community groups and so on. Finally, in relation to the presentational relationship I have talked about, it is very important for me that our venues in some way support creativity. At the most basic level that might mean giving an extra two or three days for shows to be in production before opening. There is an additional excitement which audiences and staffs respond to in terms of that first act of creation. If we are able to raise money then we can also get into co-commissioning work, commissioning work, co-producing work, and hosting residencies. Those areas of work are essential in one respect, but they are also the first things to go as soon as the money isn't available, and that's a continual problem. The other area of creativity to look at is the interface between the professional and non-professional; work where community groups, professional artists, or dance in schools can work alongside each other, so that there is a creative interchange around performances rather than simply the core activity of sitting in a theatre or playing on a stage.

Ron McAllister

I am going to talk from the perspective of managing more far-flung venues away from London, because of the problems that distance creates in terms of hosting residencies or performances from dance companies. Perhaps I can start with just a few practical examples. The first was a relationship I developed when I was running the Maltings Art Centre in Berwick-upon-Tweed, which is what you might call a rural community, a town of about 10-12,000 population. The nearest cities are Edinburgh 65 miles to the north and Newcastle to the south, which again is about 65 miles. Consequently, the amount of dance teaching and the level that is reached there is very modest indeed, and there isn't really the teaching infrastructure for a very strong, regular community programme of dance. One of the things I tried to set up very early on in the history of that particular organisation was a dance residency, and I looked for a company that could provide a very broad base so that we could have strong teaching skills in a variety of styles as well as an involvement in community productions and the creation of their own work, side by side. So we turned to the David Massingham Dance company because he had dancers there that could teach everything from Tai Chi to Tap, and not many companies can offer that!

We found that there was a tremendous response to all the classes. We designed a programme of work which involved David Massingham Dance moving up from London to Berwick for about four or five months at a time over a period of two years. This was a huge act of faith between the venue and the company, because the dancers had to give up all their London teaching, to surrender leases on flats or find people to sublet while they started more or less a new life in our very small community. There were obvious teething troubles to do with, for example, the studio accommodation and heating that dancers need. There were all sorts of practical things like that, but once the series of classes had been established, - and that meant that the dancers were working every night, teaching classes as well as creating their own work through the day, a fantastic bond with that community began to develop. At the first tap dance session we had open enrolment and 200 people turned up, and the hall that we had we could just about manage a mass tap dance session, and even for Tai Chi we were getting 30 or 40 people on a regular basis. Having those regular classes meant that there was bedrock of interest, then in addition to that the company were creating their own work and there was an audience developing for that work. There was a genuine curiosity; people were talking in the pubs about this company. It does help when the company like visiting a variety of different pubs, because dancers tend to walk in a different way, they look a bit different, people begin to wonder who they are.

The next stage was to involve the company en masse in a production of *West Side Story*. Now that really was the break through! The whole company was involved at a choreographic level in some way, they shared the workload, and as it is a very extended dance piece anyway there was a lot of work to be covered. They broke into groups, all the dancers could be involved in the process and David Massingham directed the show. I musically directed it and our own technical team built the set and lit it, and we brought Marcel Batik, a sculptor up from London to work on making the whole venue into a New York underground. The Maltings is actually three levels down under the ground and so it really was like going down into a New York subway station and all the staff were involved in spraying the graffiti on the walls, it was a really a totally involving experience. The demand for tickets for that production was so great that people were on the radio offering twice the face value to get a ticket, and by now the David Massingham Dance members had become local celebrities. After *West Side Story* their next production had almost a fan following; audiences were cheering and stamping, and that doesn't happen often in Berwick, believe me.

So that was one model of a dance residency. Of course, it was enormously expensive and required huge investment from the Arts Council, the regional Northern Arts Board, and Northumberland County Council as a three-way partnership. Even then there was an enormous amount of pressure, because grants were slow in coming through and David was very stressed by the tardiness and the pressure of administration problems. However, as a venue we had the opportunity to involve the community out there with *West Side Story*, the opportunity to run classes and the opportunity for the company to have a very focussed time to work on their own projects.

My second (and more recent) example of a dance residency is at the Lawrence Batley Theatre in Huddersfield, with The Featherstonehaughs. They followed the typical model of coming for a few days, doing pre-production work and then launching the *Egon Shiele* tour, but there was a fantastic amount of excitement and it was to do with the personalities involved. Venues change very quickly and personalities move on, but at this time we have a very committed marketing person who loves dance and I am an enthusiast, and this commitment does transmit itself through the organization. When Lea Anderson came up, she would sit in the bar chatting to bar and house staff, because that's the kind of personality she is. After the first performance everybody went into the bar to talk to the company and say how much they had enjoyed it, how they felt about it, including the stewards, and that's why the company felt supported. Really it was that feeling that the project meant something to everybody in the building. We had also been quite successful in building a reasonable audience; over the two performances we had 250 per performance which was a significant improvement for us in contemporary dance.

The third thing I'd like to mention are the young choreographer's platforms initiated by Yorkshire Dance. These involve promising young emerging choreographers from the region being given space to work on a piece at YDC, doing a public performance and inviting promoters or people from the marketing side to look at the work. We meet perhaps two or three days later and talk about what kind of relationship could be built between their work and audiences. It is an interesting model and something I am keen to see develop. Venues can offer much in terms of talking through that process at a very early stage in a choreographer's career, and I think the National Dance Agencies have a major role to play in helping build those relationships.

One last practical example is an exhibition we hosted early on in the life of the Lawrence Batley Theatre, with a local artist called Duncan Mosley. I felt that there was something about the work that could stimulate some kind of dramatic or dance response. I asked a very promising young dance student at our local technical college to think about putting a small company together to respond to the work, which he did. That was very interesting because it was very much to do with the space that it was in, the artwork that he'd seen and his personal responses to those elements. And just through giving a slightly unusual opportunity like that, venues perhaps can instigate-something to help progress the career of a choreographer. The choreographer in question, Sean King, has showcased at The Place recently and he is beginning to establish quite a reputation for himself. Venues can bring time and enthusiasm, and venues can initiate creativity, as well as offering technical and marketing experience.

Many venues struggle to find the fee for one night of dance; if you quote £1,250 for one night of dance it seems like an insurmountable obstacle because we know what a struggle it is to get that back in the box office. If we tackle educational initiatives we may have to reduce the ticket prices-to £2, so actually just covering that gap is difficult. But if a company can work in partnership with a venue, there are ways of exploring joint funding through regional arts boards, and through dance agencies which can give support, not necessarily with cash but in kind, with mailing lists, giving time and effort to creating workshop opportunities. Local enthusiasts may put some money into dance as well. We have a small group of three or four people, who may put as much as £500 of their own money into a performance, and that can make the difference between something happening and not happening at my scale.

The last contribution that venues can make is in finding a dynamic in the relationship with an audience, in finding a relevance within the community. That can be through marketing, education and long term audience development. It's important to built that relationship with the venue first though, whether you are a company or a choreographer, and to do that I think it's important to know a little bit about the venue, what its facilities are, its track record, and the personalities involved. So many companies still phone me up to say, "We are touring between January and March with this project". They don't know what they are going to be doing after that project and I can't see how that will fit with my work or how they are developing as a company. I think when you are making contact with venues as a choreographer, you might demonstrate the relevance of your work to that venue, not simply discuss your immediate short-term project. So we need to hear ideas for long term strategies. For example, RJC got in touch with me recently about a millennium project which involved a huge set for roller blading, and I could immediately see that young people will find that combination of speed, the thrill of danger, quite an intoxicating blend. I can see that we can get new audiences in for that kind of project. We can also nourish emerging choreographers in partnership with dance agencies and regional arts boards, but we need to be aware that venue personnel can change very quickly. As each venue manager or director moves on, a whole range of experience moves with that person, and that's the last thing I'd like to say - that this is all about people and making those connections.

John Ashford

Now what are we talking about, is it promoting or presenting, or programming or producing or commissioning or … because there are all these confusing words, aren't there? We're supposed to be talking about promoting, but we've heard the words presenting, programming, producing, co-producing, commissioning and residencies, and these all represent a range of engagement of the people who are stuck in the middle between the artist and the public as so eloquently described by Nigel. That's what I think we do as well, but I have another form of words, which is to represent the views of the artist to the public and to represent the views of the public to the artist. You are never thanked for this, incidentally. If the thing is a success then it's because the art was terrific and it's because of the strength of the choreography, and if it's a failure it's because it was badly presented, badly promoted, so you are never actually praised for this role which is really quite invisible. To add to what has been said, I just want to tease out one or two, sort of scales, from this to that, just to get a slightly wider picture as to how we fit into the arts generally. One piece of information missing from my biography in the programme, is that after I was a critic, my first job in the theatre was to be a very active manager of the Theatre Upstairs at the Royal Court at the time when we were producing 12 plays a year from scratch. The writer in residence was Sam Shepherd, and one of the works we produced was *The Rocky Horror Show* so you can imagine the diversity of work. At that time in the 1970s, new plays were really only presented at the Theatre Upstairs at the Royal Court. The National at that point hadn't started doing new work, and the RSC just did Shakespeare. So there was enormous focus of new work happening at the Royal Court, and I do have experience of working in a producing theatre.

I then went to work at the ICA where I thought I could raise enough funds to produce from scratch two plays or experimental shows a year. During the time I worked there we were a presenting venue of other people's work and we also produced work ourselves. Finally, on entering the dance world, I found that nobody really produces dance. Probably the only producer you have listened to at this conference is Robert Cohan, who is a brilliant producer of dance. Over 20 years of triple bills in the London Contemporary Dance Theatre, and he had the capability to make them work. But not many of us have a chance to present dance; what happens in producing dance is that it is primarily produced by the artist.

Now I have to repeat something I have said before because I think it is still a truth and still interesting to think about in this context. If you look at the act of producing the performing arts, it seems to me to be absolutely clear that the greater the strength of the producer, the more popular and better attended is the product. The producer rules; he commissions the scripts, he decides who will direct, he actually decides who the star will be, and if the director doesn't like it, he finds another director. At the end of that whole process the producer is a party to those dreadful Hollywood try-out sessions where they show it to the audience and the audience don't like the ending so they make another whole ending, so that also is the responsibility of the producer. What do you get? The art form of the 20th century and the most popular performing artform in the world! That is at one end of the scale. In television and theatre the producer's power gradually gets whittled down, and at the other end are art forms like poetry, where the poet writes the stuff on his or her own word processor, photocopies it, staples it together and sends out 500 copies to friends. Maybe it goes on a library shelf, maybe in a hundred years time that brilliance will be recognised, maybe not … Where is dance on that scale? If there is a problem about the resonance of the work being produced now in dance in terms of attracting vibrant and extensive audiences, then I think we have to think about the way it is produced and about those examples I have just mentioned.

In the scale of confusing words that I mentioned earlier, 'presenter' is probably at one end of the scale; if the company turns up you make sure the technician is in the theatre, they complain that the posters haven't been put up and you go home at 6 o'clock because audience figures are low and you're embarrassed to be there! That's the very worst end of presenting, like writing and publishing your own poetry; at the other end of that scale is producing the work from the beginning where the producer takes the responsibility for all of those creative aspects which are arranged for the production. When it comes to working in dance, as I have done for 12 years, my job has been principally that of a presenter because the nature of funding for dance is such that the Arts Council provides funds directly to artists to create their work. This is clearly absolutely crazy; it doesn't really happen in theatre, where a few companies are directly funded and they are independent, but the great mass of theatre work in this country is produced venues like the West Yorkshire Playhouse. Here Jude Kelly decides that there's going to be a show called *Lively Rabbits* or something, and she decides that Ian McKellan is going to be in the company this year and she is generally instrumental in making decisions about what is produced and presented in this theatre. That seems to me to be a model that produces avery exciting theatre system in this country and is absolutely no doubt that regional playhouses like this, the absolute lifeblood of the West End. If anyone has read the Winden Report, which talks about the contribution to the economy, artistically and financially, of the West End theatre then you will see to what extent this very stage we are sitting in is important to that great creativity. Surely we've got something wrong then with dance? Why is it that all the funding goes directly to the artist, without that intermediary role of the producer, which seems fundamental to the creation of other art forms? I don't quite understand it, but that's coming from a perspective of having worked in theatre.

So when I started to run a dance theatre, my aim was to gradually strengthen the reputation of the theatre and the work that it presents, to the point where we began to meddle in those difficult areas of producing. We've heard in the example of *West Side Story* that it's absolutely crucial to the establishment of the regional venue within its community to bring about that kind of excitement. It's a hard thing to do because nobody wants you to do it. The artists don't want you do it because they would rather have the money, and make the decision to work with the boyfriend who happens to have written some music rather than a proper composer... And the Arts Council doesn't want you to do it, because it's much more interesting as an Arts Council Officer to sit on a committee and give away money to artists ... So it's a constant battle to get funds which can be used creatively to make venues work properly and make dance companies connect more securely with the public. It shouldn't be a huge battle but it is. However, when you begin to tread along a line of transforming a presenting venue into a performing one you do come across several difficulties.

Nigel mentioned one, and it's one that we all need to consider. It is the kind of relationship that exists between the work which you present and the work which is associated more closely with you through working with artists in commissioning or producing their work. Once you have made a choice to work with an artist and offer some kind of residency, association or money to do something in your theatre, then you are committed to it. It may be that the resulting work is not what you would have chosen as a presenter, but nevertheless your commitment to that artist has to remain secure for the period contracted. If that is an interesting subject for discussion then we should tease it out a bit.

I don't want to give a lot of examples but I will just refer briefly what we do at The Place. What seemed to me to be a good thing there was to help the audience understand the kind of things they were likely to see on the stage by embracing various annually repeated seasons of work. So twelve years ago we started 'Spring Loaded' which is an annual season of British work roughly 11 weeks long. Soon after that we initiated a season for younger, shorter works, now called 'Resolution', a season for International work called 'The Turning World', and a specialist season in the autumn for work from the Asian Pacific called 'Reorient'. We discovered that the annual repetition of these seasons helped to get publicity, to get coverage in the press, and give structure for a very fluid dance scene so that there were clear areas that you could aim for or suggest that your work be appropriate for. Resolution, Spring Loaded, the Turning World, Reorient - they all have some kind of sense of what you might expect I hope. These umbrellas seem to be very useful devices by which the audience have a certain kind of expectation which develops as you repeat that device each year, but at the same time I hope that it is capable of surprise. One other thing I want to say about producing, which we are beginning, at last, with the help of Lottery Funding. The word 'co-production' is a very strange one; I think what it means is co-financing. Often you hear the term European co-productions, and you get a list of famous venues in Europe who have actually put money into the work and are committed to presenting it, but that's actually really all they've done. I think a work can only be produced by one venue, and then there is the relationship between the producer, choreographer and the various elements of the work that is particular to that venue. These responsibilities are quite different from those that might exist in other sites where the work is actually not made. If the venue is going to produce a work, either from the point of view of having the company in residence for a week and putting the production on the stage, or from the perspective of making all the choices as to who the choreographer, the composer, and the dancers will be, then that has to be a personal relationship with the Artistic Director or alternative. This form of promotion is a difficult one, which binds people or divides them, but it is the stuff of the making of the theatre. In the end, dance is a theatre art, and I think that when we are discussing these issues we can take some lessons from theatre as to how we should proceed in the future.

Points raised in discussion:

- Promoters/producers are seldom asked for their artistic opinion, yet they have built up a knowledge based on experience of how audiences react to work.

- Venue producers try to produce a programme which will encourage audiences in their areas to come and see dance. It is not necessarily work about which they are personally fanatical, but work which can be promoted to the audiences for whom the venue is working.

- The difference between producing dance and theatre is that in theatre one begins with a script, which can be pre-cast. Dance is made in a studio, and on the first day of rehearsal often nobody knows what the dance is going to become. Dance needs a longer period of gestation than theatre, and young talents may need longer still.

- The producer is not an unnecessary level of beaurocracy, but an income-generating engine. The work of the producer may be able to result in a longer gestation period being financially available.

- Venue producers have a responsibility to their resident companies/artists. John Ashford stated that the policy at The Place Theatre is that they are led by the artist they choose to serve.

- When artists approach venue producers it helps if they have done a little research on the venue. Producers will generally meet artists to discuss projects if they feel that it is appropriate to their venue.

- The promoters' table is generally reached by invitation for artists. Young artists can begin to be noticed by applying to festivals such at The Place's Resolution! Promoters and producers come to the festivals to see new work, and word spreads if there is good material there.

- In some countries it is recognised that groups of venue producers/presenters choose to promote artists by arranging tours to all their venues. Such circuits exist informally in Britain, but it was suggested that the models in other countries are not always as effective as they might sound.

Session 7
Vocational Training: Current Practice and Future Needs

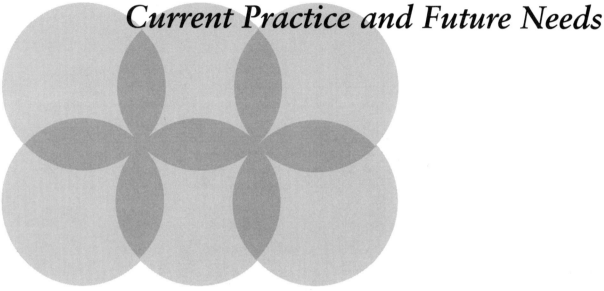

Keywords:

vocation   student   skills   training   professional   teachers

The demands made on professional dancers today can cover a very broad spectrum; they range from requirement for specific techniques for the work of particular choreographers, to the ability to improvise, complete tasks and share the process of collaboration in the studio. What effect are current demands having on those who offer vocational training? How do vocational schools ensure that their students engage in preparation for the current job market? What skills and capabilities will professional dancers require in the next decade?

The speakers in this session were Thea Barnes, Ann Stannard, Veronica Lewis and Antonia Franceschi. The session was chaired by Jo Butterworth.

Thea Barnes

Each school has an outcome of 'the dance practitioner' that will emerge at the end of their course. This practitioner will have a range of skills that are shaped by the experience lived in that school and which is limited by their individual potential. The outcome of a course of study is also shaped by the delivery of the course and the environment in which the course occurs. The classroom is a special place where varied teaching and learning strategies determine final outcomes; courses are not about teachers or the talents of students but a combination of attitudes, ideologies and expectations about student and teacher. The courses are also about the school's view of its dance context and the value it places on technical practice.

What I have observed in my experience of various courses on both sides of the Atlantic are ideologies and perceptions of what is needed or desired in the context of dance practice. They are doubled edged and most at times are both positive and negative:

· Emphasis on performance on stage without reliable and knowledgeable estimation of student potential

· Narrow approaches to movement skill and dance making, despite the obvious diversity that exists in the present context of dance practice

· Reading about dance and not writing about dance which is needed not just for dance research but for the survival of any dance practitioner in view of the existing avenues of communication for administration, governmental, commercial and private sector support

· Reading and writing over rigorous and determined pursuit to experience on a visceral, corporeal level, an assortment of movement vocabularies that include various idiosyncratic and codified dance making practices

· Neglect or not seeming to allow the time to insist that students see and observe as many varied expressions of dance as possible

The profile I require from even my youngest dancers is a range of skills that are integrated and not just about physical prowess. I need dancers who are accomplished in several technical styles; ballet and Graham being at the top of list for dexterity and dynamics; jazz and vernacular forms for earthiness; dancers who are physically fit aerobically with a better than average upper torso development. This does not mean I change dancers, it means I encourage dancers to add to their potential, not deny what they were born with or where they came from. So what I want is flexibility, openness. I want professionals who are aware of the issues that impact on their art practice culturally, economically, socially, and politically. I want professionals who use survival tactics that are tempered with entrepreneurial skills and opportunism but are still respectable and sensitive. I want professionals who are self-disciplined, and most importantly self-motivated. I want professionals who will question because they themselves have done research past their own personal experiences and are active participants in dance making because they start from a point of thirst, desire, and adoration of dance, of movement, in all its manifestations.

Depending on the choices made in teaching and learning strategies in schools that offer dance and its many subject areas, because dance is more than just performing on stage, teaching dance or choreographing dance, the profile I have just described could be and most times is sabotaged. This is one of the main reasons for the development of the Phoenix apprenticeship and for encouraging an environment for dancers in the company to explore choreography of their own choice.

I know too well about economics and the availability of expertise for a school. I suggest networking, shared resources, and elimination of parochial attitudes that close lines of communication between schools and isolate dance practitioners and keep them from ascertaining what is really happening in the field. Something like the Greenhouse Effect and what it is seeking to accomplish this weekend.

In the field is where the school outcome will be tested. There is nothing worse than a student who has achieved the outcome but cannot survive in the context. What is the use if the dance field is flooded with a particular kind of outcome and there are no places in companies, no value or relevancy to communities? Why have an outcome that does little more than pacify a talent or a specialised singularity but does not encourage future insightful and articulate advocates in dance art for the future?

It seems impossible for any one school to encourage the most all around technical skill, open mindedness, contextually astute professional that I believe is currently required for dance. The current context of dance practice is not just one high art form, elitist clique of expression, one dance scene or one or two idling vernacular forms. I firmly believe in encouraging students to know and recognise those forms of dance making that got dance to where it is today. Where would we be without Louis Horst and his modern dance forms, just like where would we be without Louis XIV, Laban, Judson Church, British New Dance, Tudor, Katherine Dunham, Peter Badejo? I think we need to be careful when we say as teachers that we don't want to use the old stuff and let's be innovative and take leads from other art practices, other intelligences, to make dance. Being lucky enough to have arrived at a point of informed choice does not allow being jaded or condoning ignorance of the past 90 years of the dance practice continuum. We do need to look at creativity and imagination but I would choose to do the investigation corporeally, through the body; describe creativity and imagination by detailing lived experience. Perhaps we measure product when maybe we need to look at process and our singular ideas about form.

Dr. Pearl Primus has left me with two lines of advice that I have cherished and will share with you: 'Discipline is Freedom', (this is a Martha Graham advice also) and 'there is movement in everything.'

So to summarise, I would like to see dance training that encourages tomorrow's choreographers, dance makers, dance practitioners by encouraging

- Exposure: being aware that no one has ever seen it all

- Observation skills: to know movement is as big as the cosmos and as small as my figures coming together, to acknowledge difference, and recognise singularity for what it is and the context we live in as a plurality with lots of difference

- Responsibility: to the frontiers that have already been crossed and the will to cross today's and tomorrow's frontiers; also respecting responsibility to self, identity, and community especially when it comes to a person expressing their own particular lived experience

- Synthesis: to love to investigate, explore, rediscover the known and then go on to do your own thing.

Ann Stannard

My contribution is in three parts:

1. my perspective on vocational training

2. vocational training specifically in Central School of Ballet

3. a few of my thoughts for the future

Vocational training has a broad context within which dance artists are trained and educated for a wide variety of roles in dance. This variety is a strength. It can also be a weakness because there is, too often, a lack of clarity about what it is and where the training will lead.

No discussion on current vocational training can fail to refer to the plight of training organisations and schools. A report on the matter, several years ago confirmed that 'the current funding system of support is unable to provide an adequate system of support to meet the training needs of young people wishing to pursue careers in dance and drama'.

The disappearance of student grants has meant for Central School that as a percentage of income local authority funding has shrunk from 70% in 1991 to 25% in 1998. The effects of the difficulties of holding on and trying to see students through is that many people feel crushed and dispirited.

Schools survive through fund-raising and through parents who already put in far more money than government is asking of university students. We have survived these last 2 years also through the lifeline of the Interim Funding Scheme, the IFS, which is lottery money and DfEE money, distributed through the Arts Council and fought for so hard by the Council for Dance Education and Training. There are many irritating restrictions on it but we are very grateful and it does help us hold on.

We do know that the problem is now on the government's agenda and that very soon announcements will be made by ministers about a long term solution - so there is some hope.

This solution is not likely to be a bag of goodies but hopefully it will contain an opportunity for schools to make *their* case for *their* training.

I hope that everyone will have the courage to define criteria that are clear, accurate and unambiguous. Last time we had a go at Accreditation, this was lacking. For example - 'fit for purpose' seems to me a useless phrase unless there is consensus on the 'purpose' and on the interpretation of 'fit'.

We have all watched British business these past few years turn itself around - it stopped believing in its own propaganda that British was necessarily best. It took a good honest look at itself and at its competitors - and it turned itself around, raised standards and is learning to be competitive in international markets.

I would like to see dance training take the same position - for the good of dancers - so that they can be more competitive in the world market.

How does one school, Central School, tackle training now?

We provide for those who wish to be highly skilled performers and who will commit to a somewhat intense course. Students come at age 16, sometimes 18, and study for 3 years.

What we do is determined by the belief that:-

· the vocational training and education we offer must prepare students for work as performers

· and for work that exists

· and that requires School to try to keep in constant contact with the profession where they hope to work

There are two main aims to the training:

1. The need for good dancers to have the physical and technical skills to enable them to respond to the range of movement required by Choreographers, Artistic Directors and Ballet Masters/Mistresses. To be professionally acceptable these skills must be competent and consistent.

2. Secondly, the need for young people to be educated, nurtured and developed intellectually and emotionally equally with their physical development, which is considerable.

In short, so that they can do and so that they have something from inside to do it with. We aim to help them develop to make a contribution to the profession, to life beyond dance to society and to be fulfilled personally.

The course that they study has nine components:

1 & 2.   the range of skills required by the profession in Classical Ballet and Contemporary Dance. Both forms are much more demanding than used to be the case. The former, from Bournonville, through the 19th century classics to neo-classical work and as quirky as you can get - it contains Pas De Deux, Character Dance and all the Repertoire. The latter was entirely Graham work, 20 years ago, and now it includes Cunningham, Limon, Horton and Release.

3.   Jazz - gives rhythm, co-ordination and speed

4.   Music - to develop musically expressive and sensitive dancers

5.   Voice   - singing and spoken
  - opens up the whole personality, develops confidence

6.   Choreography   - in this setting
  - we do not claim to graduate trained choreographers
  - this is a huge subject to put in perspective for young inexperienced people
  - it will be an intrinsic part of their lives as performers and so they develop knowledge and skills through making pieces
  - As with everything there is huge pressure on time, money and space. In the First Year their experience is through 'A' Level Dance which they complete in one year with in-house performances. Second Year is a collaboration with student designers and musicians and results on 6 or 7 ten minute pieces which are presented in public performances. Students who wish to continue in Third Year are given space to prepare a piece for the performing group and sometimes the piece goes into the programme.

7.	Academic Studies

At this age there are 'A' Levels. In an ideal world one might dream of a more relevant course of study - but they do make a valuable contribution to development and give university entrance. In-house academic work is completed by an in-depth written project.

8.	Performing

When the technical skills have been built and the academic/intellectual aspects of the course are complete, the focus can be on performing experience and finding a job. The final five months provide some 30 performance opportunities in venues which demand true professionalism. And with career advice added - the plan works - we meet our target of 80% of graduates in employment within 6 months of completion.

9.	Dancer's Health

The ninth and final component is crucial to everything else. We work with a Physiotherapist, Pilates Trainer, Nutritionist and Sports Psychologist. Students learn to look after themselves in this highly specialised profession. They need anatomy, prevention of and recovery from injury plus the psychological approach to recovery from injury, goal setting and personal achievement. Body Conditioning is important and Nutrition also, even though or because it is an emotive and sensitive area, needs attention.

We believe that this way the whole person is developed and as a result you have real people on stage - not automatons.

For The Future	**- I have three concerns**

- students
- teachers
- dance in general education

1.	With students, I confess I'm proud of what we do developing real people who are highly skilled who are helped into careers.

But when we look around internationally we see higher standards - these are usually produced by serious training over a longer period than 3 years - it is considered that it takes 6-8 years to absorb the work soundly.

I would like to see government willing to work with us to determine what is really good training and education and agree to fund that realistically. An informed Accreditation system with clearly defined criteria for good training would help.

Also to help students I would like to see closer co-operation with Artistic Directors. We work very closely with Northern Ballet Theatre. School and Company share the same Artistic Directorship of Christopher Gable. Students know what Christopher expects of his dancers. Their course contains the elements of drama, the development of emotional availability Christopher requires and so they are well prepared to fit into the Company.

Not everyone can go into NBT and it would be good for everyone if other Artistic Directors would make some time to share their needs with us.

2.	Secondly, the needs of teachers. Good teachers of dance at the highest levels are rare and precious. Good teachers deserve and need recognition and above all support. Where can you find that support in dance? Although a successful performing career is no guarantee that one has the ability to be a good teacher it is from this group that teachers of the highest calibre will emerge. So I plead for a good teacher training organisation to at least match what is available abroad - and within that teacher support and development. Only then shall we be able to get down to achieving more in less time because we will have addressed quality.

3.   Finally - for dance in general education.

I want to make a plea for children in state schools to experience more dance - more physically demanding dance opportunities alongside and relating to their academic work. Our education system, it is acknowledged, is failing many children. The time is right for radical ideas and proposals. The discipline, commitment and self-confidence built through dance can permeate the remainder of children's lives. Research in other countries shows that academics plus arts achieve more than academics alone. Howard Gardner has shown the importance and value of recognition of plural intelligences.

Leeds is a city developing itself in all directions. It has inner city problems; it has dance training and professional dance. With Northern Ballet Theatre we continually try to work together to make an impact reaching out into the community. We believe Leeds is the obvious place to be radical and lead the country in the development of young people's lives using dance as a catalyst-to develop achievement and meaning to life. It would also identify untapped raw energy and talent for the profession.

Veronica Lewis

I started ballet classes at the age of two and a half, and finally learned to plié at the age of twenty-two. It is not a matter of how many times you plié, but whether you do it properly, and I think back now of all those wasted pliés.

As teachers in vocational establishments, we need to ensure that the dancers of tomorrow are equipped with the right clothes from which to choose, in what we might call their wardrobe. I would like to make six points about vocational training in dance.

1. Dance teachers share a great responsibility to both dance itself and to the young dancers who come to them for training. Then, behind every student who arrives for training are their previous teachers, their inspirers, their parents, and to all these we bear responsibilities. Another awesome responsibility is to our teaching staff. Teaching has a poor image as a profession, and dance teaching suffers still more. We need to respect and nurture great teachers in the making. There is also a responsibility, as teachers, to the institutions which have given us the chance to be part of their development. My final responsibility is to the future, which is the basis of this conference. We are here to think about the best way of moving dance forward and ensuring that we aid dance and dancers of the future.

2. The media portrayal of dancers is always from a similar angle. They see us as all being badly done by, down trodden, having to take our clothes off to earn a living. The seedier side of dance is of great interest to them. In fact most of our dancers are not reduced to such a state to earn their keep.

Wayne Sleep was depicted as embittered and hurt by his colleagues, but still as a brilliant performer, by a TV programme on ballet training. This caused much discussion, showing dancers as psychologically damaged by our training, and we have only just survived through until Ann's calm, clear vision redeemed us.

The media perception of dance training is poor and does a disservice to us as dancers. Dance training has altered radically and, from my own personal experience and contact with others, it no longer has the old 'put up and shut up' image that it once had.

3. I do believe vocational training has changed, both because it needed to and because it had to. Instead of the 'put up and shut up' training, we now have students with huge bank loans, who expect every penny's worth of their £8,500 tuition fees. There must be some middle ground, in reality, where we should be training dancers in the long term. We need to strive to train thinking dancers, or perhaps to train dancers who are also thinkers. The profession has changed and we cannot afford to be complacent. We no longer just teach dancers to imitate.

4. The fourth element is a balance of training. The balance should be clear in each institution, and we should not be trying to duplicate each other. We need to each define our own purposes, and be clear about what we are aiming for. The balance must be continuously under review, to adapt with the times. What worked well in 1967 did not work in 1976 and certainly will not work in the future. The dancer's wardrobe needs to include technique, improvisation, composition, choreography, repertoire and an increasing amount of something called choreological studies. Also, crucial to the development of a well-educated dancer is the contextual work, including music, history, analysis and notation. We continue to strive to understand the inter-dependence of dance, the dance performer, the dance community development worker, the dance teacher and the whole purpose of dance.

5. Important underpinning elements include a safe, secure teaching/learning environment, which can help all students to achieve their best. It is important not to programme our dancers to fail. You do not have to undermine a student's confidence to ensure survival in the big, tough world. This has been a great shift in dance training, in which we need to celebrate even the slightest achievement in our classes. This nurturing of the balance between mind, body and spirit is essential to our training.

6. Training dancers is so exciting. Unlike training a pianist to play Beethoven, even with a new Millenium interpretation, dance training prepares the dancer to perform works which we do not even know about yet. To achieve this preparation, we must look at the frontiers which have already been crossed and think of the training behind the successful dancers of today. Then we must find a way of preparing the next Gill Clarke, Wayne McGregor, Rosie Lee. The balancing of training and training institutions must reflect this awareness of and adaptation for the future.

Antonia Franceschi

I am not necessarily involved in the vocational establishments at the moment, but I do have some observations. I have seen many of the dancers which these people have trained and/or worked with, and I have noticed most that they cannot believe how much concentration is involved in daily work. When I go and teach company class, with some exceptions, the dancers are almost in shock at how much work and focus is required in terms of daily technique or barre, in order to facilitate a career.

The most important element is to have a great teacher. If you have that, then you will reap the benefits for the rest of your life. It will train you to work with a choreographer, to audition, if you are just given the bare bones of how to approach a barre or a sequence of steps. You must work hard with your teacher, and appreciate it. The way you approach your classes is the way that you will work for the rest of your life. You can see in a class when someone is really focussed, and that also applies in audition.

When I began teaching in London I was attending open classes. There were a group of girls who wanted to get into a ballet company. Between the ages of 18 and 22 is the most critical time for ballet and contemporary dancers. If you are not in a company by the time you are 22 then your career in that area is over. These young dancers had just graduated and were on their own. They came into an open class, and worked to their limits. So I decided to help these young dancers. I was preparing myself to work with a choreographer, so I rented a studio to train myself and invited the girls to join me, so that I could help them at the same time.

To work with a choreographer, you must be functioning at your highest potential. If they ask you to do something, you must be able to try your hardest to do it. It is much harder to work with a choreographer on a new work than to learn repertoire because it is the great unknown. You have to be able to do contemporary dance and to move in many different ways. It is not possible to just be a ballet dancer anymore.

I have done every form of dance, and I was prepared because of my initial training. Well-trained people learn to find freedom as artists because they do not have to be concerned about their instrument, their body. People believe that to dance with the New York City Ballet, say, you have to have the right kind of body. In fact, it does not matter what shape the body is, but whether you can dance. The most important factor is having a good teacher.

How do you prepare dancers to go into the professional field? You must give them the tools early on, and provide them with encouragement. Repertoire is important, because if as a dancer you are learning a great piece then you will learn through your body. Your body will know what is good, because good choreography will improve you as a dancer. You will learn about choreography through the experience, through your senses.

Points raised in discussion:

· At dance schools which are connected to a company there is a great advantage in seeing the company rehearse and working with visiting teachers and choreographers. Schools which are not linked to professional companies need to try to get international choreographers and artistic directors to come and give classes to give those students an opportunity and an insight into the professional scene.

· One of the training levels which Britain is lacking is schools which cater for 11/12 year olds to 18 year olds. Other countries have such establishments, and young people often decide early on their direction in life in dance. Then they can work to achieve in their art form over several years, rather than trying to squeeze it all into three years professional training.

Session 8

Artists Programming Artists:
The Finnish Model

Keywords:

artists' programming committee
independence

performance space
choreographers

Ismo-Pekka Heikinheimo shares a project developed in Helsinki that involves dance artists in the choice of programming for dance performance spaces. The session was chaired by Aimé de Lignière.

Ismo-Pekka Heikinheimo

In the last ten years contemporary dance in Finland has gained tremendously in terms of more public, more makers, more dancers and other people who are involved in dance like designers, architects, and musicians. It has changed the whole Finnish arts scene, particularly in Helsinki. Helsinki is the capital of Finland and has about half a million inhabitants. The surrounding district numbers about two million. In the whole country there are only five million people. There are six dance companies in Finland that receive funding throughout the year from the government. There are many independent dance artists who get very little, if anything, in the way of funding for their work. In response to this situation, the Zodiak Centre for New Dance was created.

Five young Finnish dancers and choreographers founded Zodiak Presents Dance Productions as their joint dance arena more than 10 years ago in 1986. Since then Zodiak has worked actively as an umbrella organisation and dance association for freelance dancers. Zodiak has imprinted itself on the conscience of the Finnish dance field and dance audiences as a free association, performing original, ambitious and experimental dance, and whose productions, almost without exception, have represented the artistic peak of contemporary dance. Evidence of this includes a number of prizes: the Government Prize for Dancing 1993 and the Suomi Prize for Young Art in 1996. Since 1990 Zodiak has had its own performance, rehearsal and office spaces at the Cable Factory. The Cable Factory is a huge complex about 2 km out of town by the sea, housing hundreds and hundreds of artists working in all fields.

At the beginning of 1997, Zodiak took a new step forward by redefining its role and becoming a more extended forum for audiences, called the Zodiak Centre for New Dance. When fully developed the centre will be a unique performance, production and happening space offering the entire freelance field in Finland a joint, uniting forum for action. The Centre functions primarily at the Cable Factory where it received a 100 seat performance space, rehearsal space and office in the autumn of 97, but performances will also be produced for other spaces around the capital, and both Finnish and foreign performance visits will be arranged. There is a café in the premises where matinees, meetings with artists, and other events can be arranged. At the same time, the Centre for New Dance will organise visits by foreign productions, dance artists and teachers. At its full volume the Centre will be able to produce and host 20 to 25 different dance works and dance evenings a year, with 130 to150 performances. The Centre employs annually and on a production basis 130 to 150 dance artists and associated professionals.

The artistic policies and profile of Zodiak are set by an artistic Committee of 10 freelance choreographers and dancers, with the Centre's director. There are two people working in the theatre full time. One is the technical manager and the other is the director, who is the only person working in administration. The administration is kept very small and flexible in scale to allow sufficient funds for the production programme within the annual budget. The Centre receives its funding from central government and from the city of Helsinki. The group members at the Centre change all the time, but it has a structure which maintains the group ethos. We are attacking the heavy bureaucracy in the arts where people who are not artists themselves select work and dictate where the money goes. The Committee of artists meets about five times a year and there is a policy of totally free submission of work. Because the Committee members all are active choreographers and many of us also teach in the colleges and schools, we know where new people are coming from, who are the new dancers, new choreographers and we all see a lot of dance.

Proposals are received in the form of papers giving details not only of aesthetic concerns but also of practicalities, including details of dancers and other staff. In addition, some people choose to submit videos. The Committee considers the proposals in terms of our own space, which is quite small and has some specific problems although it is very intimate, and also in terms of other spaces in the city. We have all been working for so many years that we know all the other spaces and the programmers and directors of those spaces, and sometimes we suggest to them that they programme a particular performance. Our space is too small for large productions and so now we have done works with the National Gallery; with the Old Russian Opera house, Alexander's

Theatre; with Kiasma, the new contemporary arts museum designed by Stephen Holl, which opened in May; and with STOA, the East Helsinki Cultural Centre. So we can also direct choreographers into the other spaces and this has been working very well.

So we come to the next part, which is what do we give the people with the little bit of money we have? We can give them rehearsal space, which is about the same size as the Zodiac theatre itself and we can give them that space for quite a long time - two to three months even. It doesn't mean that they get the whole day but maybe around four hours a day. For new premieres which are coming here we try to give about a week or ten days in the space for the artists to make it exactly how they want it with the lights and sets. We would like the situation where people can make work without pressure, so that they have time to experiment, so we are also trying to enhance the quality of that way of working. We also assist them in the technical aspects e.g. sound, lighting. Our technical director is actually a lighting designer by profession and she sometimes designs the lighting for companies if they don't have any funding for their own lighting designer.

Our director, Raija Ojala, deals with the press and advertising, sees to the printing of leaflets, brochures and programmes so that the artists do not have to worry about this. Raija is the ex-head of Theatre Magazine so she has experience in this aspect. And this year is the first year that we can give all the artists, choreographers, dancers, designers (around 130 artists) one month's salary, which is quite amazing. In Finland there has been a study of people's earnings and dancers were the poorest group of all. Unfortunately we cannot give more than that, so if artists work with us longer they still only get one month's salary. It is tricky because most of the dancers are on unemployment benefit; they work for three months and they get paid for one month so they lose two months benefit. Then for outside productions, which we produce for just a couple of evenings, we only pay £70 per performer. If there are people coming from other countries then we help them to get funding from international bodies. If a British group was coming then we would contact The British Council in Helsinki to see if they could help us. But there is always the possibility that the group will only receive £70 per person. It is our work. We need to be able to afford to pay ourselves. This is not our hobby any more!

Aimé de Lignière
Do you change the Committee often, and do non-choreographers or artists from other fields also get the opportunity to be members?

Ismo-Pekka Heikinheimo
We have our artistic Committee which is made up of choreographers and the director, but we also, as an organisation, have on the Board two choreographers, a lighting designer, a museum director, an administrator and a producer, but we don't have people from other fields. The Board is only responsible for the money, and for help with developmental plans. The Committee makes only artistic decisions; we outline the programme.

Aimé de Lignière
Is there any possibility of finding sponsorship from businesses in Helsinki?

Ismo-Pekka Heikinheimo
In a small country like ours we don't get business sponsorship coming into dance. Private funds like the Finnish Cultural Fund has been very sympathetic towards us, but business is not interested.

Aimé de Lignière

How does the Committee come to a decision on the programme? What procedure do they use?

Ismo-Pekka Heikinheimo

Personally at the last Committee meeting I brought a list of my own criteria for myself. My idea was that we should cut down on the number of productions so that we could achieve better quality of work. I only selected 14 of them and then we had the meeting to discuss it. Everybody comes with their own selections and we see which ones are the same and which ones are not. We all come from such different backgrounds and we are interested in totally different things.

Aimé de Lignière

People from the directorial side of the arts tend to say to me that artists can't make the decisions because they are compromising the integrity of the art form.

Ismo-Pekka Heikinheimo

This was one of the big issues in the dance field in Helsinki when the whole idea of the Centre came up, but I think we have dispelled those doubts and fears in the last two years. I could easily do without Zodiak for my own choreographic work. I have opportunities elsewhere but I want to speak for dance in Finland and I'm active in that way. It's not easy and you get complaints of course. It's like any funding body. But at least we can show the Minister of Culture that we can do this big thing without a big administration and we can do it ourselves.

Aimé de Lignière

I think it dispels the myth that artists aren't good at being objective. Actually I think artists are incredibly objective and not subjective, and also that we have a built-in integrity and self-regulation that somehow directors don't believe we have, or aren't capable of administering ourselves. But then all the directors are doing, really, is administering for us in their own subjective manner. I'm a firm believer that the dance business in this country needs to harden itself in some way and one of the ways to do that is to put more artists into those sorts of positions.

Ismo-Pekka Heikinheimo

I would like to introduce Victoria to answer that question. She is a very good example because she was a dancer and now she is a director of a festival.

Victoria Marangopolou

I feel very strongly that artists have trained themselves to understand the administrative side of their work. It is important that they should be able to communicate with their administrators. The administrators also have to understand much more about the artistic muse. It is very important to me that both sides should meet somewhere. But I would like to ask one question. You say you have an artistic committee that decides about the programmes, and the supporting details such as the promotion. Who makes the decisions about how a performance is going to be promoted?

Ismo-Pekka Heikinheimo

Everybody gets the same opportunity. The choreographer or his designers will have a vision of how things should look for his production. Everyone has a certain amount of money allocated to him, so the promotion and production group can decide what they want to do with it. If someone is not particularly interested in publicity then they get the normal press releases and contact with critics for previews. They get their leaflets but they all have to decide for themselves what kind of leaflets they would like. The administration does exactly the same for every programme but then if one group is very active, of course, they can contact the TV and anything else they want to do.

Speaker from the floor

I'm involved in a model that is very similar to Zodiak here in Britain. It is called Chisenhale and it is fairly new. I'm on an artist's panel like you. But our system now is that artists apply to us for process rather than product for various reasons. Are you able to support an artist just for research or for process or are you tied to the box office and your funders in order to make products all the time?

Ismo-Pekka Heikinheimo

In the first two years we have not been able to do that although it is our hope to just enable processes and not to require end performances to get the ticket money. However we have just started and we have to show the government that this is what we want to do. In 1998 we had 156 performances, and 10,200 audience members. This is what the government requires. Then when this has happened for a couple of years I'm sure we can start with something more experimental in that way, so that we can provide space for process and not product. We had one person who worked on a series of performances of work-in-progress. She worked in the late evenings and mornings, and in the evening performance she showed what she had done and the audience could interact. But that is the only performance of this sort which we have had so far.

Aimé de Lignière

Who decides who will be on the artistic committee?

Ismo-Pekka Heikinheimo

I was invited to join the committee. The original five founders of Zodiak invited five more. Only one person has left since then, and we invited someone else to replace her. We agreed to work for a three-year period. Then in three years there will be new people and the annual meeting for the organisation will take proposals for new members. Then, to my knowledge, it will be the Board's decision.

Aimé de Lignière

The members are very different, because otherwise the situation could develop that only one part of the whole landscape of contemporary dance would be able to set up production in Zodiak. I think it is not easy to find the diversity.

Ismo-Pekka Heikinheimo

If there were only three people then this could be problematic, but there are ten of us so the number of people already guarantees something. If it happened that the committee became biased then I think the money would not be available anymore. It is regulated from many angles; the dance people look at us very carefully, and so do the government and the press.

Aimé de Lignière

One of the things which people say to me in Britain is that artists don't want to be responsible for other people's art or indeed don't want to be responsible for their own administration even. That's why we have the system we have here which, I think, is one of dependency. So can you comment on whether the Committee get fed up of having to make decisions about other people's art when they think they should be working on their own artistry? Do they give willingly of their time?

Ismo-Pekka Heikinheimo

Yes. We all prepare ourselves for meetings and read everything carefully so that we know what we are talking about. We are all choreographers, we all have to organise ourselves. We know how to use our time, we have all these skills, but we are not administrating anything. The administration person does it. She writes out the papers for us but we read them and we comment on them and make the decisions. But it is not only the papers. It is what we see, the people we meet.

Aimé de Lignière

Do you have a strong international policy?

Ismo-Pekka Heikinheimo

No, we haven't had, but as we prepare our Autumn programme, we can see that we have started to go international. We have a French group and a Danish group, and then we have the project that was held in Belgium this summer, the Choreo-co-ordination Project by ELIA Dance Section. We started an audience education project this Autumn as well. The artists have to meet the audience after one performance out of ten. Previous speakers here were talking about having people taking care of an audience. This way if the choreographer comes in contact with an audience, you can get feedback from the audience. Sometimes the feedback is very interesting. At the beginning of August there was a pig farmer who came to see all the performances at the Full Moon Dance Festival and he was the best of all at interpreting dance and intellectualising about it. It was quite amazing, so the artists really get a different kind of feedback on the way they work. This Autumn we are starting with someone who has worked for thirty years as a choreographer, and she is doing a little workshop for the audience on movement expression, a basic course so that they will understand something about movement.

Aimé de Lignière

I'm still pondering on this question about objectivity in the artists and artists being generous enough to want to talk about each other's work. I know that you have some experience of this country as well as Finland. This situation seems very generous and very wholesome; why do you think it is differentfrom programmes in the UK? Do you think it is because of the size of Helsinki, or is it a difference in attitude?

Ismo-Pekka Heikinheimo

I think the attitude has also changed in Helsinki. Previously everybody worked on his own but now people understand that if you talk together you have more ideas. The whole thing is based on organisation where people come together and actively exchange thoughts. With only one voice you are not heard easily. So we realised that the dance people have to join together to do something, and not just complain.

Aimé de Lignière

I think the whole issue of programming by committee, whether it is an artist committee or a committee of producers/programmers, is quite a difficult one. As you said you still have problems, you still get some criticism because eventually it is seen as a group of people who are either looking after their own work or selecting their friends or only choosing certain people. It is open to criticism. I just wonder whether inevitably it becomes more bureaucratic, because you have to have a committee that looks after the committee. You have to then start having very clear criteria and before you know it the central idea of artists selecting artists' work disappears and you've created another bureaucratic system. Also as it grows the artists involved, quite rightly, will say 'I can't keep giving my time and energy to this because I'm trying to make work.' Then eventually it comes round to saying that maybe what we should have is a director to feed all of our views and before you know it you've come full circle again. But I think what is interesting about Zodiak is the model. The idea of having a committee that only sits for 2 or 3 years and then you find new people, seems like a very good one because then you don't get stuck with the same institutionalised group.

Ismo-Pekka Heikinheimo

We have been criticised because our programme is very diverse and we don't look for themes or titles or whatever. But because there are so many people working in Finland who have no opportunities, we wanted to make sure first that they get a chance to show their work. I think now we are going towards the idea of having fewer performances per year. We can, however, show how successful our programming has been by ticket sales; in 1996 we sold 3,400 tickets in the season; and in 1997 when we opened the new theatre we sold 6,552 tickets. Now in 1998 we have sold 10,210 tickets so far... I don't care much about numbers for myself. The value of art is not counted in numbers and we would do this anyway if we didn't get a single penny, because it is our passion to do it. We don't care about the numbers but the numbers enable us to have the opportunities that we can take.

Points raised in discussion:

- Artists need time to learn about programming, in the same way as promoters do. They will not get it correct immediately.

- There should be more models of this and other kinds in place so that artists and promoters can see alternative methods of working and learn from them.

Session 9
Craft, Skill and Application: The higher education sector

Keywords:

choreography   higher education   assessment   development

Choreography is now taught in a large number of the degree courses offered by Universities and Colleges. What is the nature of what is being taught? How do the aims, course modules and required assessments of the HE sector effect what is taught and how it is taught? What are the anticipated applications and career structures, and how does this interface with more traditional methods of learning one's craft as a choreographer?

Participants in this session were Professor Christopher Bannerman from Middlesex University, Karen Greenhough from London Contemporary Dance School, Evelyn Jamieson from the Liverpool Institute for the Performing Arts (LIPA) and Valerie Preston-Dunlop from the Laban Centre. The chairperson was Stuart Hopps.

Stuart Hopps

I am a freelance choreographer working mainly in film, television, theatre and opera, but I have in the past taught in higher education. More importantly for me, I studied in the United States on a Master of Fine Arts in Choreography, under the great tutelage of Bessie Schönberg. I am convinced that that study period set me off on this on-going career of 25 years so far. I'd like to introduce Valerie Preston-Dunlop, who is mainly a freelance practitioner, but is also adviser in Postgraduate Studies at the Laban Centre; Professor Christopher Bannerman, who is Chair of Dance at Middlesex University; Karen Greenhough who is Coordinator of Choreographic Studies at the London School of Contemporary Dance; and Evelyn Jamieson who is the Director of Dance at the Liverpool Institute for the Performing Arts (LIPA). I have asked the panel to talk about their philosophy and approach to craft, skill and application in the teaching of choreography. From this we can perhaps learn about the differences which will inevitably exist between the various institutions. I am told there are over 35 courses now teaching choreography in higher education. It's fantastic when you think back that not that long ago there was very little happening.

Christopher Bannerman

First, I should say that I would prefer to speak from a personal point of view rather that from an institutional perspective. There are a number of people teaching choreography at Middlesex University - we welcome the diversity which this brings, and I feel that this is an important aspect of our work.

Another factor which will impact on what I have to say stems from my own personal learning history and it is something that has become more apparent to me in recent years. I have reached to the conclusion that while I have learned an enormous amount through my engagement with Higher Education and through interactions with colleagues from various disciplines, nonetheless the learning which took place in the Dance studio has been absolutely fundamental to my career. Of course I was fortunate in that I was able to benefit from a relatively long career in the profession and from the teachers and choreographers with whom I worked.

I am clear in my mind that the studio is a centre for learning and that the processes of art making are, or have the potential to instigate, profound learning experiences. I mention this in part because of Stuart's introduction in which he reminded us of the phenomenal growth in the number of dance courses in Higher Education which include a choreographic element. This sudden growth followed a late introduction to Higher Education and I remember only too well a conference presentation I made to HE colleagues in 1989. I was asked to speak to the statement: 'The Role of Dance in Higher Education' but I was told that title should be 'Is there a Role for Dance in Higher Education?' However, ten years have passed and much has been achieved; I feel that we should be confident about our progress and that we should no longer feel any need to justify our presence, or our art form.

Perhaps I am overstating this matter, but by acknowledging the numerous learning opportunities provided by dance and dance making, from practice-based methodologies to critical perspectives, we begin to contribute to a broad range of provision. Of course this also means making clear decisions regarding our values, while recognising that they are are not the only ones which are valid. In other words I feel that we, as individuals and as institutions, are occasionally at risk of attempting to be all things to all people or of attempting to justify the superiority of a particular approach when in fact the dance ecology benefits from the diversity of approaches.

Can Choreography be Taught?

So, as you can tell from my previous comments, when considering the teaching of choreography I feel that we may lose sight of the importance of the learning of choreography, in other words the student experience. I feel that this is especially important, as in an art making process, the engagement of the learner is absolutely essential - it is a prerequisite. So, teaching can take place in all sorts of circumstances, for instance lecturing to a group of 300 people; but whether they learn anything or not is another question. In choreography, however, the experiential involvement of the learner is surely paramount. The title of this session however, does direct us to some specific areas, and while this is helpful in narrowing the field of concern nonetheless it still leaves a potentially vast terrain. So I will focus the rest of my comments on aspects of this which might sometimes escape comment, not because they are obscure, rather they are so obvious that they are in danger of being taken for granted. Some of these aspects also serve to reflect a concern in Higher Education for skills which are not only specific to a single discipline, but can be transferred to other contexts. I believe that dance making offers these opportunities, but that it is also a subject worthy of study in itself.

There are a number of key skills in choreographic processes which could be considered in a wider context: they are skills of looking, and more importantly seeing, in remembering, in reflecting. There are skills in organising - organising our internal world of thought and conceptual engagement, and in practical skills of organising the external world of studio bookings and managing dancers. There are also skills involved in finding and maintaining inspiration as well as recognising when a new path is unfolding which offers exciting potential but which means that the original inspiration must be abandoned. The choreographer Siobhan Davies once noted that the original idea for a dance is 'like a faint breath behind you' but that the choreographer must discover while making the dance, 'what does and does not work'. [1]

There are of course the skills in generating movement material. I use the word generating and not creating as the use of the creative contributions of dancers and the use of found movement have become important tools for the choreographer. This highlights the importance of the choreographer as facilitator and that reinforces the importance of the communication and interpersonal skills which are essential to this endeavour. This is followed by the skills needed to select and to manipulate the movement material; to shape, mould and edit it. On a macro level, this involves working with time and space and locating overarching structures within this continuum, as well dealing with the structures and dynamics which are internal to the dance.

While I have identified skills which are involved in these aspects of what might seem the craft of choreography, much of this is underpinned to a large degree by the individual creativity and inspiration of the choreographer. This may seem to be the most elusive area to the choreography teacher, but I feel that there are ways to unlock creativity and inspiration and students, teachers and professional choreographers must always look for them. Often, for me, creativity is enhanced by the process of problem solving, whether it be a problem stemming from the translation of a concept into movement, the joining of movement phrases or the achievement of a particular dynamic. So, while the old adage indicates that art is 10 percent inspiration and 90 per cent perspiration, nonetheless the inspiration is critical and each aspiring choreographer should develop strategies for releasing it. The distinctive creative voice sometimes needs encouragement and sustaining it requires care and attention.

Often the making of a dance for performance involves collaboration which might come about through the use of sound, design, lighting design and setting. I believe that dance has gained enormously from its engagement with other disciplines and so the skills needed to sustain successful collaborative partnerships are also important to the choreographer today.

You might notice that I have stressed the interactive aspect of the choreographic process and this is not meant to ignore or to minimise the importance of solitary research by the choreographer or the use of such things as notation, video and digital technologies in the making of dances. I have selected the aspects which depend on human interaction because they continue to be central to much, if not all, choreographic practice. This is perhaps understandable as the realisation of a dance work involves interaction between the spectator and the performer and the ways in which the performer mediates the dance is of utmost importance.

Today choreography teachers face an increasingly diverse dance world and a cultural context which is calling out for greater diversity still. This is one of the most daunting aspects of working as a teacher in a creative field. Of course the opportunities for creative expression and exploration are increased, but this vast array of choice can be confusing. In the face of this changing environment, I believe that the teacher must be intellectually clear about the direction of the choreographic course and clear in the values which underpin it. It may be that each choreographic course cannot deal effectively with the entire range of dance today and that we must be honest about that. However it is clear that the future development of dance as an art form rests with the contributions which the students of today will make, and I feel that this places an obligation on those who teach.

So we endeavour to equip the students with the tools which we feel they will need, while allowing them to chart their own direction, applying the tools as they see fit. The recognition of the essential nature of many of the tools and the skills which are developed, allows the student to adapt and apply them in a variety of contexts for a variety of purposes. The distinctive choreographic voice emerges through the interaction between the intellect and intuition, the intertwining of craft, skills and inspiration which forms and informs the dance making process.

1. Davies, S. "Rigour and Warmth", Dance and Dancers June 1992

Karen Greenhough

Every time I hear people speak I realise how much bigger the picture is than what I've got on my little sheet of paper. I work primarily with my colleague, Sue MacLennan, and the two of us do most of the teaching, thinking and talking about the composition and choreography classes. I am making a distinction between the notions of composition and choreography. At the School, the composition classes are mandatory for all students in the first two years, and in the third year choreography is an optional subject. We also have a small but very devoted MA in Choreography as well; I am talking about devotion in the students as well as the teachers. So I think there is a logical strategy, perhaps a philosophy, behind the way we work. Sue and I work very differently, although we complement each other and fill in for each other, but we are only two so I am sure there's lots of holes left there. I'll try and give you a rundown of how we have thought about the education of composition and choreography.

Composition and Choreography

First of all, I would like to preface this by saying that as long as I have been teaching, the more I teach, the more I discuss, the more I think about it, the more I talk with other people about composition and choreography, the more I realise what a messy business it is. I never seem to be able to find a particular method that lasts for all time or for all students, and it changes from year to year, from student to student, from moment to moment. It's really something where I get in there with the students and we wallow around together, and out of that comes hopefully some kind of knowledge both on their part and mine. So I'm going to try to make it coherent here, but I think it's a bit misleading to think that it might be that coherent at the School.

The logic behind the notion of people taking composition for the first two years is that we think that compositional training is not just an important part of a choreographer's training, but it is important for everybody who wants to make a contribution to dance as an art form. Therefore, we think that our students coming out of this situation need to be very knowledgeable about their artform. They need to understand the nature of dance, the nature of the materials and tools with which they are engaged. They need to be aware of the big questions about how dance fits in to a larger socio-political context, how it fits into a larger art context, and then what specifically are those dance issues. Those dance issues in themselves are huge because there is so much involved in forming them.

The Critical Eye

When students get to the third year, the focus is more on what their own particular voice is, not just about the kind of basics and discovery of the nature of the art form. I think central to the teaching, or central to the education is this thing that many people have mentioned which is the critical eye. It's the development of an informed understanding of the dance work which, as I said, is based in a larger critical context and of course in the art and dance culture which contributes to the meaning of the work. In other words it's not just about making work, it's about the receiving of that work and if we understand the culture that we live in, if we understand the culture that informs that meaning I think we understand more about what we have to do to communicate clearly to our audiences. Another reason for developing this educated eye is because it's the thing that allows us to be critical about our own work and critical about other dance work. It also makes us better advocates for dance. For a long time dancers avoided trying to be articulate about their art form, and I think that's left us in a very disempowered position in the bigger cultural sense. It's very good now that people are starting to be able to observe and understand what they're seeing, to be able to articulate what they see, and to convey those things to a bigger population. I think that is one of the ways in fact that dance will become more significant and make a bigger impact on the world at large.

Practical/Conceptual Learning

The training, especially in those first two years at the School, takes two forms essentially, and this is probably not so different in other institutions. The first part is practical studio investigation, which takes the forms of directed improvisation, and solving compositional problems. This is very much as a means to an end, and not an end in itself. When we explore something improvisation-ally, when we create studies, I think of the analogy of students going into a weight-training room and strengthening certain muscles. They are given certain limitations and certain focuses, and that's hopefully going to strengthen certain compositional, certain choreographic muscles which they need if they are going to continue choreographing or if they are really going to understand their art form. The other thing that is significant and important is the critical observation and discussion of dance work, and that happens in the classroom about the pieces that the students make. It also happens in the context of them going to shows and talking about and even, dare I say it, writing about dance work. The writing about dance work is not just an evaluation of the dance, it's about trying to identify what it is that that choreographer is trying to do. I firmly believe that choreographers, like all artists, are trying to communicate something, and so it is incumbent upon the audience as well as the choreographer to try and be as conversant with those things that it is possible to communicate through dance.

The training tries to educate students about the art form, and we are talking in this context about Western contemporary dance art traditions. We are trying to encourage the development of compositional skills which I have already talked a bit about, to get them to resource the materials at their disposal, and to construct these in some kind of coherent, clear form, which certainly involves making choices. Everything is out there to be chosen, from the costumes you wear, the music you choose, the movement that you're generating. Everything is a choice and that choice is really dependent on what it is you're trying to do, what it is you're trying to communicate.

The Responsibility of Creating Dance

The last thing I think that's really significant is that we are trying to give students the opportunity to understand something about their own creative powers, and to give them the courage to access those things. It is your own personal voice and you're putting it out there to share with other people and that is a huge responsibility really. I try to encourage the students to take that responsibility very seriously. It's not about getting up there and showing off, as much as we might be like moths, which are attracted to a flame, and that may be the thing that initially got us dancing. Really it's a far more adult kind of thing that we are doing out there, and I think that we need to be as wise as well as resourced and as skilled as we can in communicating that. Now of course you can't take full responsibility for that communication because the rest of that responsibility lies with the audience; the audience completes the picture. So I think that even in this compositional training we may in fact in some instances be training good audiences as well, hopefully. The big dilemma which I wrestle with all the time in teaching choreography is trying to find a balance to encourage a kind of rigour in the approach to the making and seeing of work, and at the same time trying to give students permission and support them in that attempt to explore something much deeper and more vulnerable. So in a way I am asking them to abandon themselves to something and at the same time I am asking them to use a lot of control. That is a very difficult thing to balance. Maybe one of the keys to it is something that Rosemary Butcher mentioned yesterday, about having a number of parallel tracks so you are never just approaching it from one direction, but are trying to find a number of ways of recognizing that this is a very complex and awesome thing that you are trying to do. So I think that choreography can be taught in that context. I think it's also possible to learn to choreograph through careful observation and practice on your own, but I think what an institution tries to do is to package that to create a safe and really stimulating environment for that kind of learning to take place.

Evelyn Jamieson

There's something a good number of people find contradictory: many of us here teach people to make art. Included in this teaching is the development of creativity. Can creativity be taught or does it simply pass from generation to generation by way of DNA? I don't think so. All rhetoric aside, I personally have recently embarked on another seemingly contradictory challenge, the forming of choreographers and performers for, amongst others, the cultural industry as Head of Dance at the new Liverpool Institute for Performing Arts (LIPA). Do popular dancers need a degree in Higher Education? Again, I think this can be most useful.

This very brief talk concerns the following:

- Finding a balance between craft and creativity in dance tuition at HE level.
- Choreography as it is presented in the undergraduate dance route tuition at LIPA.
- The need for clear assessment criteria as a means for supporting the above and how this can be achieved.

I am contextualising these points with some observations summarised in my handout.

Choreography at LIPA

Dance at LIPA is part of a holistic performing arts degree. The course includes a core programme which provides a firm base upon which students can build their specialist skills. The dance specialist route emphasises vocational and performance aspects of the dance profession, offering students the entire spectrum from the commercial/ entertainment industry to highly innovative contemporary dance.

The dance specialist route is not a pick and mix cocktail. Students follow a planned path through their three years which has been developed to enable each individual to receive an intense but complete dance education and training. (That is, there is not a huge selection of modules for them. Instead, the course has defined the majority of their path very clearly.) Students study various dance techniques and styles: for contemporary dance examples include Limon, release and Graham-based work; furthermore there is jazz dance, musical theatre and street dance as well as classical ballet and Pilates/body conditioning.

Alongside their daily technique classes other areas are covered through modules that are designed to extend the student creatively. Choreography is not seen to be an added extra as many who are not acquainted with the course content may think. They might be expecting a performance-only training course. At LIPA, for example, choreographic modules are not optional for the dance specialist student; they exist alongside the technique modules in Years 1 & 2. We feel at Year 3 there should be the opportunity for students to decide and select modules that are most appropriate to their individual skills and capabilities.

For the first time in my H.E. career I am dealing with a wide breadth of choreographic style. This is indeed exciting and challenging and some might say - schizophrenic. That is: can one combine contemporary and popular choreography in one course? I do believe that the principles that underline the craft of choreography are the same whether it be within the contemporary dance or the popular dance genre. Learning how to choreograph is just the same in my view; to be really successful in either you need to truly understand the mechanics of the choreographic process. I am discovering with my colleagues that assessment within our context doesn't raise any problems either.

This is an exciting time for us at LIPA as the course has just seen its first set of graduates through the course this year. We are still discovering better ways of delivering the programme - not just in terms of facilitating practical choreographic study but also in the essential theoretical base of analysis and evaluation so important in supporting practical development.

How choreography is 'taught'
(Please note: the following refers to the dance specialist students who are on the dance route of the LIPA performing arts degree, not our minor study students.)

Students are given the opportunity to explore and develop their choreographic skills a) individually, b) collectively and c) through what I call imposed direction. Modules are designed to give the students ways of developing their own movement material and then ways of being able to make well judged content selection alongside the shaping and forming of the entire work.

With this in mind, year 1 choreography is about understanding and developing: a) dance content using a number of methods to facilitate the process of material generation; b) forming and placing the content into some kind of logical and workable structure; c) improving the stylistic and physical mastery of execution; d) the projection of all the design and collaborative elements, and last but by no means least e) the expression of the overall piece.

Students at this first year level are also given the opportunity to work on a choreographic project in their second semester. This project is one of a collaborative nature and gives students the opportunity to work with other students from other disciplines. Although this may seem a bit optimistic at this stage in their development, it does seem to work very well. I think the key to the success of this collaborative exercise is down to the fact that the students do have cross-disciplinary lectures and sessions from the onset of the course and are in dialogue even before they start this project in their second semester. In short, several problems of vocabulary or dialect difference have already been encountered in cross-performing arts sessions during their first semester.

Choreography is therefore continued throughout the year. Their second semester module really begins to get them to understand and use different processes. Group devising is encouraged and a number of tasks are created throughout the module to enable this sharing of ideas, dance material. This of course works hand in hand with the development of the decision making elements which form part of their personal/social interaction as well as concerning the form and structure of the work itself. Small group work is encouraged at this stage, affording them collective devising opportunities and choreographic craft application.

So where do the students go from that foundation?
Year 2 consists of a more personal diet enabling students to be given a choice in terms of the kind of choreographic study they wish to follow in the first semester. (This is the first time within the dance route that they have been given any kind of choice.) One particularly interesting choice concerns choreography which can be studied in relation to other contexts. Students who take this module look very closely at and gain 'hands-on' experience of making choreography for a very specific brief/context, e.g. film. The other option is to study choreography within the musical theatre genre. This first cross-roads enables the dance students to start making decisions about what kind of performer they would like to become and which area of the profession they wish to enter.

In the second semester of Year 2 choreography continues and the students are all brought back together. In this final choreographic module before the third year allows no choice in what they are to do. This module addresses the more complex choreographic issues related to development of style and more detailed approach to construction. The evaluative side becomes much more considered at this stage which is vitally important to the young developing choreographer. At this point, the students should begin to have some "knowing and feeling" as Jacqueline Smith-Autard puts it. They are thus perhaps more able to evaluate some aspects of a work than the more intuitive parts.

Having given them the 'tools' of the craft of choreography over a period of time - in this instance 2 years, the student is then in a favourable position of being able to choreograph a piece of work. Their work may or may not have a strong intuitive/artistic leaning; this of course varies with the student.

Choreographic development concerns finding a balance between being able to make work well - let's say 'the nuts and bolts' as I often refer to the craft, and the element which not everyone possesses equally - the artistic. Can artistry be 'taught'? I think it can to a degree. To simplify a lengthy discussion, my belief is that the discovery of individual focus and uniqueness can be translated into a form of personal expression. This in turn plays a vital part in terms of the process leading to the acquisition of the central component of any choreography. The degree of discovered 'uniqueness' may be linked to a sort of 'talent barometer', those being born with a great deal of talent being 'the blessed ones'. Whatever the level of talent, experience plays a significant role in developing artistic prowess; if students are given the right stimulus and experience on their course they can develop this alongside, or better said, holistically with the learning of the 'how' of craft.

The final year
Year 3 for dance students at LIPA is geared towards getting them ready for the industry/profession. Although it is heavily weighted towards the dancer as performer, they choreograph a fair bit nevertheless. Choreography can be taken as an assessed part of their Year 3 if the student so chooses. Ability feeds choice by the student at this stage which I believe represents a successful strategy. By this stage students and staff are aware of the capabilities within a group and through a process of self-selection and guidance, students decide whether they choreograph a major piece on their own, collectively, collaboratively or not at all. The last point really doesn't happen in actual fact as even within a dance performance module, students are often required to devise material for elements of a directed piece of work. It is the degree to which students are expected to create work according to their abilities and the requirements of the module in question that determines the extent and types of choreographic input in the final year. Assessment obviously reflects these specific choices.

Assessment
Criteria for assessment need to be transparent. Students need to understand what they are being assessed on and how. Choreographic assessment should be about identifying the protocols from the making process:

a)   **Content** - intent, development of dance material, the use of space, dynamics, time etc.

b)   **Form** - transitions, sequencing, layering, compositional structures and the overall form of the piece.

c)   **Style** - cohesion in terms of overall style, technical/physical mastery, the uniqueness of the style, are all the dancers in the piece confident and capable of expounding the style demanded of them?

d)   **Projection** - landscape of the piece, that is, set/theatrical design and music/sound - is the balance right?, costume and colour, and obviously the dancers' physical expression of the work.

The above list cannot be properly prepared without first articulating the expected learning outcomes of any particular project or module. The name of the game here is: 'What exactly do you want to have the students learn?'.

Now every choreographic process contains the elements stated above; therefore the assessment/choreographic criteria should easily be translatable into classification according to the level to which each piece or project measures up to the clearly presented protocols. In other words, criteria for assessment in my experience do not differ from project to project in terms of how to assess the choreographic elements; the difference occurs in terms of the specific aims and objectives of the assessment and their relationship to the intent and context of the work in question. Once this has been clearly defined and identified then specific assessment protocols particular to the task can be formulated and given to the students. This makes the criteria extremely clear and transparent to both the student and the examiner.

In the form of a conclusion, in my previous institution, University College Bretton Hall, I had the fortune to spend most of my teaching on the choreographic modules in Years 2 & 3 particularly. These included Concepts in Choreography and Performance - a substantial 5/6 hours a week module and Year 3 - Contemporary Dance Theatre - creation of individual 15-20 minute choreographies for performance. What I developed in the programme were the ways in which students 'learned' how to choreograph and I spent a great deal of time in getting them to develop their own individual movement signature. Finding innovative ways of producing and delivering their work, I became passionate about trying to get students to develop their individual styles whilst being able to shape and form contemporary dance at a sophisticated level. At LIPA we as a dance team are currently finding our way of giving students the opportunity to develop as choreographers in any field if they so choose. As our course is only three years old, we are still only at the beginning of our journey.

I will continue to explore new ways of facilitating choreographic learning. My modus operandi leads towards student dancers' discovery of their creative abilities along with essential skills development. The assessment criteria my colleagues and I use help the students discover strength and weakness assisting them in terms of their focusing on their key strengths and bettering weaknesses. Using devising techniques alongside more traditional imposed ones - actually the devising techniques are even more traditional as they are as old as dance, itself, an often forgotten fact - is the approach I shall continue to pursue until I discover a better model. Yes I can choreograph and do it all the time. Without this experience, I would be an 'armchair facilitator'. Still, the greatest and most exciting challenge of all for me is the making of choreographers.

Valerie Preston-Dunlop

Let me make it clear from the outset that I do not teach choreography, nor can I speak for the choreography department of the Laban Centre London, as the introductory remarks to this session might suggest. What I teach is Choreological Studies and in these remarks I focus only on those aspects of Choreological Studies that are relevant to the making of dance works.

What do I teach? What do I hope the students learn?

Choreological Studies takes as essential the study of the mismatch between the experience of those closely involved in the making of the work, that is the experience of the performers and of the choreographer, and the experience of those who view/listen to the work. They are not the same and this causes no end of problems, particularly in appraisal of emerging works where discrepancy of view is the norm. To study this the triadic perspective of making, performing, appreciating is unravelled in that the notion that choreographers make, dancers perform and audiences appreciate is seen as simplistic and reductionist. Choreographers do all three, so do performers and, often, so do spectators.

The processes of appreciating can be taught. They are artistic skills. In choreological workshops appreciating skills are learned by all who participate in the processes of dance making and performing works. Appreciating skills are not only for spectators, or classes called Dance Analysis, or Criticism.

In order to do that adequately for up to date work, a choreological studies perspective takes as problematic the commonly stated notion that movement is the medium of dance, period. Movement is the medium, of course, but so also is the sound of the dance with which the movement has an inevitable relationship, the space in which and with which the dance is made, the performers with which the work is created and through whom it is mediated. Current choreographic practice evidenced in the works of such leading artists as Lloyd Newson, Pina Bausch, William Forsythe, to name just three, shows that these artists are not only dealing with movement but with all four of the strands of the dance medium. They both choreograph and direct the work.

What is also problematic in current theory is that even when the four mentioned strands of the dance medium, the performer, the movement, the sound, and the space, are recognised as in the province of the choreographer, the nexus between them is touched upon but not dealt with as a crucial feature. In Choreological Studies therefore the nexus of the strands of the dance medium is a central focus. Nexial methods of integrating the strands as Bintley might do, methods of juxtaposing them and contracontextualising them as Bausch does, methods of co-existing them as Cunningham and his disciples do, are starting points in a Choreological perspective. They are not afterthoughts just as they are not afterthoughts for the artists concerned.

In theatre, or performance arts, the works will communicate whether there is an intention so to do or not. As soon as people watch and listen they expect to get something from the experience and they hope to understand the work, whatever that phrase might mean. Therefore in choreological workshops and seminars the notion of communication in dance is addressed and unpicked. People fall into the trap of thinking that communication is a one-way process, from the artists to the audience, when it is in reality a two-way process, including the ideas and imagination of the spectators who will see what they will see in the work almost regardless of, or at any rate in addition to, what has been put into the work's material by the artists. Jean Jacques Nattiez's use of Molino's research on the semiotic layers within a music performance gives a starting point *(Music and Discourse: Towards a Semiology of Music* (1990, Princeton University Press). He recognises the poietic layers which the processes of making put into the work, the layer of the trace (which for him may well be a score), and the aesthetic layer added by the appreciators or interpreters. Study of these layers as they function in dance makes it essential to focus on the medium and its nexus for it is in the medium that the semiotic layers are placed by the artists. They are or are not seen by the selective perception of the spectators. Distinguishing these layers is learnable. Distinguishing them in your own work is difficult but also learnable.

People also fall into the trap of believing that understanding work entails looking for its story line, or its references. Of course references, even stories, might be present but so too are a host of non-referential elements which go towards the meaning of the work. Here the research of Jacobson as discussed in Pierre Guiraud's *Semiology* (1975 Routledge) is a starting point. He shows how (1) the aesthetic content of the work means, gives value, in works with and without a narrative element. You see, for example, order and disorder, formal and informal structures. He shows how (2) the artists' attitude to the codes of their art is evident in the material form of the work and gives off conforming or innovating, both of which have a value and a meaning independent of references and aesthetic content. The codes of theatre which lead to expectations of how one and all should behave during a performance may be disrupted, intentionally, or the codes of different styles of dance material or dancers' relations with their audiences may be adhered to or played with. He shows how (3) the performers add their own layer of meaning through the nature of their commitment. He shows how (4) getting a response from the audience can be a function of the work, not by a narrative means but by sorting out what in the work will arouse and the nature of that arousal, anger, tears, amusement, admiration, reflection... And he shows how (5) setting up the possibility of communication and either maintaining that or subverting it is a meaningful act.

In choreological teaching these things are not only discussed in the lecture room but are meaningful in the studio. Attempting to recognise the various layers of communication which might be in the very material you are making and/or dancing becomes second nature to a choreological studies student. The ability is developed and becomes a resource that the dance person can use as and when to accompany the intuitive creation of material as well as the conscious construction and editing of material.

At the Laban Centre London the choreological programme for undergraduates is a three year one. For postgraduates it is one year although some prefer to audit year one and take the course with all its assignments in year two. Assignments are in the main multi-stranded in that students are expected to present corporeally, verbally and in some written form, possibly using symbol systems where words fail, with video or computer assistance as appropriate.

Choreological studies is not teaching anyone how to make a dance but it is teaching how to look at what you have made and are making and it is giving you the skills to choose to work that way over the unfortunate but often used appraisal: I like it, I don't like it. It hopefully teaches you what to expect from other people's views of your work and gives you straightforward knowledge of possibilities which you can incorporate into your working process or which you can recognise need to be edited out of it.

Preston-Dunlop V *Looking at Dances: A Choreological Perspective on Choreography* Ightham, Verve Publishing, 1998

Points raised in discussion:

· The panel were asked to describe their assessment procedures and criteria. At LCDS, procedure and criteria become more specific as students develop, e.g. at first year level measuring the level of engagement with a task rather than/as well as its physical results. At LIPA, students' progress is measured in several ways but broadly in terms of skill areas in which they show development since arriving at the institution. Middlesex University seeks to give informed judgement based on specific criteria. The Laban Centre use peer assessment to help to set up criteria for tutor assessment.

· Other methods of assessment offered by delegates included the following:

1) Students at Scarborough University negotiated a set of intended outcomes with their tutors and wrote them up in the form of an abstract. Their achievement in terms of their finished choreographic work was therefore measured against their own criteria, rather than imposed ones. Assessment is carried out by more than one tutor to discourage favouritism.

2) A delegate from the University of Lisbon commented that she had used a similar process and found that it discriminated against students who found difficulty in expressing themselves in written form. Sometimes the most sketchily-described intentions produce the most successful finished work.

3) A delegate from De Monfort University, Leicester described a similar process of assessing students which allowed extensive scope for in-depth student evaluation and negotiation. This proved highly enriching for students, but immensely time consuming and was reluctantly abandoned.

· The panel were unanimous in their opinion that the "nuts and bolts" of choreography can be assessed regardless of style.

· The panel was asked how far they felt that their courses were designed specifically to produce choreographers. They responded by emphasizing that choreography is part of a general education in dance at HE level, and that Higher Education is just one stage of any dance professional's development.

· The panel felt that students made clear choices about the kind of training they were getting before embarking on particular courses at the stage of reading prospectuses, visiting and auditioning.

Stuart Hopps ended by advocating the increased input of professional choreographers into students' experiences at HE level.

Session 10

Funding Dancemaking: International Perspectives

Keywords:

funding   grants   choreographers   development   companies

In the UK we have learned to be resourceful in terms of the funding required to support and nurture dance making. Other individuals in the USA, Europe and Australia, working in different contexts, have been equally inventive in the quest to find monies. This session will pool the resources of presenters and funders who have had experience of working internationally. The speakers are Nancy Duncan from Pentacle, New York, Sue Hoyle from The Place, London and Jerril Rechter from Australia, and the chairperson was Gregory Nash from The British Council, England.

Gregory Nash

The British Council does not fund the making of dance but one of its functions is to fund its worldwide distribution, so as Drama & Dance Officer at the British Council, I have some role in the process.

Our panel members play much greater roles in this process. The first is Sue Hoyle, General Manager of Contemporary Dance Trust, formerly a colleague at the British Council and also formerly Deputy Secretary General of the Arts Council of England. The second is Nancy Duncan from the Pentacle Agency in New York, who has quite a lot of experience of the UK dance scene and was recently involved in the very successful British dance season in New York, the British Invasion. The third is Jerril Rechter from Australia who is a Dance Fund panel member of the Australia Council and is in the UK at present on a placement with Ludus Dance Company in Lancaster.

Sue Hoyle

I am going to concentrate on talking in particular about funding through Regional Arts Boards and the Arts Council of England. It is very interesting coming back from France and realising that, apart from the lack of money, there are many positive points about the British funding system. That is not how we thought it was in 1989, which is when I became Director of Dance at the Arts Council. There was report called *'Stepping Forward'* which held up the French way of funding as a model. It talked about the year which had just happened, L'Année de la Danse, in which the French Government with Jack Lang as the Minister of Culture had spent an enormous amount of money boosting dance in promotional terms.

Funding for Creating and Touring in France

A lot of us were looking at the models which the French had instigated such as implanting choreographers in centres in different parts of the country. We could see that there was money being invested directly in the training of dancers by the Minister of Culture and Education, and we were envious of the fact that there was money at local, regional and national levels. Going back to France now, things have changed. It was a year or two after *'Stepping Forward'* that the Delegére de la Danse, Brigitte Lefèvre, who now runs the Paris Opera Ballet and who was then the Director of Danse at the French Ministry of Culture, came with a group of French people to the Arts Council and met with the Dance Panel. Brigitte Lefèvre said that the problem in France was that they had money for creation but not for touring. I said that the problem in England was that we had money for touring and not for creation. The investment in dance in France has not been completely successful, and I could see that for myself when I saw what was happening on stage. There is some interesting choreography, but it doesn't surprise you in the way that choreography here surprises you. I am much more interested in seeing work here than I was in France. Across the channel, work is wonderfully presented on the big stages, but there isn't the same choice of promoters that I think we have here. A single promoter and his family directs one of the large dance theatres in Paris, and also a smaller equipped space in the north of Paris. Outside Paris there are few opportunities for dance to be presented for more than one night. Dance is often only presented in England for one night also, but France is a large country with quite a lot of investment in dance. Apart from a Maison de la Danse in Lyon, which has a policy of presenting for more than one night, almost everywhere else it's one night and then you're on to the next place, or usually back to base.

The French are going through radical changes just as we are. Catherine Trautmann who is now the Minister of Culture announced last year a brand new policy of increased decentralisation, emphasis on access, balancing creation and promotion, reducing ticket prices. As well as the changes which are happening nationally from the French Minister for Culture, there are local developments. I was very aware when I was living there of some of the things the National Front was saying in France. There were real threats in some cities to the local investment in culture which the National Front call 'the cultural dictatorship of the left'.

Positive Points in Britain

There are some good things here in Britain, but we are going through a period of extraordinary change, the like of which we have not seen since 1946 when the Arts Council was set up. For a long time in dance we complained that there was a stranglehold on funding, and that there was no chance of increased funding for dance. The case was made, and certainly during the '90's there has been an increased proportion of funding available for dance. Now the Arts Council spends just under 19% of its arts budget on dance. It is not enough, but it's better than it was. There are other changes which are happening also. There have been the well-publicised changes at the Royal Opera House, which receives the biggest dance grant for any organisation in this country for the Royal Ballet. Things are going to change a lot but if there are some improvements, such as a greater proportion of performances at the Royal Opera House for ballet, cheaper ticket prices and a bigger emphasis on education, then that will be for the better.

There are other changes which we have all seen such as money being spent on improving buildings for the benefit of dance. Certainly everyone is looking forward to the reopening of the new Sadler's Wells Theatre which should present fantastic facilities for dance. But Lottery money for buildings is being reviewed. Everything it seems at the moment is being reviewed. Arts for Everyone has enabled many people who felt excluded from funding to receive some money. In fact, in the last financial year, the very fast light-footed scheme, Arts for Everyone Express, gave £1.35 million to over 300 dance organisations, and the main Arts for Everyone programme gave £3.8 million to dance. That's a lot of money when the total spending on dance through the revenue grant is £23 million. The Lottery has helped in other ways too. Over 500 dance and drama students were helped through the new Lottery funding scheme. Revenue funding has been on standstill or cut back for the last five years and things were at a crisis. The Arts Council decided it was going to look at ways of integrating Lottery and revenue spending and making more money available at a regional level, closer to where artists are based.

The Government has just done a comprehensive spending review which means there will be an extra £125 million for the arts over the next three years. They state that they want it to be used for particular things, and they haven't said how much of it will come to dance or indeed to the performing arts. There will be other areas of the arts included among the beneficiaries as well. The Government promises that the extra money is going to be used to stabilise organisations who are at particular financial risk, and to encourage access and promote educational work. No wonder that the Chairman of the Arts Council in the latest Arts Council report states that the arts never stand still and nor does the society in which they take shape. Radical change, like much good art, is bound to please some and discomfort others. We are all feeling uncertain about what is happening and how we can help dance to make a case within this context.

Even the British Council has been reviewing itself. What I did find when I was in Paris was that the British Council's budgets for the arts which are very modest indeed are fantastically effective. It wasn't very difficult to persuade the French to programme British dance if you gave them some advice. That is what they needed more than money. The money was usually available from the British Council for about 10% of the cost of a British Arts event in France, and the other 90% would be found from French sources.

The 'Tipping Point'

I have been reading a report from the USA on dance audiences and on the national task force that was set up for dance audiences. Bonnie Brooks, former Executive Director of Dance USA, talked about the 'tipping point', which is something which has been learned from the way in which diseases are transmitted. A 'tipping point' is a catalyst, a small change which can bring about drastic alteration. Big changes may have just a small effect. The important thing to decide is what you want and to tip things in the way you want. We tend to think in linear ways, we do this then that happens. It's not like that. You push one bit and the whole structure can change. I think that this is a really important moment for us to decide how we want things to change, even within this time of flux. One example is that the French decided they would put a tiny amount of money (by French standards) into trying to encourage the ballet companies based in regional opera houses to be more creative. So they had a strategy for creativity in ballet. We have tried other things here, but the French example is very telling. Which of our ballet companies commissions the likes of Bill T Jones, Stephen Petronio, and many others to create works for them? They have done this in France and I think it was as a result of encouragement and investment. Sometimes scale isn't important but what is important is being clear in your aims. The purpose of the funding is central and artists need to be clear about this. They have to know what they want to do with their money and to argue the case for it. I think it's important that those who have control over resources, such as buildings or funds, realise that flexibility is important.

Finally I wish to reiterate that this is a time of change and in my view it is a time of opportunity. We should recognise that the funding for dance has increased a great deal. Now that the Government and the Arts Council are reviewing the way in which the Lottery funds and revenue funding is used, we have to decide what we want and go for it. It is a good moment for dance. Dance has spread its tentacles at local level, and we can make an impact there as well at national level. We should be looking not ten years ahead as we did in 1989, but 20 years ahead. I was very struck by Dance Theatre Workshop's brochure, produced 2 or 3 years ago, which talked about the first 60 years of Dance Theatre Workshop. I thought they couldn't have been going for 60 years. No, they were covering the period up to 2025. We have to do that as well. We have to look back, and also look forward at the same time.

Nancy Duncan

A lot of the themes that Sue just mentioned regarding how funding priorities are changing – such as promoting access and education and helping organizations stabilize - are happening in the U.S. as well. However, for this presentation I would like to give an overview of arts funding in the United States particularly as it relates to dance. As I talk about the U.S. I think it is interesting to keep in mind the size of the U.S. in comparison to England. The U.S. is comprised of 50 states and my current home state of New York, is geographically similar in size to England. Hence, in comparison to what you have here, the amount of funding allocated by the U.S. federal government to support artistic endeavors may sometimes seem like grassroots funding. I will first give the national perspective and then talk about New York State.

Early Funding in the USA

Prior to the late 1950's the U.S. had no formal funding system for the arts. In particular, dance as a performing art relied on what we refer to as sole proprietorship. If you wanted to get paid you relied on theater managers hiring you and paying a fee for your performance. There was no other support structure. Pioneers in dance had to find their own theater, produce their own concerts and hope that a theater producer would see it and want to promote it. It was not until the late 1950's that the Ford Foundation created the concept of an arts grant. Along with the creation of the arts grant, The Ford Foundation established the concept of a non-profit organization, which still dominates how we fund dance in our country today. What this means is that in general, for an artist to receive an arts grant they must either form a non-profit organization which requires creating an institutional structure with a board of directors or find a non-profit organization that will serve as a fiscal umbrella for the funds. If an artist chooses to work with a fiscal umbrella, they almost always feel very pressured to form their own institution as soon as possible. The Ford Foundation also created the concept of 'leveraging' which still governs most of our foundation and corporate giving. Quite often, dollars granted to an organization are expected to help leverage matching funds from other sources.

In the early 1960's, with the coming of the Kennedy and then Johnson administrations, there was an incentive put in place to create a national funding profile in the arts. The first national, federally funded organization for the arts was created in 1965 entitled the National Endowment for the Arts (NEA). The NEA was perhaps one of the first funding organizations to create grant awards in the 'purest' sense – awards that could be given directly to individuals - called Artist Fellowships. Artists were able to receive money directly from the NEA without having to be an established non-profit organization. When you applied for a fellowship from the NEA a panel of your peers would review your application and if funded, the artist would receive a grant of $7,000 for one year, which is about £4,000, to be used for developing their work. Unfortunately, there was no guarantee that the artist would be funded again if they re-applied for a fellowship. Each year a different peer panel would review the pool of applications with no requirement to fund past recipients.

In 1995 the NEA went through a major restructuring and the discipline-specific funding categories, which included fellowships, disappeared. I will speak more about the restructuring later. There are still a few fellowship opportunities left, but they are primarily on the state level. Just prior to the appearance of the NEA in 1965, New York State created the first state arts council called the New York State Council on the Arts (NYSCA). By the time NEA was created there were four state arts councils in existence. The state legislature in New York did not allow NYSCA to give funding directly to artists. NYSCA grants had to go to charitable organizations that had non-profit status. In the 1970's, to address this restriction, NYSCA created a separate organization called the New York Foundation for the Arts (NYFA). NYSCA re-granted a portion of their budget to NYFA, which then enabled them to give fellowship grants directly to artists. NYFA still awards fellowships, each amounting to about $3,000. Again, the fellowship awards are decided by a peer panel review and there is no guarantee that a past recipient will receive support in the future.

So, in general, most of the funding in the U.S. for dance, and the arts overall, continues to be based on organizational stability and continuity over time. Because of this our choreographers have been driven to form companies quite early, perhaps before they are really ready artistically or institutionally to do so. I think because of this factor, coupled with the fact that U.S. funding structures, both public and private, have suffered drastic reductions in funding levels over the last 10 years, we are constantly looking for alternative ways to support the art of dancemaking.

Four Funding Initiatives
In 1995 the NEA's funding structure was changed, eliminating all discipline specific programs. It is now comprised of four funding categories: creation and presentation; education and access; planning and stabilization; heritage and preservation. Under this structure all art forms decide which category addresses their artistic programs and then submits an application. What this program structure means is that a panel for creation and presentation will be looking at applications from the Metropolitan Museum of Art, a company such as Stephen Petronio Dance Company, New York City Ballet, and emerging dance and theater companies all within the same application review.

Over the last 15 years national funding initiatives have been developed to address the artistic needs of the dance community that were not necessarily being met at the national and/or state level. These initiatives were usually created by several funding organizations joining together to pool their resources. This kind of collaboration reflects the entrepreneurial thinking that exists in the U.S. The first one of these initiatives was called the National Choreography Project (NCP) which was a funding partnership between the Rockefeller Foundation, the NEA, and the Exxon Corporation. The project was initiated by the NEA and administered by Ivan Sygoda, Director of Pentacle, a non-profit service organization for dance based in New York City. The objective of the NCP was to support the commissioning of new work primarily by ballet companies, though it did expand to include some contemporary dance repertory companies. The NCP had funding commitments from each funding partner for three years and after the three years the program was discontinued. Under the NCP, CoDanceCo, a company I had founded, had the wonderful opportunity to commission and perform a work by Eiko and Koma. It was the first work they had ever set on dancers other than themselves. It was a very exciting and rewarding experience for all of us. Pentacle, the administrator of NCP, then administered a new initiative called the National Dance Repertory and Enrichment Program which was funded again through a partnership with several funding organizations, the Lila-Wallace Reader's Digest, the NEA, and Philip Morris Companies. Again, this initiative was funded for three grant cycles.

Soon after the National Dance Repertory and Enrichment Program ended Pew Charitable Trusts, a foundation based in Philadelphia, created a new initiative entitled the National Dance Residency Program (NDRP). Pew chose the New York Foundation for the Arts to administrate the program and it too, was funded for three years. The NDRP was created specifically to strengthen the relationships between choreographers and companies. Pew designed the NDRP to be more flexible in terms of how the choreographer would use the funds. The grant was not contingent on creating a new work, but rather on supporting the creative development of the choreographer and the company. This initiative was also created to have a life of three funding cycles.

A fourth national initiative, one that is still operating today, was created shortly after the NEA restructured its funding programs. The NEA had a sum of money called 'set aside funds,' or discretionary funds, that could be allocated toward leadership initiatives and I believe this is still true today. In consultation with the NEA dance program and with counsel from Dance/USA and the Association of Performing Arts Presenters, Sam Miller, Executive Director for the New England Foundation for the Arts (previously director for the Jacob's Pillow Dance Festival), created the National Dance Project (NDP). This initiative was created to support the commissioning and touring of new dance work. With the restructuring, the NEA would no longer support, in particular, choreographic fellowships or national touring seasons in the way it had in the past. NDP, as a production and touring initiative, was awarded a leadership or Chairman's grant from the NEA (I think approximately one million dollars) to create a five-year initiative. Again, these funds were expected to leverage additional funds from other foundation and corporate sources.

Most recently, the dance field has benefited from the creation of a new foundation that is dedicated to supporting, among other areas, dance. Doris Duke, one the wealthiest woman in the US and heir to a tobacco fortune, died a few years ago and left a great deal of money to be used to finance her foundation. Over the last year the Doris Duke Charitable Foundation has given several million dollars to many of our premiere dance organizations and programs. The NDP is one of them and as such, will be able to continue its program for several more years.

In summary, dance has survived in the U.S., not because it has been overwhelmingly supported by the federal government, but because everyone passionate about it from artists, managers, administrators, presenters, and funders continually find resourceful ways to survive each problem as it arises. The dance field is constantly changing, constantly reinventing itself not only artistically but in its funding structures as well. Sometimes through its own choice, sometimes because the funding structures have changed, the dance field in the U.S. has had to find new ways of working. Going back to something Sue Hoyle said earlier, what is important for all of us to focus on is how we can effectively respond to and use change.

State Arts Councils

In terms of state funding, each of the State Arts Councils is very different in how they structure themselves. When it comes to how we work within each state I sometimes feel the U.S. is behind in our thinking as compared to England. In particular, I am thinking of the National Dance Agencies that have been established here.

Recently however, the dance program for the New York State Arts Council, working in partnership with Ivan Sygoda, Director of Pentacle and David White, Director of Dance Theater Workshop, created a new program originally entitled the New York State Task Force on Partnerships in Dance. Sygoda and White identified a group of individuals from around the state who were dance 'activists' and invited them to come together as a task force to determine new working methods which would increase dance activity within the state of New York. NYSCA's dance program was able to grant the task force, now called the New York State Dance Force and jointly administrated by Dance Theater Workshop and Danspace Project, approximately $110,000 per year for the last four years. This is about £60,000. The task force is comprised of artists, presenters, managers and educators from around the state who have proven to be activists within their local communities. Each member is re-granted around $10,000 to support dance projects they create individually or in partnership with organizations in their communities such as presenters, colleges, and other arts organizations. The money can be used in a wide variety of ways in order to deepen the dance infrastructure i.e., supporting dancemaking, presenting, education, and audience development programs. The New York State Dance Force has been able to leverage funds from other funding sources recently and we hope it will continue for a long time.

Just a final thought. This conference is entitled the 'Art and Science of Nurturing Dancemakers' and yet I don't think we have addressed what we define as dancemaking. There is a major move in the U.S. for the dance field, and in all the arts, to embrace the diversity that exists in dance, all forms of dancemaking, not just the contemporary dance form. As a result, our funding structures have to focus on supporting the cultural diversity in dance. Also, outside of the funding perspective, there are many other ways of supporting our dancemakers.

Jerril Rechter

I am the Artistic Director of a Youth Dance Company in Tasmania in Australia and I'm a member of the Dance Fund, so what I am going to say might seem a little dry, a bit of funding-speak. However, I want to be able to present a clear picture of how dance in Australia is funded. From my own personal perspective, I believe that the arts can threaten the status quo. Art can be provocative and troublesome. Art rightly calls into question how we view the world. Art has the capacity to change people's lives. It offers an insight into the experience of someone else's world and a gateway into the journey which they have taken. In Australia it celebrates what is uniquely and powerfully Australian, particularly at the end of the 20th Century when it is our desire as a country to question our governance and federation. Art explores and creates icons. It is linked to the thinking and probing of our history, and is integral to the creating of balance between the traditional and new. So today I am going to try to provide an insight into the Australian context.

The Australia Council

In Australia the main sources of funding for dance are at federal and state level. States share many aims with the Australia Council and co-fund many artists. But how that funding takes place between those very different organisations, the Australian Council and all the state bodies, is very different. The Australia Council underwent a review a few years ago, and some quite massive changes to its overall structure occurred as part of that review. The Dance Fund became Australia's main support for dance. But within Council there is also the major organisation fund which supports six dance companies. Maybe the ones which international audiences know best are 'Bengara', 'Sydney Dance Company', 'Merryl Tankard Australian Dance Theatre', 'The Australian Ballet', and two of our state ballet companies.

As part of Council, the audience development and advocacy division supports dance market initiatives and some international promotions. These add other resources and strategies to dance through indirect funding. Federally there is also the Department of Communication in the Arts supporting Australia's touring programme. That is becoming more important to dance. Half-a-million dollars per year, which is about £250,000 per year, goes into a programme called 'Made to Move', and this programme supports the venues. The venues choose the contemporary-based companies for their season. In the Dance Fund all the grant decisions are made by arts practitioners, such as myself, who are appointed by Government to sit on these panels. The policies are determined by the arts practitioners based on their knowledge of the art form through formal or informal consultation with many artists. Fund members also seek advice in assessment and policy development from a new group called the Artists' Register of Peers. Nominations for inclusion in the Register are called for periodically by Council and are open to anyone who, by virtue of their knowledge and experience, is equipped to make a fair and informed assessment of artistic work and grant applications. This group are an incredible help when it comes to the funding decisions.

The Difficulties Facing Australian Funding

The Dance Fund has taken a major role in the ongoing development of the broad dance and movement arts field. The Dance Fund's aim is to encourage artists who excel in and are developing their area of practice. We encourage explorations and innovations in a variety of forms. Clearly we cannot directly support all dance, so we don't try. I believe that one of the Australia Council's major strengths is that, unlike state funding bodies, it will fund a project. If you submit a project to the Council they will fund either the whole thing or they won't fund it at all. This is often very difficult, but it also means that artists are encouraged to put in a realistic budget and that budget is respected by those members on the fund. Artists are given the full amount to produce their work, produce their season, develop their ideas. At State level, often applications for $10,000 Australian dollars will receive $5,000, which means the artist has to cut back the creative process or cut back on time, which is very difficult.

Over the years in Australia, we have developed a fair degree of Federal and State support. However, the balance between the resources of our agencies is shifting quite dramatically, compared to 10 years ago. Federally, the budgets are reducing and this year dance has 10% less than it was granted in 1996-97. Also prior to that dance took an enormous cut, so over the last three years the Dance Fund has had an incredible reduction in its funds. It is also important to consider that we have a shifting political climate at the moment, with a Federal Election at the end of this month which could change funding policies and dollar allocations dramatically across the country. As the budgets are reduced, more critical and occasionally more painful decisions have to be made. Currently the Dance Fund distributes about £900,000 of Council's total budget of around £22 million. But it also has access to special initiatives money such as the Government's Emerging Artists initiative (see below). This brings the fund for the dance budget to around £1 million. Adding all the other components across dance federally, the total is around £2 million nation-wide. Still our budget is very tight and getting tighter. Dance funding assessed and allocated by dance professionals represents about half of the Federal support for dance. This allows some structures to survive on the basis of the greater momentum even if the real artistic initiatives of the time are being generated by the smaller companies or independent groups of artists.

The Dance Fund

The Dance Fund has seven specific categories to which artists in the field may apply twice a year, but with reducing budgets we cannot sustain the expected support. Through the Fund's triennial category we will find that in two years the already relatively small dance infrastructure will be about 12 to 15 companies across all of Australia, including the major organisations. It is a significant reduction across the Australian dance landscape. Both at Council and at Dance Fund level we will be watching what effect this supposed strategic change will really have. In essence the network of dance companies is a fragile over-stretched net with each company representing a kind of post holding the net in shape. With the loss of one or more of the remaining companies, the shape of the whole dance field can change, losing entire pathways for different kinds of performers. This is a real concern within the Fund and within the broader dance field.

The next category is the Commission and Partnerships category. It aims to increase and broaden the pool of external resources for dance. For example an investment of 80,000 Australian dollars in partnership with the Australian Film Commission and the Australian Broadcasting Corporation was only 20% of that entire project budget. The Fund has just supported a partnership between the National Library of Australia and the National Film and Sound Archive in Ozdance which will see other significant resources going to dance. We are also entering into partnership with the National State Ozdance branches to help emerging artists. Through these partnerships Council is trying to improve its funding of the arts. The Fellowships category is a once-in-a-lifetime two-year funding allocation. It is about 40,000 Australian dollars. It is awarded to artists who currently excel in or have the potential to develop a significant and unique area of practice. The Presentation and Promotion category is potentially a small touring programme which is artist-driven rather than venue-demand driven as opposed to the Made to Move programme which is absolutely venue-driven. We try to support artists deciding where they want their work to go. The

Development category covers individual professional development and industry development through conferences, journals, master classes, and programmes. We have a New Work category and we've recently divided its support into two sub-categories. One aim of the project is to explore and develop one or more choreographic ideas, in essence to develop the work up to a workshop stage. The other sub-category aims for full production, where marketing and production management and clarity of performance aims are critical. This has been a really important step for the Fund in the more outcome-focused Government environment in which the Australia Council has to work. Additionally, the Australia Council and State agencies are supporting a range of different models, such as choreographic centres of research and development, subsidised space to ensure new work has a chance to be performed, companies led by an executive producer rather than a choreographer.

Funding Young Choreographers

Under the section of Youth and Emerging Artists, which is all-important, there are four distinct categories. Education and training of dancers is an area which the Fund does not support. Emerging artists, professional practitioners working with young people in youth dance, and dance and education by professional companies are the three areas supported by the Dance Fund. Youth dance applications have two different criteria but overall the applications must compete for funds alongside all other applications. Dance and education models are similar to the British education model such as Ludus which I'm working with at the moment. We've found that the pattern of the last three to five years, particularly with the disappearance of company structure, has been that young graduates are applying for funds to make and present work. They basically want to dance, so they form a company and apply for funds, but unfortunately a lot of them do not have the depth of skills or the body of work behind them to compete at that level. To combat this, Council introduced an Emerging Artists initiative. These are special funds allocated for young choreographers between one and five years after graduating or wherever they can justify being an emerging artist. There is no age limit as such. These grants are to develop their skills and craft without the pressure of a performance at the end of the process. All the states within Australia have Emerging Artists start-up grants. In Tasmania we have a start-up grant for young choreographers to apply for specifically, so they are not competing against those more established artists for funds.

The Dance Fund wants to ensure that they are encouraging new initiatives and diverse forms in dance and movement practice. The Fund has a national overview and a responsibility to the expression of the changing Australian identity in its contemporary cultural diversity. The Fund wants to work with other parts of Council, Federal counterparts in Canberra and State agencies to develop dance as an industry. This covers audience development through broadcast and touring, community participation and access to dance, and interesting international markets. But just to go back to my opening section which I call my 'art factory'. Art is delicious, intoxicating and resonant. There has to be a reason for producing and creating a work of art. It is not just that it's new or innovative and the hope is that as arts funding agencies intervene in the Australian arts environment, they allow for more good work to arrive and thrive.

Points raised in discussion:

No discussion points were available due to a recording error.

Session 11
Mentor Models

Key Words:

creative process   devising process   funding   role of the choreographer,
apprenticeships

Peter Boneham of The Danse Lab in Ottawa introduced to the UK a particular and very personal model of choreographic development, working with individual, experienced choreographers to challenge preconceptions and to nudge them out of habitual ways of making work. This session discusses the original model, identifies the ways it has been used in this country, and shares views from those who have participated in related projects. The speakers were Assis Carreiro, Kevin Finnan, Wayne McGregor and Katherine Watson. The session was chaired by Ken Bartlett.

Katherine Watson

I spent ten years working with Peter Boneham and probably know him well enough to be able to discuss his work. The Danse Lab was founded thirty years ago as a touring dance company in Canada. The company had a supportive structure in terms of choreography. It encouraged and supported the creative development of the dancers and choreographers. About ten years ago Peter Boneham decided that he no longer wanted to tour. He talked to funding agencies about creating what he called 'a lab.' The base for The Danse Lab was in Ottawa. Ottawa is not a mecca for dance, and The Danse Lab is in fact the only professional dance organisation in the city. Peter felt that he could provide choreographers with somewhere to research ideas and develop work intelligently and sensitively. The company only works as a lab. It has not changed a lot; the values and ethos have remained constant. We invite choreographers to come and work in the Lab which provides dancers, rehearsal space and technical support. There is also a structure whereby there can be an exchange of work to a small audience. Choreography is presented not as complete but still in the creative process. Dialogue is critically important, and occurs throughout the process between choreographers, dancers, audience and the person whom Peter calls 'a third eye.' That leads into the title of this session - Mentorship.

We have always struggled with this term and we tend to refer to mentors as choreographic monitors or 'third eyes'. Surely a mentor is someone who has known you for a long period and who knows and understands your work in-depth? A monitor might not necessarily know you as well. Perhaps this is the best kind of 'third eye,' someone who is not deeply attached to the process and who can offer a fresh and honest perspective. There is always a monitor for the work. Choreographers from around the world are invited to work at the Lab; the next step is helping facilitate that partnership between choreographer and monitor. We talk to the choreographers about who they are interested in working with, who they feel is the right person to work with through this process at that point in their choreographic development. The monitor does not necessarily need to be a choreographer or a dancer, it could be someone from theatre or even architecture, but there does need to be a valid reason for the choice. Peter sometimes suggests a suitable monitor or even acts as the monitor himself. We try to maintain flexibility, both within the working environment and between the choreographer/monitor relationship.

We try to facilitate early dialogue between choreographer and monitor before the choreographer's residence at the lab. The monitor tends not to visit the studio on the first day of work but waits to see how the choreographer starts working and what they would like to achieve. Many monitors have commented on how challenging it is to observe another artist's creative process, and to support and challenge the choreographer. The partnerships do not always work - sometimes monitor and choreographers find it difficult to communicate with one another. In these instances, it is still possible to see development in the choreographers' work so being part of the process is still important.

Assis Carreiro

I am going to speak from my personal experiences of running the dance mentor lab in Birmingham at the DanceXchange. Our aim there was for regional based choreographers to have the opportunity to be able to reflect, experiment and take risks with their creative process under the guidance of a mentor, so when choreographers were stuck in a rut or lost sight of their creative process there could be someone to offer feedback and provide debate. Our mentoring schemes were devised to question the artist's intentions, methodology and practices and to offer new possibilities and ways forward. I do not think there is a right way for setting up mentoring. There is no template. I think part of the success of mentoring is the notion of flexibility, and learning by doing. Perhaps the most crucial element of mentoring is finding the right combination between mentor and choreographer. There is no point in forcing two individuals together who do not feel comfortable working together. Each project is unique unto itself.

I will briefly discuss three partnerships to demonstrate the different formats of mentoring. Rui Horta, artistic director of SOAP was very interested in combining the two elements of Dance and Light. We invited Rui to run the lab over a five-day period. We sent application forms to dancers, choreographers, designers and architects around the country. The chosen applicants - half dance artists and half visual artists - first spent a day watching a technical rehearsal of Rui Horta's performance so they could observe how he directed his company. They spent the rest of the time developing material. It was very collaborative, completely creative, no strings attached, just a safe place in which to experiment with ideas. At the end of the week, the participants shared some of the work. I know some of the artists then went on to develop the material further for their own works.

Another lab we organised was with Mark Morris. He worked with about twelve choreographers. Again, artists had to apply to be considered for the lab. The final selection was a mixture of quite senior artists with regional based artists. They spent three days working with Mark Morris and his accompanist. Mark would set tasks for participants to devise work. It provided an opportunity for the choreographers to develop new ideas and material. Mark would then talk to them and question them about what they were doing. Mark Morris loved the experience, he liked the privacy and safety of it all, having the time and space to play with ideas without having to show work. It was a very relaxed environment throughout the process.

The third project took place with Peter Boneham. Peter has a very strong personality; he can be a bit of a handful. I realised I could not force this relationship, so needed to consider which choreographers would best suit this project. I approached Russell Maliphant and Javier de Frutos as I felt such a project would be beneficial for them. Unlike The Danse Lab we did not have a company of dancers available for the choreographers to work with, so instead I approached Ricochet Dance Company who had worked previously with Russell Maliphant and Javier De Frutos. Before the project, the choreographers discussed with Peter what they wished to focus on. They then had two weeks in the studio with as many dancers as they needed. At the end of the project a small audience was invited in. It was specifically advertised as a choreographic lab rather than a performance. Peter and the choreographers discussed the process and then showed sections of work created. Many choreographers were interested in being involved in further labs, whilst others felt it to be just too exposing. Peter came back to work with regional choreographers another three or four times at the Dance Exchange. It was important that the artists who were involved in this process had already developed a relationship with the Dance Exchange, so they had continuing support before and after the lab. It was also crucial that the artists trusted ever one involved because they put themselves in a vulnerable and exposing situation.

Kevin Finnan

I think mentoring is an experience that is rich in opportunity, has fantastic potential and a lot to offer. It is, however, fraught with pitfalls and difficulties as well. The first responsibility of the artist is to be clear about what you are going into and what you want to focus on. I had been making work for a long time and had started to feel unhappy with my movement language. I decided that I would focus on this with Peter Boneham as my mentor. He completely tore me to pieces each day but I realised that this was a way of provoking new ideas. I could well imagine a lot of people finding it an utterly destructive experience but I was prepared for it mentally and knew I wanted to go through with the process. With hindsight the experience was very beneficial. I learned a great deal particularly about structure. During the mentoring experience, I had real difficulty in making movement. I see movement as a vehicle for imagery and am particularly concerned with content. I did not do this at the lab. Peter encouraged me to create abstract-phrases, which is just not what I do as an artist. People have their own influences and aesthetics. Peter was very concerned with movement language, notions of beauty, logic and form. Whilst I can appreciate where he is coming from those are not the main concerns of my own work. However this experience has since greatly influenced some of my work. I was recently commissioned to create a choreography for a company called Blue Eyed Soul where it was sufficient for the movement to be the medium. The work I learned with Peter really came into the fore, and I am very pleased, and proud of the piece I created.

Two years later Chisenhale asked me to be a mentor to a group of young choreographers. The choreographers understandably seized the opportunity of having space, dancers and a showcase provided. Rather than use the time to experiment with new ideas, the choreographers all decided to create new pieces and use the showcase to platform their completed works. I got the impression that the choreographers felt I was getting in the way of their work. With hindsight, I feel that those choreographers were extremely vulnerable due to the pressures that they felt they were under. What they needed was support and positive feedback. They certainly did not want any critical questioning or practical interaction in their process. There were some positive aspects to this project but the way it had been set up and organised led to it being more problematic that it needed to have been.

Mentoring provides opportunities for artists to experiment with the creative process. It allows choreographers who quite often feel isolated to gain support and development. Mentoring has however become a panacea in terms of opportunity, and yet it does not suit every choreographer. Surely, there are other methods of providing support, facilities and time? Mentoring projects need to be specific to the individuals involved, and to cater for their needs. For example, it may be appropriate for a dance artist whose work is image-based to have a contemporary filmmaker as their mentor. The thought that a mentor has to be another choreographer is very limiting. Another idea is to bring together groups of people working in the same particular field. For example, you might bring together music, theatre and dance companies who are all exploring a particular way of working. An exchange of ideas, working practises and creative processes could be beneficial for all involved.

Artists tend to feel the need to present themselves as unique and individual. The ultimate insult is that they are derivative. Yet it actually decries the natural order of learning by influence and inspiration from other artists. Originality is the sum total of everything that has influenced you, everything you take from other people plus the bit you put in yourself. Mentoring encourages the notion of young artists developing through the influence and experience of more established artists.

Wayne McGregor

The notion of mentoring is already part of our dance ecology. It forms part of the broader continuum of on-going choreographic development. We are re-packaging something that has always existed in various forms. For example apprenticeships and the notion of learning through influence. There are so many methods of mentoring that can empower the artist. The Dance Agencies and funding bodies need to be interchangeable and fluid with the range of mentoring possibilities available to artists.

I will briefly discuss my experiences of mentoring. I was involved a project called SKITE based in Lisbon. It was a completely open and free structure. The mentors were from a variety of disciplines - architecture, theatre and visual arts. Rather than specific tasks being set, we all collectively decided to work together on particular ideas that were then either developed or discarded over the four weeks work. It was almost like playtime but that interchange of possibilities was really important and beneficial.

I was on the ECF European Programme that had a completely different agenda to that of SKITE. We started with an intellectual premise before embarking on practical work. Choreographers acted as dancers for each other that resulted in quite different relationships being formed. The intellectual rigour of this project resulted in a different kind of observation and critical analysis.

I chose to work with Peter Boneham as my mentor because he is simply not afraid to offer his total opinion. In general people only offer superficial feedback. Yet honesty of opinion can open dialogue and can really offer you the opportunity to grow and develop artistically. I would suggest that this type of monitoring is only appropriate at particular times of your career. Timing is critical because as artists we go through massive cycles of confidence. When I was working with Peter, I felt I was quite confident and had resistance. Sometimes I could feel quite sure about the work I was making but after speaking to Peter I was not too sure! He did not strip away my confidence but at a different stage of my professional life I may have found it a far more difficult experience.

Mentoring should be funded so that it going to be beneficial for the artist, providing a route that is specific to the needs of the individual rather than conforming to predetermined criteria. I have personal experience of how flexible funding can be beneficial for the development of the artist. The Arts Foundation Award gave me about £17,000 to develop my own research and development programme. There was absolutely no agenda or long application forms and instead I was able to focus completely on exactly what I wanted to do at that time.

I think artists can generate their own mentoring. It is a self-agenda. It is about finding an agenda that empowers your work. I do not believe that we are so fragile that we cannot cope with honest opinion. It is the engagement of open dialogue and the understanding and development of ideas through discussion that can challenge work and provide a new way forward.

Points raised in discussion:

- The role of the mentor was discussed. What skills are necessary to be a mentor? Suggestions included - generosity, flexibility, openness, objectivity, honesty, supportiveness, and the ability to provoke, stimulate, challenge and question. Not all these skills need to be implemented in each situation.

- It was proposed that Mentoring could be divided into four categories.
    1. Workshop - An individual artist who works with a group of people

    2. Dramaturgy - An artist who works alongside a specific project and who constantly challenges and provokes the artists involved.

    3. One-to-one - An individual relationship between two artists.

    4. Open forum - A group of artists working together.

    All four models have different functions and benefits.

- Concern was expressed about the way in which mentoring projects are managed. In some cases, mentoring is seen as a form of prerequisite for funding. The artist may not have a choice of who acts as their mentor. It can also imply the notion that the mentor's role is that of quality control which can place added pressure on the artist.

- It was agreed that other forms of mentoring need to be explored. Suggestions included platforms for 'work in progress,' greater interaction with audience (post performance talks, open rehearsals), apprenticeships, work experience alongside established artists, cross-arts mentors.

Session 12

Choreographers Interviewed: The Choreographic Debate

Keywords:

choreographic process	research and development	product	space
light	continuum	working model	

This session offered an opportunity to share in discussion about the choreographic works performed in the Conference Gala, which featured pieces by Jonathan Burrows, Rosemary Lee, Wayne McGregor and Russell Maliphant. Each of the four choreographers discussed the making and production of their work with a colleague of their choice.

The speakers were Jonathan Burrows and Alistair Spalding, Russell Maliphant and Christopher Bannerman, Wayne McGregor and John Ashford, Rosemary Lee and Alistair Spalding. The interviews were chaired by Allen Robertson.

Allen Robertson:

I'm the Dance Editor at Time Out, and I feel a kind of an interloper here. What we're going to be talking about is the process that happens before I ever get involved. That is, what happens before the work gets on stage, and the nature of the relationships between the people who make it, commission it, provide space for it and those who provide time and money. We have four choreographers; the first, Jonathan Burrows is talking to Alistair Spalding from the South Bank.

Alistair Spalding

Jonathan rather disconcertedly said to me in the bar before we came in, 'I don't really like talking about my work', but I'm going to make him.

When I first saw the solo that you performed last night, at the first performance in Newcastle, there was a moment where you stood right in the corner of the stage and you had the whole stage in front of you... It was a really special moment for me because it felt like we didn't know what was going to happen next, and you didn't either... And so my first question is about your process. It seems to me that your process is about discovery, about trying to find things out as you are making them work... Is that true?

Jonathan Burrows

Well first of all what I meant was that choreographers seem at the moment to be asked all the time to talk about their work, and sometimes I feel a little like I want to pause for thought. But yes, in a way the process is one of discovery, and its ongoing. For instance, this solo is part of a longer piece, and I'm discovering that performing it alone like last night, changes it. It's been a piece that has unfinished business about it, which has been both interesting and frustrating.

The version of the solo in the group piece is different, and when we perform the group piece it starts the same way as when you saw it the first time. But it's been a piece that has unfinished business about it, which has been both interesting and frustrating. Last night was very educative, in that at one point there was a possibility to split the piece up into its consecutive parts, but last night convinced me that we'd made the right decision to keep on trying to hold on to the larger picture.

I think that in starting to work on a new piece, it's often that you haven't finished with what you were working on previously. When you start work on a new piece, and the memory of why you were moving in the old piece is of no help at all, because that would only take you to the old piece. So the first thing you have to try and do is find out why you're moving at all, where you might start. And usually the reason ends up being both really important and something that's completely arbitrary and I think that's something difficult for people who are not making dance to try to grasp, because what they see is a completed picture.

Alistair Spalding

Is that why you always start with a kind of formal problem?

Jonathan Burrows

I don't always start with a formal problem, but sometimes I have, yes, and for that reason.

Alistair Spalding

Can you give me an example of when you haven't started with a formal problem?

Jonathan Burrows

Yes. We've just finished making a trio, a nine-minute trio, called *Altogether* which we made three attempts to make. The first two attempts we threw away after a week's work, really a lot of work and we just threw it away. The third time, we just had all this accumulated movement memory and rhythmic memory from all the discarded work, and that took us straight into the piece in a non-formalistic way.

Alistair Spalding

So where did you start then? How did you start that next bit?

Jonathan Burrows

I sat down with Dana Fouras, who was working with me, and I said 'Look, this isn't working but what have we got?' We had been trying to do a lot of preparatory work which was complex, and though it seemed truly fascinating, it ended up being completely invisible... - and I think she said 'Let's throw the note book away'. When she came into the studio the next morning my notebook was, quite literally, in the bin.

Alistair Spalding

I'm interested actually in what happened then, because I still can't quite understand. Do you mean it was a kind of intuitive thing?

Jonathan Burrows

Well no, it was another example of going in one direction to end up in another direction. A year ago I was trying to make an installation piece, but it wasn't seen by anybody. But something about it interested me, and I realised that that was my unfinished business. As soon as I realised that, then I had somewhere to start, which was the material from that installation piece. As soon as we started with that material, we shifted on to things that were new and that we hadn't expected, and pretty soon the material from the installation piece got left behind. But that was the door we needed to open and that was the unfinished business. It's very contradictory and also some of it's very hard to grasp but you do have to go in that direction to end up in this direction.

Alistair Spalding

Yes, and I presume that's quite difficult when you are working with dancers as well?

Jonathan Burrows

Yes, it's hard sometimes for people to orientate themselves through the contradictions.

Alistair Spalding

What about when you are working on your own?

Jonathan Burrows

That can be difficult too, but at least then I've only got myself to annoy.

Alistair Spalding

The other thing I'm beginning to understand about you is that in the working process you like to work on a daily basis almost, rather than in blocks of time. I wondered if you are always able to do that, if that's the best way to work and whether the infrastructures that exist allow you to do that?

Jonathan Burrows

No, it's really, really hard, but I'm not a manager, I am not a producer, I am a choreographer; so when I get up in the morning I want to choreograph. The more you practice the better you get, and if you take three months off then you are just going to be a bit rusty when you start out again. But no, it's been quite difficult. I've only been able to establish a working pattern like that by people being very generous with space. The only way I could afford to make that solo was that I had a key to Greenwich Dance Agency and I went in from 8 till 10 in the morning for two months.

Alistair Spalding

So that's fine when you're working on your own but presumably when you're working with dancers it becomes really problematic, not the time of day necessarily, but the funding?

Jonathan Burrows

Dana Fouras and Ragnhild Olsen, who I'm currently working with, are very smart, and have encouraged me to realise that we can spend 7 hours working in a day or we can spend two hours, and that if we really focus in that two hours we get more done than working the 7 hours.

Alistair Spalding

And then going further on, in terms of the presentation of the work, that must be difficult too, is it? If it's always in a stage of development, do people worry that they don't know what they're getting, or that they're going to get something that is fairly vague?

Jonathan Burrows

Guy Cools from the VZW Voruit Kunstencentrum in Ghent wrote an article recently which I agreed with, in which he said that the prevailing model for the working process in dance is still a theatre model. He suggests that we really have to try and find out more about what a genuine model for a choreographer might be. I am working with Julia Carruthers who is managing me, and together we're trying to find a way to stay flexible for things to shift and change, and at the same time try to be practical. And sometimes we get it right and sometimes we don't, but it's a constant negotiation, and I think the main thing for dance producers who promote to remember is that there aren't any rules, that everybody's individual and that everybody needs something slightly different.

Alistair Spalding

Yes, a kind of flexibility?

Jonathan Burrows

That's the absolute key.

Alistair Spalding

How do you know when the piece is finished then?

Jonathan Burrows

Because there doesn't seem to be any more unfinished business to be dealt with right at that point.

Alistair Spalding

So there is actually a stopping point?

Jonathan Burrows

In a way, yes, you get as far as you can, or there's a deadline, or sometimes you just find a good ending so you know it's over for now.

Alistair Spalding

Thank you.

Allen Robertson introduced Russell Maliphant talking to Christopher Bannerman from Middlesex University.

Christopher Bannerman

I thought I would start with a question about a time before the work we saw you performing last night. I remembered as I was watching, that you came to Middlesex once during the summer when no students were around; you wanted to do some research in the theatre and I thought that was a bit odd because of the dark and low ceilings. Then you said you wanted to try something with light now I'm beginning to see, I think there was a rich vein there to be explored.

Russell Maliphant

Over that summer I wanted an opportunity to work with Michael Hulls, the lighting designer who designed last night's piece. We wanted to research a situation where he would create a rig and then I would explore working with those different lights. I think we had three weeks to explore and to gain trust in each other. We've been working together for a few years since then, but that was the first time that we had an extended period to get to know each other's work in depth. *Shift* was made the following year; we only had a week together to make it, but those periods of time in research and development that we had at Middlesex has influenced all the work that we have done since, and Mike and I have quite a strong base formed from those periods.

Christopher Bannerman

It seems to me that we tend to think of light as being an added element to dance, but you reminded me that everything we see is reflected light. If there is no reflected light, we don't see, and so therefore there's no theatre dance. But juxtaposed with that is a very deep sense of embodiment, and you appear to be bringing a number of strands and some very deep body knowledge onto the stage for us. Maybe you could tell us a little bit about that?

Russell Maliphant

My journey in dance has been reasonably long. For one thing, I've been dancing for over 25 years, and in quite diverse styles, having had classical ballet training alongside tap, modern, jazz and many folk dance styles as a boy involved in dance - when I was at Comprehensive school and should probably have been out playing football and rugby. Over the years I have studied Tai Chi, Pilates, Capoeira, release technique, contact, also trained in The Rolfing Method of Structural Integration, which is a bodywork with the fasciae, yoga and a few other things which I have tried to explore with my body.

I try to synthesise these ranges of information or integrate them to a certain extent so they're not individual practices, but they can feed some help into my personal practice with my own body. So I like to have those techniques to draw on and not to be limited. When I worked with DV8 straight after the Royal Ballet, I found that having a classical technique, at that time, in that situation was more of a limitation than an asset; so I wanted to be able to try and drop that technique and move into softer styles, softer techniques. But then later on I found that I would also definitely like to draw on classical, I wanted to be able to pick up the technique but also be able to drop it, as and when appropriate, so that it is not residing in my body against my will. So that's been part of the process.

Shift - as a piece of work is also fluid in how it's choreographed. Where I am in space is set, and where I am in relation to the music is set; the essence of the movement and shapes are known and from that place it's an exploration every time of doing it, so it can still appear different. I mean it's relatively the same piece but it can be harder and sharper sometimes, it can be softer and calmer other times, I'm looking for a state where I can work and feel authentic with myself during the piece.

Christopher Bannerman

And you look for a structure within which you can respond in the moment, just exactly in that second? You don't decide before you come on whether it's a particular kind of evening for you that your body has indicated a certain kind of engagement, it's right there?

Russell Maliphant

I'd say the warming up process is beginning to feel where you're at, what you're body is taking on that day, and then the performance continues that process.

Christopher Bannerman

It's interesting the amount of time and knowledge that is necessary to achieve and elegance and simplicity that is illuminating. I think it was an art critic who said 'Well Monsieur Matisse, how long is it going to take you to do that?', and he said 'Twenty-five years'. Good lesson for us. You mentioned previously that the music was something that was known before this work started. Is that an unusual way for you to work?

Russell Maliphant

Yes. That's the only piece where I've explored the process of having the music completely set first. I heard that piece by Shirley Thompson once, didn't know what it was, I think I was preparing for a show and someone played that piece of music and I enjoyed it. And then I had a commission from Assis (Carreiro) at the Dance Exchange and Jane (Greenfield) at Nott Dance to make this solo; and I thought what am I going to do, and remembered that piece. Shirley Thompson agreed that I could use the piece; I started to work on it and the music was quite formative because it has a certain kind of sensitiveness; I wanted to work a little away from that and the timing of it, but it began to kind of colour some of the vocabulary and the process was quite quick. We had a week working in the studio theatre to bring that together. I had had some time at The Place's Choreodrome earlier that year, so I already had some kind of material up my sleeve to draw on. Mike came in with some ideas in which boxes appeared on the back wall but it wasn't this, just the boxes, and then over the course of that week it became clear that the strongest thing was the simplest thing and that was having just the boxes, and from there it all came together reasonably quickly. But yes, I think if we didn't have the known asset of the music it would have been very difficult, I don't know if it would have been possible, to make something in a week.

Allen Robertson then introduced Wayne McGregor and John Ashford, Director of The Place Theatre.

John Ashford

Wayne, you didn't even train as a dancer did you?

Wayne McGregor

I didn't have a formal dance training until I went to College, no.

John Ashford

And you're a local boy from Bretton Hall made good?

Wayne McGregor

Yes.

John Ashford

What I really want to pinpoint are moments of choreographic development rather than looking at development of a recent choreography. It must be interesting finding out which points lead you into wanting to make dance; that always fascinates me. Was it during your more general performance training that you knew you were interested in dance?

Wayne McGregor

Yes, I think I started from a theatrical background so a lot of my earlier experiences in dance came through theatre. But I was always very attracted to the more visual aspects of theatre, to the things that I thought actually provided me with some sort of kinetic connection basically, the things that I thought visually really moved me but in a kinetic sense. And I think from there that I started to think about the motion of the body and how I could work with that choreographically. When I found out about the choreographic course at Bretton I thought that it would be a really good way to experiment with some of those ideas, but in the context of experiencing a wide range of other things which you were able to do there.

John Ashford
So you weren't going to put all your eggs in that particular basket?

Wayne McGregor
I put most of my eggs in that basket. I just kept a few away. I did a subsidiary subject for two years working with devised processes in theatre, and I think that's really fed into the ways in which I think of the choreographic material.

John Ashford
So you were considering working with movement prior to engaging in a specific training course, but you chose a route which was less formal than a traditional dance training.

Wayne McGregor
Well yes, I have never been attracted to a formal sort of training. I hadn't, for example, thought that I wanted to go do several years of balletic training. I have always had a very strange way of moving normally; when I went out dancing I always had a quite unique way of moving and I always had. I knew I could feel it.

John Ashford
So have you always wanted to be a choreographer in a club?

Wayne McGregor
I think I really wanted to! I felt that I had some physical language that was interesting, that this was a way in which I could express something physically which was very integrated into the fabric of my personality. And because my body type dictates - it dictates quite a lot of articulation for example - I thought of using that as a basic resource... Not thinking about a technical training and putting this body into that technical form, but seeing how I could excavate some of the body information and take it into some form of communicative language.

John Ashford
Were you as clear as that when you left Bretton Hall?

Wayne McGregor
I was. After I left Bretton Hall I went through a period of uncertainty, as I felt I wanted to do choreography but I didn't quite know how I was going to do that. So I went to America to really try and gain some more resources, to get technical resources, to try and feed into thinking about choreography. Then I came straight back to London and made a piece.

John Ashford
And I saw it... it began with a solo and then it went on to group work. And I felt there was a great disparity between what you were doing with your body in its uniqueness as a soloist, and what you were getting the rest of the group to do. Whereas now those two things seem to have come together in ways which are absolutely right, and that's been a five-year process.

Wayne McGregor
Yes, I don't think I've got it right, I'm still on that journey... it's a very difficult process of discovery. It is to do with the relationship between someone who has very individualistic characteristics in their own performance persona if you like, in how they actually employ physical material in performance or choreographically, and other dancers. What type of dancers then can you work with, not simply to understand it but to give it a different type of dimension? What is really interesting for me is not to get clones - I don't want bodies that actually are going to try and become and have the same kind of physicality - but I am really interested in a kind of

transformation where a different individual can actually take on board that language so there is a coherence to the piece, but also take it into a different direction in a way. That's why I wanted to work with Antonia (Francheschi) in the piece that I made for this Conference. I know it is suicide to make a dance piece for a dance conference in three days, I realise that, but it was one of the challenges I wanted to push myself through... I wanted to work with a body and a technique that's really alien to me, not to try and make that body fit particular characteristics but to try and celebrate that individuality itself. I tried to celebrate in the history of that body, and to try and take that material and transfer it somewhere else specifically for this piece. I think what I've tried to do with the company now is to choose dancers who have real adaptability and flexibility in terms of the language, but who can then give it an articulation and a dimension that I couldn't provide.

John Ashford

The journey over about four years from there to here has involved a degree of mentoring, in Canada and perhaps elsewhere that I don't know about.

I think ideally the time allowed for the production of a dance should be about 12 weeks. Only nobody seems to get 12 weeks, they get 6 or 8 if they're lucky. Now, they get this bit that's knocked off that's called Research and Development, or mentoring or some other scheme. I have a very brutal question which is, would you rather have had the mentoring or another 4 weeks?

Wayne McGregor

I think I would rather have both actually. I see the work as a continuum and don't want to compartmentalise myself in that way. I don't think - OK, I'm now doing R&D, now I'm making a piece, now I've got an odd week of teaching, or really concentrating my energies on production... I really think about it as a fluid continuum in which all these things happen, sometimes simultaneously, sometimes in isolation. So you have however many weeks you have – 10 weeks or whatever, and you're thinking about that rehearsal time, but within that time there are moments of R & D, or big points of discovery if you've got questions... And sometimes you can come some way to resolving some of those ideas, and sometimes you shoot off in a completely different direction. I think of it as a very fluid interchange. I can identify certain mentoring times when I felt confident enough artistically to have a brutal interchange of experience and receive opposing views, and I have had times also when I don't have that confidence. So I really try and find it for myself, I try and empower myself to negotiate that journey so that there's some clarity to it. Sometimes it's by accident, sometimes it's by design.

John Ashford

You produce a phenomenal amount of work, not only with your own company but also with the National Theatre and with opera companies abroad and in community and education work over the last 4 or 5 years. To what extent does that external work influence the basic task of making dances for your company?

Wayne McGregor

I don't think it's external, I think it's part of the same journey. I genuinely get as much from working with a group of young men at The Place, creatively and choreographically as I do working with the dancers. Again it depends; things come into focus for a certain period of time you grow in that time and then you come away and you work more with the dancers, you know it's a very fluid interchange. For example, my experience of working with the Shobana Jeyasingh Company wasn't so much the quality of that piece but what the information exchange was. For both Shobana and me it was that articulation rather than the view of the piece. I think we're still in the position of being product-centred and we think all the time only about the product and not about the journey. And I think one of the things that is great about this Conference is that so far, in much of the discussion, we are really thinking much more about the fluid continual journey and actually trying to watch pieces with much fresher eyes. Not looking at arrival, but looking at that notional journey.

Allen Robertson then introduced Rosemary Lee, in conversation with
Alistair Spalding.

Alistair Spalding

I know you were slightly worried about the context last night and I can see why, because I think your work is coming from quite a different place. I think that's partly because of where you're starting out from which is more of a personal starting point. Is that true?

Rosemary Lee

Probably. I've been trying to work that out, listening to the others. I think most recently, while I've been working on solos my starting point has definitely been the performer. So for *Galliard* my particular starting point is Gill (Clarke), there is no question that it's made for her. At the moment I seem to have a focus on a one-to-one basis, having in the past made pieces for 200 people - my biggest piece up to now was 237 participants! But for the last four years it's been more or less solos. So I seem to get really interested in one person and how I deal with their essence.

Alistair Spalding

To stay with this idea of starting points, if you don't know the person who is dancing for you then there must be something that started before hand? If you walk into a room full of people that you don't know, does the piece start then, or does it start before?

Rosemary Lee

No – it starts before that because of the way I work. I've never wanted a company or to tread that route of regular touring and a regular working pattern. I've wanted to be able to keep trying different contexts and different working models. That means that my starting points are often reactive – commissions for example. However, I also try to self produce a large project at least once every two years.

So for instance going back a bit, I knew I wanted to make a work that was accessible to a different kind of audience, a promenade audience. I don't often like the proscenium kind of setting, I prefer investigating the relationship with the audience in a different way. Then I found the site, and the site led me to the piece, and then I met the people... So there lots happened before meeting them. But when I'm actually dealing with an individual, that's the bit that is similar. With *Galliard* it was a desire tomake a solo for Gill so that was my starting point.

Alistair Spalding

Going back to *Galliard*. What else was there at the same time? Why the Queen?

Rosemary Lee

Ah, that's because of Gill. What came before was that I was commissioned to make a piece with the Balanescu Quartet, to work specifically with Alexander Balanescu. The piece was made in 1994 so it's four years old, and perhaps once I knew I was making the solo for Gill, I started to have a strong hunch about what I might be working on and the regal, queenly ideas came then.

The other thing that is interesting about *Galliard* is that for both of us, this is the third revival. It was made in '94 and performed once, and then it was revived last year for a tour, then it's had a rest for a year and it's been revived just for this conference. It's been a kind of case of 'chinese whispers' as Gill would say, and things have changed and shifted. We've actually gone back to some of the original ways of interpreting particular bits of movement or a particular phrase and bypassed the one in the middle. It's been very detailed and interesting to see how it's grown.

Alistair Spalding

What kind of performance was it last night for you?

Rosemary Lee

I found it astounding, it was wilder, more abandoned and I was completely enthralled. Normally I'm a complete gibbering wreck watching my own work, worrying about things, but I suddenly realised that I had gone on a long journey with her, and it ended in the blackout, and I hadn't lost it anywhere with my own worries. I was amazed that I was able to do that, and that she was able to take me on that journey. We need to ask Gill really, but I thought there was a wonderful edge of abandonment and control that she was treading and that was something that was integral to the piece. It was even more exposed to me last night.

Alistair Spalding

So once you're in the studio and you are working with the performers of whatever kind, then do you start using formal techniques or problems to begin?

Rosemary Lee

Galliard was slightly different from usual because we had such a short amount of time, and I knew Gill and her training so well. With other people I'd work on body work, sensing and release work and imagery. I want to get people as comfortable as possible, into a state where I can see things unfold and where there aren't any barriers. So I work on that whoever I'm working with, and talk a lot about body and sensation and then introduce imagery. With Gill we improvised with many different images, setting up different tasks with different kinds of qualities and words and trying to put the two together. I remember one was 'passionate Morris dancing' and another one was 'knife-edge' and that made 'passionate Morris dancing on a knife edge'! I was trying to layer what I already knew about Gill, and trying to add other qualities that I wanted to draw out. Gill is an exceptional dancer with a flow and a way of making transitions in her body which I find extraordinary, and I wanted to chop them up every so often, and then at other times just let it go like the circular sections.

Alistair Spalding

And a similar question to the one that John asked, where does this take you when working with different kinds of groups? Does your working process change or do you see it differently, or does one form the other? Does this include your film work?

Rosemary Lee

Film work has to be different because of the way you work with the camera, but in general I'd say it's very much like Wayne's description, it's a continuum. With Gill and with the Richochet dancers, who've had more training, I was able to work at things in a more detailed way, to maybe approach the work with more refinement than I would with other people. But the actual core and foundation for what I am doing comes from the same place. All my pieces are equally important to me whether it's a BA degree piece for students or a piece for children.

Alistair Spalding

What about making work for yourself, is that different?

Rosemary Lee

I think that the process of making work for myself is different. I find it's longer, it's much more difficult, there is more self-doubt, and I can't make decisions so quickly. The last two I've made I felt that I was really exposing myself in a way I was concerned about, so I had to do it all privately and then just get out there. I don't like mentors and people coming in and seeing me. Usually the only person I'll let in is Sue MacLennan. And because I feel it's so hard, and then I just get it out there, I don't go through a process of discarding, I just work away and then just present it. I've worked with videoing myself for the last few years, and I'm beginning to think that I've got to chuck that out too. A solo that I made about the same time as *Galliard* took just ages to create using video. It's got about five motifs, but to get to those five, to get to that minimalist choice, I went through them time and time again and thought I'd got it, the came home, looked at the video and thought it was emotional rubbish. It felt authentic but it didn't look authentic on the video, and then I realised that the video wasn't telling me what people would see, because it's not a live performance. In the end I decided to put myself on the line and try it and see if it worked.

Alistair Spalding

Just one last thing because again this is about choreographic development and I know that you're currently in an R&D year. I think that's probably going to mark a sort of change in the way you work, or is it a kind of watershed?

Rosemary Lee

How can I tell beforehand? It's because I said publicly that my last piece felt like a kind of culmination for me, because I decided consciously to use old material in it which is something I've never done before, perhaps like a kind of finale. I don't know whether this year is going to affirm whether I carry on doing what I do or whether it's going to help me branch out. But I do know that I was missing performing and once you get labelled as a choreographer nobody else asks you to dance. I love performing and so during my R&D period I am asking people to choreograph for me so that I am performing and interpreting again. It's tough because I'm not in shape, but I feel in shape in other ways, intellectually and emotionally.

Allen Robertson

What has emerged throughout all of this is clearly that time schedules have to be flexible and that people do need the time that they need. Or as Jonathan said, two hours can be as good as seven hours if you know that the two hours is all you've got.

Points raised in discussion:

No discussion points were available due to a recording error.

Session 13

Urban Culture and Dancemaking

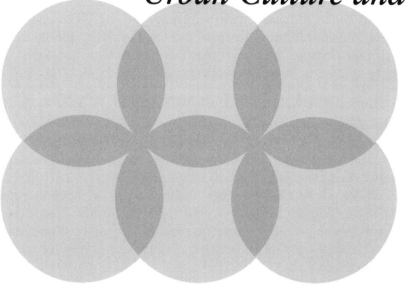

Key words:

Workshop Festival tradition	hip-hop technique	break-dance	African dance

Dick McCaw from the International Workshop Festival introduced Germaine Acogny, a choreographer and dancer from Senegal and France, and Abdelaziz Sarrokh, Artistic Director of HUSH HUSH HUSH based in Ghent, Belgium.

Speakers' contributions have been translated from the French and Flemish.

Dick McCaw

Outside our workshop space at Yorkshire Dance each day there were rollerbladers. They had incredible steeply banked platforms almost like ski jumps and would zoom down one ski jump, over a ramp in the middle, up the other side, turn round and sit down. There was a tree on the near side ramp and one lad swung from a branch down the ramp and they were all egging him on. Yesterday the police arrived and put defensive iron fences around the big ramps as Germaine and I were walking into work, and that was the introduction to Urban Dance for me. When you look at what these kids are doing for about four to five hours a day - the grace, the agility, the skill, the co-ordination, the joy, the energy of this activity - we agreed that this had to be called dance. It was everything that we were trying to communicate in our workshops.

Every year the Workshop Festival has been dedicated to exploring one particular theme, so when I asked Germaine and Abdelaziz to give a workshop this year it was to answer the theme of rhythm. Again what astonished me about these 12-15 year old kids was that they were doing that, engaging in something completely bodily. Perhaps these kids come from broken homes, perhaps they have social problems, but this was no talking cure, this was no video screen experience, it was with the body. For ten years the Workshop Festival has been dedicated to understanding the body, the body's rhythms, and how the body functions as used by a performer. I was very pleased to see the body almost taken to its peak of perfection with these rollerbladers. It's no huge move from roller-blading to the street dancers where Abdelaziz began at the age of eleven dancing with friends and doing Hip-hop and break-dance.

At nineteen he met Alain Platel, and was introduced to 'serious dance' or 'art dance'. He started making dances which synthesized Hip-Hop, break-dance, Electro boogie, and art dance. I will start by asking him about the passage between Hip-hop and contemporary dance.

Abdelaziz Sarrokh

For me it is experimental. I have not been hugely original in using Hip-Hop in my contemporary dance, because for the past eight years there have been dance companies using Hip-Hop in France. The difference is, here is a serious dance company doing Hip-Hop and then doing their contemporary work, so there is a complete separation between the two types of dance, one done next to the other.

When I went to see the 'American Hip-Hop All Stars' it was two hours of non-stop break-dance/Hip-Hop, and while that might have appealed to me on a technical level, I felt that certainly a dance audience would be bored after about 20 minutes. When I started my company HUSH HUSH HUSH I started to use this Hip-Hop vocabulary but within a contemporary dance framework which I learned from Alain Platel's influence on my work.

When I was working with Alain Platel I was impressed by the humanity of his work and I find this humane aspect in street dance. In street dance I can find all kinds of dance which I can use in my 'mixture'. It is experimental, and the most difficult thing in HUSH HUSH HUSH has been making the bridge between the break-dancers and the professional contemporary dancers. This is because the vocabulary and techniques are very different. On the one hand there is curiosity from the contemporary dancers to learn about hip-hop, but from the other side there seems to be a more negative attitude.

However, despite the difficulties of making these bridges, in the first rehearsal process of two and a half months everybody starting opening up to each other, so one group did start learning the other group's way of moving, and this is one of my greatest pleasures in that process.

I tried to break down these barriers, tried to make the bridges. I asked the dancers to work with characters, using certain costumes for certain characters; a well-dressed person with a book, a student etc. So whether a break-dancer or contemporary dancer was just about to dance, they would be asked to start the dance with that book. It was therefore not immediately obvious when you looked at the whole group who was who; it became an integrated cast.

For two or three weeks before the production there were real problems with the breakers who would say "What are people going to think of me, my friends are going to be in the audience and you are asking me to dress up... You know, this is something I am not prepared to do. I will look foolish, I will be ashamed of myself".

In order to overcome this problem I became something of a social worker, saying "You'll be alright, its OK, you will look fabulous in that costume and its going to work, I promise you - you'll look good." Then at the première it was a huge success and they said "Yes you were right, it was a good idea, I like the costume, you know it is a good concept you have". And I wondered what would have happened if the première had been a flop. They would all have come to me saying "I told you, I told you it would not work, this costume is completely ridiculous, the idea is completely crap". They started understanding my ideas, my conception of how this dance theatre works, and I was vindicated by the fact that the première did work.

One of my anxieties is that maybe this work is something that is rather hyped up now, but in three or four years it will go out of fashion. Therefore whilst we is touring around, and whilst it is a huge success, I do not enjoy it quite as much as I could because I feel it might be rather short lived.

Dick McCaw

We have established Hip-Hop and where it fits in - now let us turn to Germaine Acogny. She first came to the Workshop Festival in 1992 in Nottingham to a project called Stamping Ground (the name was borrowed from a piece by Jiri Kylian for Nederlands Dans Theater). We had very many different accounts of what is traditional dance and I was completely shocked when Germaine said, "What is this 'African Dance' that you keep talking about? What is this place called Africa? There are 44 different countries that have had influences from three main colonising European countries. There is Lucitaine Africa, Francophone Africa, and Anglophone Africa... Do you think we all have one dance in a continent about five times the size of Europe? And by the way, what is this village dance which you impose upon us? We live in towns, we have cars, we have roads, and we have skyscrapers. You Europeans are probably as un-advanced in your thinking about Africa as we un advanced in our thinking."

It was so refreshing when we were getting very bogged down in earnest white liberal conversation about black issues, hearing Germaine say, "Come on, you are just putting us in another folkloric ghetto...". The other thing she said this week was "Do you think you have dance in your blood and that white people do not have dance in their blood? Do you think we do not learn dancing, that we are born dancing? No, we learn dancing."

Abdelaziz has also commented on the fact that the workshop participants thought they would just come and break dance; they failed to appreciate that it would be very hard work. It is this idea that dance isn't taught, that African dance is something simply acquired in the blood and it is also the fact that you have said that in the context of this talk, African dance is also urban and not just from the villages. Would you like to speak about how an urban African dance draws on those traditional roots and what the relation between the two is?

Germaine Acogny

I am very happy to have heard what Abdelaziz has said because it very much corresponds with my experience and how I learnt traditional dance.

In creation Africa promotes all kinds of African art. There are different forms of African dance because there are different shapes and sizes of dancers. It is difficult to define. You can't really ask what it is. What is it? A large part of what makes up contemporary African dance is development. There is no fixed definition because contemporary African dance is always evolving. It is what is happening today; tomorrow it will develop and change.

The words 'traditional dance' remind me of taking dances from the villages in straw skirts and costume and putting them on stage. This might have been a very well intentioned thing, not just for European tourists but rather to demonstrate African dance. But obviously the dance was taken out of its social and cultural context to be put on a stage. The other thing that happened was that sometimes the women had very brightly decorated top pieces and other times their breasts were naked and there comments such as 'Are you going to see the African striptease tonight?' Whereas it is completely normal in a village to see women with their breasts naked, once you put it on stage it becomes a quite different thing. This is my personal opinion; even when I go to the beach I find it still quite shocking to see women with bared breasts, so for me the idea of putting these women on stage was even more shocking.

When I was looking at this traditional dance performance on stage I considered what these movements are about. They no longer have a social function; they are no longer part of the lives of the villagers. After all, in Dacca you do not live in huts, you live in very large buildings. So I went back to my education and formal training as a teacher of physical education in France, because dance is not formally taught in Africa.

In Africa, you learn in two ways; the first way is simply by imitation. You watch somebody dancing, and that is how you learn. Secondly, you learn through rites of initiation when you go into the Sacred Forest and there is a master drummer and a master dancer, and you are formally taught the steps which allow you the passage from childhood through to adulthood.

When I discuss my approach to dance with African colleagues, they say 'Yours isn't traditional African dance'. This brings me again to question 'What is this African Dance?' In point of fact I had huge difficulty learning African dances because some of the dances – for example the circle of the legs from the Waloof tradition from Senegal- took three years to acquire. So the idea that these dances are simply acquired or are part of some genetic code is frankly racism; it is absolutely not the case. It takes time to understand these very difficult and very different types of dances, so for me it is really a question of technique, of understanding these different dances, whether it is contemporary dance, Hip-hop or traditional dance. First technique, then feeling.

My work is also bringing together once more of two worlds of dance. On the one hand the classical dance, the western dance which I brought from my studies in Paris, and traditional dance. One teacher tried to force my body into a particular way of movement to plié but I found it much easier to access the classical plié by doing an undulation wave movement, making a wave between my sternum and pubis. Later when I was working with Maurice Béjart I was once again demonstrating the plié and Maurice said "Don't try to do it classically. Root yourself in the ground and establish a relation between yourself, the ground and the sky, that way you will be able to do your plié the way only you can do it." So once again as far as I am concerned it is a question of technique, but it is of marrying these two techniques in an intelligent way.

I would say to Abdelaziz, I feel that his work is not a passing fad or fashion, because he takes the work and makes it his. He is dancing and therefore because he is dancing it is authentic, it is life, and there is no way on earth that it is going to be something ephemeral.

The world would be an awful lot healthier place if we danced more. Of course we are intelligent sentient beings, but we were made to move, we were made to dance. And if we do not dance then the capability will start to disappear, we will start to degenerate. I am disturbed that somebody who is so young has this fear that what they are doing will perish soon. In my dictatorship it will be a dictatorship of dance! Whereas in China every morning people do their Tai Chi before work, we would all be obliged to dance because dance is life and life is dance.

Abdelaziz Sarrokh

Do you still study the traditional dances of Senegal? And if so, have those dances changed over the period since you started learning traditional dance some 30 years ago? How have those dances changed?

Germaine Acogny

Yes, traditional dance is changing. The younger dancers are changing it, not necessarily for the best of reasons but in order to gain money. Younger dancers have to dance for tourists, and in order to impress tourists they tend just to take the very quick movement and the quick beats and the loud drum music, almost to deafen the tourist. The movements become more gesticulations rather than elegant dance moves, for in traditional dance there are slow, medium and quick movements, and all of them have their own pace, their own elegance and their own sensuality. There is a distinction to be made between a dance that is explicitly sexual and a dance which is sensual. For me it is most important that we hold on to that sensuality, so in recent courses I have given (in her dance centre near Dacca) I have invited an old master aged 74 to work with the younger dancers. In this exchange, the younger dancers who can be brought back into contact with some of these traditions, and with the slower movements, which they can risk doing for a non-tourist audience. But it is that exchange between the elders, the old masters, and the younger generation which I feel will help the tradition develop, continue and not to atrophy, and of course I continue to take lessons in African dance myself.

Points raised in discussion:

· Break dancing can be exciting to contemporary dancers because it has such a high potential of energy and excitement.

· Putting social dance forms on stage, usually something done among friends, suddenly creates a 'them and us' situation.

· Everyone brings their own 'bag of tricks' to the rehearsal room, and in improvisation people will create based on whatever they are good at.

· Although different anatomical structures are associated with people from particular racial origins, people all have different body shapes and sizes. The important point is to remember the principles of the movement and adapt them to your own body.

· It is important that the artist responds authentically to the type of music being used, and that may involve adding classical steps to jazz music and jazz steps to classical music.

Session 14

Can Choreography be Taught?
European Examples (Part 2)

Key words:

choreography   teaching   assessment   auditioning   course structure
course aims

An introduction to two very specific models of choreography courses, one from the University College of Dance in Stockholm, and the other from Rotterdamse Dansakademie. How are students selected, what is taught and how are the courses assessed? What differences exist between these models and the British ones described in sessions 1 and 9?

Christopher Bannerman introduced Gun Roman from the University College of Dance in Stockholm, and Hilke Diemer, Co-ordinator of Choreographic Studies at the Rotterdamse Dansakademie.

Gun Roman

Can choreography be taught? My answer to this question is yes and no. There are things which can be done to support and nurture talents which appear, such as to educate promising young choreographers. This talk will illustrate how we do this in Sweden.

The University College of Dance in Stockholm began in 1963 as the Choreographic Instates. Among the founders were two great choreographers from Sweden; Birgit Akesson and Birgit Cullberg. In 1964 a pedagogy department was added. Our college is still the only provider of higher education in dance in Sweden. It offers several courses; for example, a three-year course for dance teachers (BFA), a three-year course for choreographers (BFA), a two-year course in Swedish folkdance, a dance therapy course, a one-year performance course for contemporary dancers, and so on. The college has about 150 students, and enjoys excellent facilities, including 13 dance studios, a theatre, 4 lecture rooms, a library and video-editing suite.

Several important choreographers have led the Choreography Department over the years; Ivo Cramér, Jean Cebron, Lucas Hoving, Renate Schottelius, Per Jonsson, and currently Margaretha Asberg, who became the first professor of dance in Sweden in 1992. We take only 3 to 5 students every third year. The students are usually required to have experience in the performing arts sector before they enter the department, and are usually aged between 25 and 30.

Course Aims

The aims of the course are as follows:

- To aid the creative dance artist in developing an aesthetic awareness based on knowledge, which can give him/her the freedom to begin a conscious dialogue with the world around him/her.

- To provide a basic knowledge of choreography, its theory and its practice.

- To provide a basic knowledge of the historical development of the art of dance, from primitive forms to the present day, in relation to art, philosophy and society.

- To allow the development of independent creative and analytical thinking, and provide verbal communication skills for the articulation of these ideas.

Year One

The first year is mainly dedicated to solo works, so that the student may develop his/her individual movement language. Thus the student's own body becomes the instrument for researching the language of dance. Alongside this personal research, dance compositions are studied in relation to the historical and social development of art, widening the frameworks for contemporary and individual movement perception. These elements are supported by a series of lectures on dance history, art theory, philosophy and cultural studies. During all three years, the students take part in collaborations, both artistic and technical, with students from the other arts colleges in Stockholm.

Year Two

During the second year, we try to further the development of analytical appreciation by requiring students to analyse every composition assignment which is shown. The students are encouraged to develop verbal communication skills, as the work of a choreographer is, to a large extent, a question of expressing ideas to other people; not only dancers, but also musicians, set, lighting and costume designers, technicians, producers. Application processes for funding are also covered at this stage, along with administration and stage-craft.

In composition studies, the students work with a group of dancers, which makes higher demands in terms of choreographic complexity. The dancers are professionals who are employed by the college for project periods.

Year Three
The third year is mainly dedicated to furthering the studies and experiences of the previous years. The students are allocated more personal study time, in which to work on rehearsals and preparations for their final performance examination. For this project, the students must take full responsibility not only for the artistic outcome, but for all other aspects of the production. Modern media, such as digital video will probably play an important role in the future for choreographers, and a fairly extensive amount of time is allowed for this area of study in the final year.

A course in dance art such as this cannot be relied upon to produce great artists. However, it can provide knowledge and understanding of the creative process and experience of production possibilities which act as a grounding for further individual development. After completing the course, students are allowed to use the facilities at the college for two years. This has been decided as we recognise that funding is usually the largest problem in the early years of professional work.

The Audition Process
The college holds auditions every year, but the course only takes a new year-group once every three years. I think this system works well, as the applicants are given feedback on the work, and they are not so nervous when they audition on several occasions. About 6 weeks before the audition, applicants receive their assignments. They are requested to prepare four compositions for the audition, including compositions to given pieces of music, inspired by a one of two given texts, and a free composition. At the audition they show two compositions before an initial selection is made, and then the remaining candidates show their other compositions. Candidates are also required to take part in a dance technique class, take a music test and be examined by the college's physical therapist. The audition ends with an interview. Students must be able to speak Swedish, which means that applicants can easily come from all the Nordic countries.

Hilke Diemer
Issues Behind the Development of the Choreographers's Course
The Rotterdamse Dansakademie has a dance teachers' programme and a dancers' programme, both four years in duration. The art schools are not connected to the universities in Holland. This can be an advantage, as quicker decisions can be made when you are not part of the bureaucracy of a larger system or university. However, the disadvantage is that because they are not connected to universities it is not possible to have postgraduate programmes at the schools. Therefore there can be no progression beyond the four year programme. One of our problems in creating a programme especially for choreography was how to include all the necessary elements within the time. In the development of the course, some basic questions were raised. One particular question concerned the definition of a choreographer. Did we limit choreography to the creation of contemporary dance work for presentation in the theatre context? We decided that the definition should be more open, so that students could learn to improve their choreographic skills within the styles with which they are accustomed, but also learn to apply their craft in different contexts, including the community context.

The next question was whether the school environment is an appropriate atmosphere for growth as a choreographer. I felt very sure that it is not appropriate to have to deal with examinations and set curriculae. The learning process for a choreographer is about making your own choices and finding your own path to achievement. There must be some fixed moments and subjects within the course which everyone must cover, but there is also the personal element of finding your own direction as a choreographer. Students must develop their own ways of finding inspiration and doing their research. So I felt that the programme should be more individual. There is the concern that you could prevent students from developing by dictating what they should learn and how they should learn it. It creates a consumer mentality that I think is dangerous if you want people to be independent afterwards and to make their own choices.

So I tried to arrange the course around what already existed in the school. The discipline remains in terms of morning technique classes. However, the course is constructed on a modular basis, so that the students have a choice of subjects for each six-week module. In this way, we agreed what should be included in the course, but the students can decide on the form of the course for themselves as individuals. There are four six-week modules in the year. During each module, the students study intensively for two days a week, and the other three days are for personal composition and rehearsal work. This approach was a revelation in the Academy, as the students had control of the paths which they took. Teachers are there to provide feedback and encouragement, but they do not need to be there every moment to nurture the talent of a young choreographer. The students must take responsibility for themselves. Students may take two months out of the school to study with a choreographer, and they return with a lot of information and inspiration. Students are expected to work on the course modules for the two years and also to create new works every 6 months. These works are presented in schools within the Akademie first and then go on tour around Holland in professional theatres. In that sense, our course is different from many similar ones as students' compositions are made and shown publicly throughout the course.

Application and Audition Requirements

Every student has to pay for his/her course in Holland, which costs 3000 guilders a year. Students who have already completed the four-year dancers' course and wish to take the choreographers' course have to raise the money for those further two years' study. We only have 9 studios, so we take a maximum of 5 new students each year. (There are 225 full-time dance students at the Akademie in total.) We cannot afford to buy in professional dancers, which limits the students to some extent, but one of the requirements for application is proof of at least two years professional dance training, so all the choreography students are also able to perform their own and other students' works. They are also requested to provide videos of their composition work, including group pieces as well as solos, and they have to send a written paper about the motivation behind their application and what they hope to gain from the course. They must also write about what inspires them to choreograph, which is always interesting. The course is there to provide for students who want to work in choreography in the wider context, and not just the theatre. There are no age limits for applicants as we try to be flexible with the course.

Selections are made based on these submissions and a maximum of 20 people are invited to audition. They each perform a solo and take part in a composition workshop to see how they work with others and in response to instruction and feedback. A maximum of 5 students are selected by the panel, who include representatives from the Academy, a professional choreographer, and department staff.

Teaching and Monitoring on the Programme

The school is now 60 years old, and some of the staff have been there for many years. This can mean that some aspects are very fixed, and it can be difficult to be creative within that atmosphere. I try to bring in guest teachers to inspire the students. The students can influence the programme by requesting teachers if, for example, there is a great deal of interest in street dance at a particular time. Some principles of the whole school are fixed, and run through the composition programme; for example, Laban is taught as a basis for analysis and cannot be interchanged with a workshop on hip-hop.

We do not work with a single artistic director on this course. I co-ordinate the programme and try to offer facilities and find the right people to teach for the course. Every student can choose his or her own mentor. Students are also responsible for monitoring each other and discussing their working processes. They are often able to help each other with feedback and constructive criticism.

Points raised in discussion:

- Students need to be taught to criticise each others' work in a positive manner, but to also be spontaneous in their responses. However, criticism of work should always be supported by knowledge and reasoning, even when it is initially spontaneous. Too much positive feed back is not always constructive, and students are sometimes happier when they are told what is wrong and how to improve it. Critical response does not always have to be positive, but it must be constructive.

- While criticism in the school situation tends to be supportive, students need to be able to cope with the kinds of criticism which they are likely to receive once they leave the school, which may not be so supportive.

- At these institutions, assessments are generally not given a specific mark and feed back is largely verbal.

Session 15

Visual Art as Stimulus for Choreography: an Interdependent Process

Keywords:

dance   visual arts   composition   motif   pedagogy

Professor Ana Macara introduced her ideas through lecture/demonstration and a practical workshop with reference to a very specific dance and visual arts project developed in Lisbon with students during the last academic year.

Introduction

This paper refers to the workshop and video-demonstration presented in the Conference *"The Greenhouse Effect: The Art and Science of Nurturing Dancemakers"*. The work shown was based on research activities developed in Lisbon, Portugal, in the Dance Department of FMH - Universidade Tecnica de Lisboa. This was developed in collaboration with visual artist Antonio Folgado. The purpose of the experiment was the search for new ways to accomplish basic composition skills among undergraduate dance students in choreography class. Our means were the use of specially created drawings to be used as stimuli for the creation of dance studies and, eventually, a dance piece.

Background

I have collaborated with visual artists since I started to work in the creation of dances and multimedia productions in the beginning of the eighties. In some cases, as a choreographer, I had to appeal to the visual artist to create the stage set and/or costumes. In other cases, a project was developed together by artists of different areas, or it was the visual artists who felt the need to call upon performers to give their work a different impact, by animating installations.

From our contact we have understood the need for a close integration of the different elements in any creation. We have also discovered that common concepts are present in works from the different fields. They can be similarly treated by different means of expression, and this seems to make us understand them better.

Either the support element is the human body or inert mass, compositions may be developed around the same concepts. As Guerber-Walsh (1996) affirms, concepts such as "dimensions - two and three dimensional", "peripheral space", or "colour" can be explained and understood either from the perspective of the visual artist, or that of the choreographer. The concepts can, in this way gain a new dimension, as they are not restricted to a single means of expression. In this kind of approach there is a reciprocal feeding that we have been understanding as very stimulating.

Motivation for creating dance

It is our belief, based on several authors and also on our experience, that in order to create a dance, different kinds of stimulus are indispensable. In our choreography program we try to develop the students' ability to develop movement material by provoking them not only with different musical incentives, but also with other types of sound atmospheres. We also use emotional or thematic suggestions, kinaesthetic or tactile sensations often induced by particular types of props or costumes, along with formal particularities in movement quality and the use of body parts in the space. All of these usually constitute good stimuli which usually help students discover new ways in which they can address dance, eventually approaching their own personal and ultimately unique style.

The project

Our particular project, was developed with the students of the Department of Dance in Faculdade de Motricidade Humana - Universidade Tecnica de Lisboa.

We have chosen to approach one concept common to composition in dance and the visual arts: the motif. Our purpose was to experiment with how to transform and develop one particular, very simple motif, such as a circle, or a ring, both in pictorial and in movement support, in order to create movement material and, ultimately, a dance piece.

Ultimately, the purpose of this project is the creation of pedagogical devices, trying to approach composition concepts, which are not always easy to apprehend, in stimulating and motivating ways.

The project has been developed in successive phases, in a continuous process which will be kept in progress:

1. **Selection of the visual stimulus**
    We have agreed on starting our collaborative work by developing, as a motif, a very simple geometrical figure: the circle, or the ring. This figure, which is full of symbolic and representational references, should have the potential to stimulate interesting work both in the paper and in movement material.

2. **Creation of visual support**
    The visual support was the responsibility of visual artist Antonio Folgado.
    Several drawings were created on paper, based on the development and transformation of the same motif. They were selected with the purpose of serving as stimuli for choregraphic creation. This series of drawings, which we present in annex, is the result of an intensive graphite (pencil) work on the paper. Black against white, black over black - where the shapes appear on the surface suggesting new shapes and new structures.

3. **Choreographic improvisation**
    Choreography students of the Dance Department of Faculdade the Motricidade Humana - Universidade Tecnica de Lisboa collaborated in improvisation classes. This phase of the work went though different successive approaches, and different sessions were recorded on video.

    a) Students were asked to improvise around the idea that was basic to our chosen motif - the circle or the ring

    b) They were asked (and oriented) to perform their own interpretation of the visual stimuli created on phase one.

    c) They developed the same kind of work in small groups.

4. **Interchange with the students**
    In order to understand how the different phases were approached by the students, each session was discussed right after it happened, and some weeks later, after some reflection about it.

5. **Analysis of the material**
    The recorded material was analysed, to serve the purposes of the project.

6. **Presentation of the recorded material to different dance students, to determine their reaction to it (use of questionnaires);**

7. **Analysis of the students response to the recorded material;**
    Study of correlations to understand in which dance studies the motif is better understood.

8. **Selection of new visual stimulus**
    The work will restart from the beginning around a different visual stimuli (e.g. the triangle) in order to deepen the understanding of the influence of visual stimuli in the creation of dances.

The workshop

In the workshop we have tried to recreate the experience developed before, in a 'condensed version'. It was our intention to confront the participant with visualised geometric figures first, and then with the works of the visual artist based on the same figures. This way, we could experiment the difference in the mental approaches going on during the improvisation/composition process, according to the type of stimulus.

The workshop went through four successive phases:

1. **Warm up**

   A short warm up is always necessary, not only to predispose the body for the movement, but also to establish a comfortable atmosphere among the participants. Simple body movements presented as a relaxing experience and movements across the space to favour the encounter of the participants were used as a departure for the work.

2. **Improvisation/composition based on visualised circles/rings**

   The visualisation of different circles in the space was used to stimulate movement improvisation. Participants were directed to imagine small, large, or medium size circles in different planes - horizontal, vertical, diagonal, one at a time. Each circle was then described in different ways with different body parts - elbow, shoulder, knee, wrist, nose... After improvisation participants were asked to pay attention to the wholeness of the body movement, and to select the most interesting findings. Finally a short sequence of movements was asked, by joining the material previously developed.

3. **Improvisation/composition based on drawings**

   In a later phase, participants are confronted with the different drawings presented in annex and asked to improvise and create dance sequences based on the images presented and evoked by a selected drawing.

4. **Same in groups**

   As an option the same work may be developed in small groups.

Conclusion

In the workshop, due to the time limitations, the work was much less developed than what had previously been accomplished with the students in Lisbon, during a much larger period of time. This work had been registered on video and some excerpts were then presented to the participants.

In these excerpts I believe that we could confirm some of the impressions from the workshop.

A main conclusion is that in the first situation, where the improvisation is based only on the visualised image of the circle, the circular motif is usually clear and entirely apparent in most of the movement studies. In the second situation, based on the drawings, the motif becomes much less obvious. Nevertheless, the improvisation seems to come much more from the inner self, with more subjective and interesting movement approaches. The psychological process in which the creator is engaged seems much more profound, bringing out much more of its individuality with all particularity and specificity.

It has also been a conclusion from our observation that, while for beginners the first approach seems much easier to motivate the student for improvisation and creation of danced movement, the second approach is much richer for more advanced students who do not need so much the stimulus to start improvising but rather to get inspiration for choreographic creation.

To conclude, and as I said before, this is an approach to a project which seems to be now at its beginning. We believe that the concepts that prevail in it may continue to be developed in different directions. We intend to keep working at it, and we hope that the participant and the reader can use the suggestions in their own way, in their individual work.

References
Guerber-Walsh, N. (1996). "Dance and Visual Arts: Procedure of choreographic creation in relation with the visual arts". In N. Bardaxoglou, C. Brack, M. Vronken (Eds.), *Dance and Research 2: An interdisciplinary approach.* (pp. 319-321). Brussels: Vrije Universiteit Brussell.

Annex
Drawings by Antonio Folgado
figures 1 through 11

Session 16

Learning to Choreograph:
in conversation with Rui Horta

Keywords:

choreography   development   training
producing   company   choreographic ownership

Rui Horta is a choreographer based in Munich. For many years he ran his own company, S.O.A.P. in Frankfurt. He also teaches a course for choreographers in Switzerland each summer, and cares passionately about the development of the art form and the need to inculcate skills and craft with young choreographers who have already demonstrated some ability. He talks to John Ashford about his beliefs and aspirations, and about models of good practice from Europe and the importance of sharing and communication.

John Ashford

Rui, I know that you are Portuguese and that you had dance training in Portugal and then went to New York. What sort of training did you have in Portugal and when and why did you go to New York?

Rui Horta

I think the way I have developed is completely atypical. I guess it had its problems, but it also had its virtues. Portugal ceased to be a democracy in 1974, so basically I was raised under a dictatorship since I was 17 years old. I come from a big family where everything was very formal. My father and mother were doctors, and there were eight kids. It was a very bourgeois system, a very intellectual family, and I had no doubts that I was going to be a doctor like my father. But then with the opening up of democracy I discovered another life, basically, and dance was a part of that. I was a physical person; I was a very good swimmer for many years. I started to study, and at I first went into architecture, and after that into physical education. And after a while I just found myself discovering jazz dance; I wanted to be a jazz dancer. So in my late teens, I went to America.

At that time in Portugal, all male dancers were stereotyped as gay in the whole stereotypical macho society. I could do jazz, it was macho enough, but then I still had problems with my friends and my family and my father. I went to America thinking I was going to do jazz because the roots were there. I wanted to dance like black people, I wanted to be black. At the Alvin Ailey School, where, by accident I discovered Graham technique, I was the only white person around, so they called me 'white bread'. I was very 'turned in' technically so I suffered a lot in my Graham classes in the fourth position sitting, spirals etc. Of course I fell in love with the techniques, but I am very clumsy, and it killed me after a while, and later it made me think a lot about my training. I particularly loved the Limon training, which completely altered my dancing, and later release technique. So I learned the old way, you know, one year, one technique. At the same time I was escaping to do my jazz classes with people like Luigi or JoJo Smith - the guy who taught John Travolta to dance. All this was a very crazy start. I was quite a horrible dancer in the beginning. I guess I only became a good dancer when I was already a choreographer. Then, after those years I became a teacher. I was quite a respected teacher at the end of my seven years in New York, in 83/84.

John Ashford

So during that time, you might have been a horrible dancer but you must have done it. Did you learn anything about choreography when you were doing that dancing?

Rui Horta

I did learn a lot, by doing and by watching. I watched always, and I knew even at that time that I would like to choreograph. This was very important for me. I was a choreographer in the sense that I knew I wanted to make dance steps, I didn't want to dance. Sooner or later I would become someone involved with staging, and I would say that this was something which became apparent very early on. My father subscribed to a French theatre magazine the *Avantscène* with text and photographs in it, and I was always amazed at the photographs. It was very clear to me from the beginning that I liked the stage, although I didn't know if I would ever do anything related to it. My first choreographic experiences were in the late-70's in the States, although I did some small projects in Portugal.

John Ashford

Did you create that opportunity for yourself or did someone offer you the opportunity?

Rui Horta

We basically did it ourselves. Everybody would pay for a venue, make a little piece and call up friends to see it. I think this was a very beautiful time to go through. I took a long time to do this part of the process because I was really self-taught. I made a lot of mistakes, my work was very stereotyped and the first things I did in choreography were horrible. I think my biggest piece of luck was to be in Lisbon doing try-outs in the mid- to late -'80s. What I made was really dreadful, but nobody knew that, because the main dance choreography was happening so very far away. Nobody cut off my legs! This is the best thing that happened to me.

John Ashford

You've just jumped a whole lot of important things as far as this Conference is concerned, because here we're talking about choreographic development. You can't just say 'I did all this horrible work and then suddenly something else happened!' How did that happen?

Rui Horta

Even starting out in New York, I still kept in contact with Portugal and I did regular dance projects there too. So, in 1984 I came back to Portugal with an invitation from the Ministry of Culture to start a small company, the Lisbon Dance Company, which nurtured a lot of the current generation of dancers. So I'm a little bit 'the old guy' and there's still a father complex in Portugal. If you ask in Portugal I'm considered old-fashioned, you know.

John Ashford

So because you're a horrible dancer, you left New York at the invitation of the City of Lisbon to form a dance company, with funding!

Rui Horta

Well, of course I wanted to do this project. Someone at the Ministry of Culture felt it was important to have a substantial project in modern dance in Portugal. At that time we were still fighting for basic things. So I wanted very much to do something in Portugal.

I must say that it was a very mainstream project because it's actually much harder to forget your background than to remember. You have so many things imprinted on you from your training and your education, and you have to throw all these things out of the window to become a choreographer. To a certain extent you have to select until you find your voice. My first years as a choreographer, in Portugal in 1984-86, were years of mainstream when I didn't reflect much; my energy was much more directed into carrying projectors, making sure that we got the right venue, and that we had the key to open the door. Because it was Portugal, not Great Britain or Germany! So my energy went into that and not into the artistic choices. I got out of that in 1988.

John Ashford

During that period were you lighting the work yourself?

Rui Horta

No, but I was learning. I learned to light by the process of being in the theatre. I became a lighting designer basically in the early 90s. Part of the choreographic experience was always to be open and see and look around at the world of theatre. It is fascinating and you learn by doing.

John Ashford

So during this whole process you haven't mentioned any single person who was significant in terms of encouraging you to become a choreographer.

Rui Horta

Everyone was important for me, but still, you are basically on your own. I was basically just on my own. I find I need a fascination to study, and there was James Truitte and Pearl Lang, Denise Jefferson and Michael Owens. They were big icons, you know. You find and you follow someone. I followed each person, and I took everything until it was almost like a Zen leader for me. I was very respectful of that leadership, but I don't want to say that there was one particular person. And when I left Lisbon Dance Company, I was in a total state of shock. I looked at my work of 1983 to 1986 and I thought I was a really lousy choreographer, so I stopped choreographing and I had a crisis here. I just had a small dance studio in Lisbon. I went every day. For a year, I didn't see a performance, I didn't see a class, I just went along every morning to the studio to work by myself, because I had to find myself, so I was just totally brutal about it.

My first independent project was with a group of dancers who are the generation of contemporary choreographers working right now in Portugal. I developed very steadily, very slowly, because I was the first generation, but they are the second, so they came on faster. They started later, but they have become mature at the same time as I did. And I guess that the third generation will be even faster.

John Ashford

To what extent did you draw from them as dancers and emerging choreographers, in that early work?

Rui Horta

A great deal. They were the only good dancers available, they were intelligent, and they were very good friends. They made me do good work in research and get myself together. So I didn't care about carrying projectors because I didn't have to tour. I was given money to do three shows, so I was relaxed and for the first time I just went to the studio to create, calmly.

The year working alone in the studio was very important to me because I almost gave up choreography. I nearly decided to stop because I felt that my work was not profound at all, it was very derivative of other things I have studied and learned. I think that year was the first time in my life when I really confronted myself with many other issues. Things also came together in my personal life, and the only thing I did was some teaching to support myself.

John Ashford

So it was more a matter of drawing breath both as an artist and a person and creating a storehouse of material which was going to be released?

Rui Horta

Yes. I needed to create. I wanted to find my own vocabulary, my own way of moving. So I went to the studio alone, not only to do steps, but also to think. That was definitely the year of change for my life as a choreographer. A lot of what I use now in composition and craft I discovered in those days. I developed a very special way of working which I have been teaching over the years, because I am very interested in passing it on.

Then came my second piece. Of course the first piece was already a little bit known, I got some attention from outside Portugal, and then the second piece got a lot of attention so it got me to Germany, which was my big chance. All of a sudden they gave me a big theatre to work in in Frankfurt with everything. I was 32 years old, nobody knew me and all of a sudden I just got this handed to me!

John Ashford

The facilities at the Künstlerhaus Mousonturm in Frankfurt which were offered to you for four months consisted of an extremely beautiful studio, video equipment, an extremely well equipped theatre of about 250 seats (which is maybe a little small for dance, but nevertheless quite adequate), and a technical team to make sets, properties, and lighting designs.

Rui Horta

It was really wonderful. Almost everybody in the theatre was below 30; it was a young theatre that just started a year before I arrived. I was a very lucky guy. I had about five gigs over 10 weeks around Europe and after those four months we put together some gigs I had for that summer and other new ones and we went on tour. Then I received a telephone call from a producer asking if wanted to do a piece on Mozart that would live in a shared programme with other choreographers, of course I agreed.

I was very intimidated by using classical music; I was fighting at that time for my musical culture because it was my weak point as a choreographer. This is an important point because as a choreographer you really have to work in an art form that is connected with other arts. The visual arts, the visual side was very strong for me because of my background, but the music side was very weak. It was a great opportunity, and we toured with *Wolfgang, Bitte*. Then I did another piece with Forsythe dancers for charity with no money, and also another project. Then I put two or three pieces together to make a triple bill, and by that time luckily we had been spotted! You don't know what happened to you, but all of a sudden you are everywhere! It's dangerous, all of a sudden, as if it happened just too fast. But I had the power at that time, a huge amount of invention and an amazing group of people.

There are several reasons why we advanced so fast. I think we were very trendy but in 1993/94, there was a succession of other things. One was a market approach to choreographers, which means that the new kid in town is immediately promoted, which is good and also very dangerous. The second thing is that I was discovered with an already substantial amount of experience because I had been dancing for 15 years or 20 years, so I was *considered* new, but not like someone of 19 or 22 making their first piece. I had done my work in a secluded place where nobody saw me. Then of course the third thing was that I had the Mousonturm organisation behind me and that provided me with a calm period which I had not experienced before. I had the studio, a warm place to go and work every day. I think it was the only place in my life when I was in the right place at the right time.

John Ashford

And that Company called S.O.A.P. was at the Mousonturm for five years, during which time you made the triple bill and four full length works?

Rui Horta

We were there for seven and a half years and made six evenings of work. And in fact the last two years of S.O.A.P. were spent simply fulfilling contracts. The Company had become so successful on that touring circuit that there was a demand even after I had left.

Leaving the Company for me closes a chapter of very crazy touring. In November 96 I decided to stop the Company but we toured for almost two years more as we had a 120-performance schedule ahead. So although it will not happen any more on that scale for me, it was a very great way to finish.

John Ashford

Going back to the project when you were asked to use Mozart, I think that's important because when someone else intervenes and makes a suggestion that can be like someone else taking an important step in your journey.

Rui Horta

I think that it was very important. I was confronted with something I had to do, that I was not used to doing, and it was obvious there was a quality there that was very strong. I had little knowledge of classical music, and I knew that this was my weak point. My work is always very conceptual and I chose to go forward not through musical knowledge but by approaching the music in that same conceptual way. I decided to do a piece about the last year of Mozart's life. I was amazed that this man died so early at 33 (as I was also 33) and I felt how could he die so early with such an amazing body of work? So I took the two pieces that he composed in the last year of his life, *The Magic Flute* and *The Requiem*. One is wild, young, full of power and almost naive, and the other is a masterpiece about death coming, and he composed them at he same time. I found that was very interesting for a piece, about that solitude in the midst of a tremendous talent, when you are a genius and you're dying. So that piece made me learn and grow a lot.

John Ashford

Having worked with classical music, what do you feel? How did that then change or influence you in your next steps?

Rui Horta

I think it influenced me a lot because I had to find a lyrical way of dancing, and at that time I didn't have one, because my vocabulary was very tough, very dynamic, and very young. It was my most sophisticated piece in years, because I had to go into pure quality of movement and so I was very radical about it.

John Ashford

I think you've actually raised something important, because what I'm trying to work through in this conversation is some sense of how a choreographer develops. It seems to me that this commission did form a very important part of your development, and that from that moment you worked with composers with a degree of rigour and with a concentration on the musicality of the work, which may have been different if you hadn't done the Mozart piece.

Just to clarify, I was a part of the commissioning process that resulted in that piece. It was a terribly crude process; four of us decided that we wanted to commission four short pieces, each from a different European country and tour them together. They would be rehearsed for the last 10 days in Munich, so the choreographers and dancers would have the opportunity to work together and would technically have to make those pieces come together into a single programme. That was the notion. In order to find some kind of unity in those four pieces we chose Mozart, partly because it was a major anniversary of his birth or death or something, so money was available. It was absolutely as blatant as that. But it's interesting how this commission was really significant for you.

So there's no point going into the history of S.O.A.P. in a sense because by then you were a choreographer. You might want to say something about the successes and failures of how that programme worked. We presented it all at The Place Theatre in London, and I think that it was important in the early days of the establishment of the company that there was not only the safe house of the Mousonturm but also a number of presenters across Europe who had made the same decision and said 'we want to follow this Company'.

Rui Horta

Having been on the independent scene for 10 years now, in Germany many people think I should now go to an opera house, but I keep saying 'No'. I want to stay on the independent scene for as long as I can. I have a very eclectic side; I like theatre, I like designing my own lights and sets, and I think that the role of the choreographer has to be very complete these days. I reflect a lot about what it is to be a choreographer now because the big chance for dance is that it is at the crossroads of the arts, it cannot exist without other arts. There's all this talk about equities and reductions, but dance has an eclectic nature, even theatre is eclectic by nature. The only way it can (and should) reduce is aesthetically. We are people of the theatre, we have to develop a visual knowledge, we live in terms of visual perception of form. There has to be a knowledge of music because we normally work with music or in silence. You have to have a strong musical culture even to be able to choose a CD, or to commission music. You have to know about your craft, about space, about composition, about vocabulary and, above all, still be inventive, and besides all this you have to know about how to bring people together which is almost psychology. Especially today, where dancers improvise and they carry the steps, the choreography is not just about doing nice steps and good steps, not even about putting them together well; choreography is about transmitting something.

Part of the education of a choreographer has to do with the education of life - you have to have culture, you have to read books, you know you have to love your art form, and it's a very hard job. And one never stops growing. The dancers that stay with me for five or six years know me very well, so they get to the point very fast and I can concentrate much more. I love to make steps, but much of my work is really at home with my books and my headphones while my kids are asleep, and I stay up until 3 o'clock in the morning, developing my ideas.

John Ashford

Let us pick on the extent to which composition is delegated to the members of your Company who have worked for a considerable time with you. To what extent is that engendering in them the desire to be choreographers? If you delegate a lot of that because you're doing the thinking about the big picture, you're almost inviting them to be choreographers. To what extent is the work yours? I believe that you have now given a duet made in this way to the two dancers who basically made it, and they can now perform it as their own?

Rui Horta

Once you are in a collaborative process nothing is mine or yours; everything is ours. That is very important when you are in a process like that. Saying that, choreography and staging are very special and they still have to be done on another level by a choreographer. I give a lot of freedom, as much as a dancer can take, and normally I think that's why dancers stay with me for a long period of time, because they feel that they are part of the process. But I must say that with that freedom also comes other aspects. I reject a lot of work. For instance, in making a piece of an hour and a half often we reject four hours of it. Along the way much of the material goes away, so the dancer, like me, knows that he has to let go. On the other hand I must say that the way I compose is very guided, it's a very guided way of improvisation. I really create almost like a tunnel, a very strong set of rules, and then within those rules you can work. It's like a flute - you have seven holes, yet within those seven holes you can play Mozart on that flute or you can play just nothing. Basically the set of rules are there from the beginning, they are the skeleton of the piece.

John Ashford

So not only are there rules, but also they're making work for you, they know what you are least likely to discard.

Rui Horta

Yes, that's why they stay with me for a longer time because they get right to the point very fast. I reject a lot of that material and at the beginning of a piece I set the movement material myself, I don't let anyone set movement material. No one improvises for the first two weeks, we just continue until they understand what movement I am talking about, what direction, which kind of body language. For instance my last piece was a really radical piece; I was really into the idea of fragmentation, of really composing movement on each joint. We worked around the body in a very special way and after a while the dancers could take over. Then I did phase 3 which is when I rearrange, recompose, and cut; I change a lot so I become very active again.

What has been wonderful over these years is that the people I worked with were on an intellectual level very close to me, which means that I do not go to the studio and work with machines. When I do an audition I talk to people as much as I see them dance, and then I sit down and interview them. It's impossible for me to work with someone who just thinks in terms of dance steps, or feet. I work on such an intimate basis with six or seven people, that it's not possible to have this kind of attitude to work.

In *Khôra* half of the sections are really very much me. I was very radical, and there are solos I changed four or five times. I lost a dancer in the process because she couldn't take it when I cut a beautiful solo. So there are casualties; I must say it's not just a rosy world.

John Ashford

Something as severe as that could be an indication of the extent to which the dancer feels ownership of the material because of the process.

Rui Horta

Sure, but they can take it. It's our duty to put it all together. I gave them the framework, the idea and they actually help me with the dance steps, and I came back and recomposed it. I brought the music in, I changed it, I made the theme clearer. But it's their body of work.

John Ashford

I think that is very interesting in terms of choreographic development, because inevitably some of those dancers who worked with you during that period wanted to take that a step further and become choreographers. I think you gave them that opportunity, or the Mousonturm gave them that opportunity as dancers in S.O.A.P., is that right?

Rui Horta

Yes, we had choreographic projects during the years. It was very exciting, and out of that some people began to choreograph. Some were already going into choreography. It is not a must, but the company was getting older, and so after a while you think 'How do I go on?' I had three female dancers who started in the company at 32, 33 years old and all had strong relationships, but they stayed with me for five years. After S.O.A.P. finished, all three got pregnant. This says a lot about how much you postpone your personal life if you are involved. And it's also beautiful, and it's a privilege for me, this is the kind of belief they put in my work for all these years.

John Ashford

So what happened after S.O.A.P. completed its contract is that you moved to Munich for two very good reasons. There is a place called Muffathalle in Munich which is a combination of a rock venue and a dance theatre, where you became the resident choreographer. The second reason is that a German producer's prize was offered to you. This is also important because becoming independent and ending S.O.A.P. as an institutional company based in Frankfurt and funded by the City of Frankfort was a leap into nothing. You say you're never lucky, yet you've actually got a residency at Muffathalle, a proper producing budget and 10 to 13 venues to tour to? Because the way in which the German producers prize works is that many theatres who have budgets and dance programmes in Germany get together and put in something like £3-£5,000 each, and the whole lot is offered to one choreographer. This first work outside the institution as it were, it's a safe haven again.

Rui Horta

Yes, but I must say, it's not such a safe haven. The main reason I left Frankfurt is because there was less money there. We had to tour so much to be able to keep going, because we were supporting 14 people - 8 dancers, me and my assistant, three technicians, one administrator - and bringing in half the money from touring. So sometimes this kind of success is not so positive. And I was always away from home, I have children and I wanted to be with them more. Also Frankfurt is not the ideal city in which to raise children; it is a very exciting city if you are single. But for a family place Munich is great, a place where your child is not going to be raped around the corner and kids don't bring knives to school at seven years old. So it's really quite a place for me to be now.

I never was attracted to do anything outside of S.O.A.P. for all those years, and then when it finished there came a few offers from bigger houses. Everybody was expecting that I would "upgrade", but to me it was very clear that I didn't want to go to a bigger venue. I just wanted to change city, and so I now have a very interesting situation. I have a rock 'n' roll venue that I love. Basically it's a beautiful theatre, a converted electricity generating station. We even played tennis there, that's how big it was, and now it's a theatre. It's just a rock 'n' roll place, and the team there is very much like this, rock 'n' roll. I don't have any big budget from the city, so I bring my money from everywhere, from a very complex constellation of co-producers that trust my work. That's why I was in France yesterday because I was at a press conference and I had to show myself there.

Staying in this independent scene is something that is almost an ideological choice for me. It's really about the fact that if I go to a bigger house I don't know if I can handle the change. If I come to London to The Place for two nights, there is a hard core of 250-300 people each night that see my work, then next I go to Hamburg and I have an audience of 400 seats for four nights. In Frankfurt we were always sold out, but that is a small venue. But if I come to a city and I take an opera house I have to do 15 nights in every two months and I have to fill up a theatre with 1,000-2,000 seats. What does it mean? How do I get to this audience? How is this going to affect my work? Do I want to make that concession? Do I want to play for that audience? I am very nervous about that, so basically what I am doing now is this. I have no money, but I live in a beautiful place, and at a time when most people are "establishing" themselves, I work on a project basis, because on a project basis I have more time. I do works for other established dance, work in a very compact schedule and make a bit more money. Then, when there is money for the next project, I will do it, and then we will see. I will try to hold on to this way of working as long as I can because it is an artistic choice for me; it is called freedom. So that's how the choreographer develops, you come back to the roots and in a way I feel very good about using the system that used me.

John Ashford

But don't you feel there is a huge pressure on you to deliver what these people who are providing the funds want?

Rui Horta

Oh it's terrible. Sometimes it makes me feel very weak, I almost feel as if I am in an exam. I always think every piece will be easier, but everyone always wants a masterpiece every time. That is the worst part.

John Ashford

And if the money is coming from all over the place do you feel pulled in different directions because you know that what the Muffathalle wants is different from the Monsounturm?

Rui Horta

This happened in my last piece. The piece before was a huge success in France, I was still touring it until a few months ago. But *Khôra* was a tragedy, I didn't sell one show in France except the Theatre de la Ville. So when it's good in Germany, it's horrible in France, and when it's good in France it's horrible in Germany. *Khôra* was very successful in Germany, it was a very hard core piece. But my last solo was very badly received in Germany, so six months ago I did a couple of gigs in my traditional places and that was it. Now I'm touring it in Japan, in France, all over. So it's like this: after a while you just have to do what you have to do.

John Ashford

Talking about choreographic development, we now know much more about your own development as a choreographer, and aside from your own work you have entered various situations where you have helped the development of other choreographers. I know that you do a regular choreographic course in Switzerland. Can you just talk a bit about that side of the work and what leads you to do it?

Rui Horta

Part of this has to do with my personality. I am someone who loves to empty and to give away. I know I'm not going to move my body until the last day of my life, so I have developed other interests, physically and also mentally, I am very curious. I would like to pass on as much as I can. This is personal, it doesn't happen with everybody, of course. I must say that I am very concerned about education, and I am very radical in my approaches to education I think. Years ago in a congress, the first year I was in Germany, I guess I made so many enemies in one afternoon. I said some really tough things about education because I think in Germany there is still a long way to go. Luckily in England you have one of the most advanced educational system in the world. Obviously you can still be unhappy about it, but it is advanced, even in dance administration. I cannot find a dance administrator in Germany but if I came here I would find an amazing dance administrator tomorrow.

I must say that passing on knowledge has been very important. The first step to forming good choreographers is to form good dancers. If you form good dancers you have open dancers, with good education, open-minded. Basically what I have been doing is teaching composition, because I think this is the hardest thing for me right now. It is about composing steps not just doing steps. A friend from New York, a very good choreographer, would say 'you know, steps just come in handy'. If you have this culture in your body you can just move, and the steps will be there. Now how to organise those steps, how to make sense of the work? So I teach a lot of composition and not in a traditional way. I teach composition and improvisation together in an integrated way that I have developed over the years. It worked for me and it works for other people I work with.

Then there's a third level that happened in Switzerland that was beyond composition and improvisation. I was really counselling a choreographic workshop, on a choreographic course and this was a huge challenge for me. This was so scary, because when I do my workshop by bringing my own aesthetic, I say 'Well, this is what I don't like, this is what I am looking for, but I don't like this', and I normally immediately criticise over expressionistic or codified work. I make the frame immediately. I believe that the body works for itself; too much face pollutes the body.

But I was the tutor to the other seven choreographers from all over Europe, and I wasn't there to instruct, I was there to give answers basically. I was trying to bring my experience without bringing my world to these seven people, because they were at a very high level already. Some of them were just as radical as I am at my worst times and I was so touched that these people were ready to take all the risks. I was there behind them just trying to listen, and I proposed several strategies. We put everything on stage after two weeks. It was also very radical and we got accused of that, and I didn't care because I presented a four-hour performance, because I didn't want to make any selections. So there were 25 dancers at the service of seven choreographers. The point was not to please people with the performance. Everybody had the right to produce the work they had done with lights, with staging, with everything, and the dancers worked for two weeks so they had the right to show the work.

John Ashford
One of the sessions here was entitled 'Can Choreography be Taught?' As a result of this experience what is your answer to that question - can choreography be taught?

Rui Horta
I think a choreographer exists already, like an actor or a film-maker.

John Ashford
That's supposed to be a very old-fashioned idea.

Rui Horta
No, I think a choreographer is there in a sense that he has a kind of eclectic mind. He looks at the tree and he sees the whole tree. If it is my friend Maria Sousa, a well-known scientist in Portugal, she will see the apple and she will work on that apple for twenty years. But a choreographer has this instant ratification, that in two or three months will produce work like a film-maker, like a theatre director. He has this global vision; this is the tree, the roots, the apple, and then he goes. So I think that kind of mind needs to already exist, but then I would say that everything from there can be taught. The craft can be taught, but then has to be discussed and Ana Sokolow told me that. She used to say, 'You know so much about composition, now go on and question everything. You know all about the strongest part of the stage and the weakest part of the stage and symmetry. Now make a piece just working on the edge of the stage'. So the craft can be taught, and then it has to be used in a very personal way. One cannot have a traditional way of composition in a new form of theatre.

John Ashford

So the craft of composition can be taught. Can choreography be taught?

Rui Horta

I think that from then on, you can attempt to produce people and give the right opportunities. You can commission music, and you can provoke choreographers. You can be very attentive, and this is the work of a good producer, when someone says 'this is the right time for this guy, I'll give him my theatre'. There are two sorts of people who produce work like this. I have had very good experiences with people who are clear and do what they do for the love of their art form, and I have had very bad experiences with people who are political and do it for the power. When you have the luck of having a boss like Dieter (Buroch), who gives you that chance to do what you want and even protects you; it's like a shield, it's a real luxury. If trust is not there nothing works on the art scene, not even with your producer.

But I don't think choreography can be taught, no. I learned so much in Switzerland about how can I bring my experience to these people without bringing my world, because I was very careful not to touch their little flowers, because theirs it is a different flower and it's very fragile. They look at me with these big eyes and if I say something I am going to impose some kind of judgement straight away. So it is about trying to ask the questions they need to be asked. It's a very good thing for a choreographer to have a very cultured friend that he trusts, someone that can help him to "distance" himself from his own work. It should be someone who is there and sits and watches and asks questions, and who is on your side. I think after a while you are on your own, you have to be very strong by the time you know the craft.

Session 17

The Artist and the Presenter:
A Positive Artistic Partnership

Keywords:

contemporary music   composer   collaboration   space

Richard Alston and Alistair Spalding discuss aspects of Alston's choreographic career with particular reference to the positive artistic partnership which has arisen between the Richard Alston Dance Company and London's South Bank theatres.

Alistair Spalding

Although I have presented the work of the company for four years now, it is only recently that I have felt in a position where I could make a proactive contribution as a presenter.

Richard Alston

You have offered support, Alistair, in whatever form it takes. To me, that is the important thing. As a long-term survivor, that is where I feel that I have been really fortunate, in the people who have given support to the company. You have looked after me from the beginning.

Alistair Spalding

Yes, I suppose what I am trying to ask is, what does it take to support a company? Getting to the point where we can actually discuss choices of programme has taken about three years.

Richard Alston

Alistair came out to see the Company on tour, and he made certain choices about what he would like us to show at the Queen Elizabeth Hall; this was enthusiasm, not interference, I might add. I was very happy, and the programme worked well. You certainly had a major input into the work that was presented, Alistair.

Alistair Spalding

So in your experience of working with me, let us be quite clear about those terms that have already been slightly defined. In terms of our relationship, I am definitely not a producer; I present the work. We have a financial arrangement, but I never come into the studio. We sometimes discuss your musical choices, but I don't suggest pieces. I am really just presenting work.

Richard Alston

But certainly, even in the three years that we have been coming to the South Bank, you have consolidated this commitment and have produced some money to enable good first-rate musicians to play. The space is a good place to dance in, but also an excellent concert hall.

Alistair Spalding

We have intervened quite proactively in the past. Perhaps we could look at one example. Let me explain the context a little. The way that the South Bank works is that there are 4 programmers: one for dance and theatre, one for classical music, one for contemporary music and a programmer for literature. When you work with the South Bank you don't just work with your own art-form programmer. When the Harrison Birtwistle Festival was being planned, Graham Sheffield (now in charge of the Barbican) approached you.

Richard Alston

They wanted to present some of Birtwistle's work, and as I was leaving Rambert they asked if I could contribute. Graham came to France to see the premiere of a piece by Boulez that I had done with the Ensemble Contemporain, and he then brought it to the South Bank with the French company, and so that was the first time I actually worked there, and with a group of good dancers and a group of good and extremely expensive musicians. So that set up a pattern straight away. I guess that's what led him to ask me to be involved again the following year.

Alistair Spalding

How did you respond to that, because that's something that I would still feel quite nervous about doing? Maybe Graham was just a bit naïve about it in a good way, but I don't feel even now as though I could say to you 'I want you to meet Harrison Birtwistle and I want you to make a piece together...' The thought of putting you in a room with a composer and suggesting that you do a fairly large and expensive project in the Queen Elizabeth Hall... How did you respond, did you feel it was imposing?

Richard Alston

Well, it's quite interesting. The project that he suggested, I dodged. The Festival was called *Secret Theatres*, and they wanted to finish with a piece of music that was called *Secret Theatre*, an acknowledged major work of Birtwistle's, and a very mature and finely judged piece of work. The people planning the Festival decided that it would be great to have *Secret Theatre* choreographed. But the point about the piece to me was that it was 'secret', so it seemed to me a contradiction in terms. Everything that you read about the way that Harry put the work together is about some kind of imaginative theatre in the mind that did not happen. Therefore I wasn't surprised that he was actually more interested in the other projects that I suggested, and the one that he got most involved in was *Nenia* which had an active dance element and a live singer. So you're right in a way, what the Festival proposed didn't happen perhaps in the way that they envisaged, because I don't think that either Harry or I were comfortable with that idea.

I could tell when we spoke to Harry that he really wanted *Secret Theatre* to be played but he wouldn't mind if nothing else was going on whilst it was being played. Whereas there are other pieces of his, like the work with the National Theatre, theatre-based work like *The Mask of Orpheus* which Lea Anderson worked on in the same Festival. I think he felt more comfortable about this piece, what he categorised as the theatre end of his work, being presented, being staged. *Secret Theatre*, conversely, is a piece of concert music, written for the Symphonietta, which as the composer he felt was a piece to be concentrated on and listened to.

Alistair Spalding

So how do you respond? Do you like being offered those opportunities or would you rather just be thinking about your own path? Do you find them useful, those suggestions?

Richard Alston

I found the Birtwistle Festival very fruitful because I had to make a lot of work for it, I had to make a full evening which wasn't entirely one kind of Birtwistle's work, as interestingly enough the Festival organisers had said very strongly what they did not want. Having taken this thing on, it made me try to think about it in as interesting a way as possible for myself and for the Company. Out of that programme, the other two pieces are now still in the repertoire and I remember also something that was extraordinary. It just so happened that *Secret Theatre* became the last performance in the Festival, and it was the most amazing audience I think I have ever seen at a performance of my work. They weren't there to see my work, I don't kid myself, but they really came from all the different art forms because it was the end of this tribute to Harry. Was he 60? Yes. So for one night only a very interesting and very different audience came, people from theatre, music, and visual arts, so it was a very different kind of concentration, quite critical I thought.

Alistair Spalding

And so working in an environment in a theatre which has that kind of music background as well as the music activity is a good thing in terms of your work?

Richard Alston

It seems to work really well I think. The only other two venues that I know of that have the same relationship are the Lawrence Batley Theatre in Huddersfield, which has a fantastic acoustic for music, so we did a similar programme there, and the Maltings in Snape. I suppose I spent so long touring with Rambert, hearing sometimes really fantastic music squeaking out of a pit! Some theatres' orchestra pits are not designed for string quartets. A string quartet sounds like a little squeaky gnat, if it's buried down there in a deep 19th century pit. Nowadays music is almost always enhanced and in some way assisted, but it is fantastic to be able to deal with music in a space where you can see the dancers move and you can also hear the music in a way that hopefully really does merit your attention.

Alistair Spalding

What about the dance side though? I know there are some criticisms about the QEH because of the actual space (for people who may not know it, it's a limited stage space with two fire exits on either side which are on different levels). So there's no real wing space; it has to be created by legs if you decide to do that. I know that it has changed some of the aspects of the work, hasn't it?

Richard Alston

Well, yes. Basically if the space is open you can only come on at the back, so performers have to come on and walk forward. In the early seasons we used to show the work first in London, therefore as I made the piece I would actually make sure that there were no important entrances from the front of the space. That is just a mundane thing but it's quite influential and we have now moved our season in the calendar year with Alistair's agreement and that's for two reasons. One is that the work that is presented in the Spring at the South Bank is aligned to Spring Loaded, the Festival that John (Ashford) runs at The Place. Since we are based there, it's good news for us to be associated with The Place. Therefore to be in the Festival that The Place presents makes sense. The other reason is actually that because I make work in the Summer and because in fact, the QEH space can be quite frightening for the dancers when they are dashing around - you think you're going to fall off the edge of the stage - it's kind of nerve racking. Every year I realised that I was presenting a bunch of terrified dancers and then going round the country and letting the work grow. So last year one of the major reasons for us changing our dates was actually to get the dancers seasoned into the movement, so it was deep enough in their body and that they had more resources. It was strategically crazy to perform first in the one place where you knew you were going to get the national press for a once-a-year quick look, and to present it at the one time when there was the greatest risk of the dancers being inhibited in the dance. It has changed the way we are received I think, because of the way they danced.

That doesn't sound too sycophantic I hope. When I was with Rambert, I had certain favourite theatres; I used to really like to see my work, sometimes on totally inappropriate stages, like the Mayflower, Southampton, where they used to close off the Upper Circle, because contemporary dance couldn't fill that, so I could actually have an entire part of the theatre to myself to look down on the space. Since then, I think that it's the people who run the theatre who are much more important than the actual desirability of the space. The fact that I feel that I have established a good relationship with Alistair, who was very clear in his support of the work, is more important to me than the shape of the stage.

Alistair Spalding

I don't want to repeat things that have been said in other sessions, but Nigel Hinds said the other day that 'You rarely get that situation where you get the right person in the right space with the right money'. I understand that and people do criticise the Queen Elizabeth Hall, but it does have money and it does have an incredible diversity of artistic interest in the people who work there, and so these kind of incredible collaborations can and do happen. You have to realise that 20% of what happens in the Queen Elizabeth Hall now is dance, yet in the early 80s that would be unthinkable.

One of the other things we should do is to try to tease out a bit what our different responsibilities are. We do work together, but my responsibilities are quite different from yours, and I know that this is a complex issue. For example, who do you think you are primarily responsible to?

Richard Alston

I don't think I can really avoid saying myself. As an artist, if I'm not responsible to myself or true to myself, then the whole thing might as well cave in. As soon as you start shifting for external reasons that you don't believe in, then you hit trouble. I am a late developer, and I feel that I have taken a long time to learn various things. My longest study period was 12 years with Rambert, but to start a company when you're 46 - or whatever I was -you have to know exactly what you want to do and there is no second chance. So it is important for me to try and push my work further, to develop the work beyond what I could manage at the same time as directing a repertoire company.

Next I feel very responsible to that Company because I really believe in an ensemble that works together and grows together. It is important that I keep an eye on who could be stretched in what way, how I can challenge one dancer or another without creating any kind of hierarchy. I feel very responsible, and happily so, to my performers because they make the work happen. None of these reasons can really be separated; the reason I make dance is because I enjoy dancers at full throttle, if you like, dancers who are really challenging themselves and performing therefore at their best, trying to push themselves beyond their best. That is a major reason why making dances excites me, and therefore it's a major part of what I want people to feel and see.

I am also responsible to the audience, because I wouldn't be doing all of this if it was just to remain in a studio. My biggest problem as a dance maker is that I really love being in a studio with a dancer right up close to me with that incredible physical energy that always emerges when people get very involved with what is happening. It has taken me a long time to keep working at making dance as detailed as I like it to be, but also for it to read and carry through space in a public auditorium. In one sense my time as resident choreographer with Rambert, going out on the road and watching works by Christopher Bruce, Robert North and Glen Tetley, was a period of study. It was like a long thinking process, and all the time being able to be in the audience. I have never seen myself primarily as a performer; I'm always very happy to be in the audience. There are definitely dancers and choreographers who associate themselves so much with the physical feel of movement that they like to be backstage, but I like to sit in audiences, hearing them like it or loathe it. Importantly, I think if you go to a different country, to a different culture, you feel differently about your work. You asked me about my responsibilities, but that's where I feel we do share responsibility.

Alistair Spalding

That's the first similarity; I think we're both equally responsible to the audience. Actually, whether my first responsibility is to the audience or the artist isn't quite clear. Many people would probably say the audience comes first, I can't serve that audience or give the audience interesting things to watch unless the first thing I'm thinking about is who to programme. So in other words, my first responsibility is to the choices that are made about the programme, because that either leads the audience or it creates the event that the audience wants to attend.

Richard Alston

And what happens when a piece of work or an artist whom you really believe in and find really exciting simply doesn't attract an audience? How does that resolve itself alongside the pressures of work you don't totally believe in but which sells the South Bank out? Is that a conflict?

Alistair Spalding

It is a conflict, yes, because the other responsibility I hold is the kind of financial one where I'm given a certain number of financial parameters at the beginning of the year, and I have to provide a certain amount of income. The way that I try to balance up both of those things is that some of the work is not to my taste but will provide an income, and I can still programme other work which I really, really believe in and will only get 50% of the house. It is possible to do both, but quite difficult to maintain support for a Company that's not pulling an audience at all. At some point I have to acknowledge that either the audience or the critics are not getting it, it's not working somehow. And that's probably more the case with some international work; British work tends to build up an audience and develop a kind of loyalty, but international work is a bit more difficult.

Richard Alston

I just wanted to mention one thing that is definitely an important responsibility to me. My Company and I have fantastic financial and administrative support, but I do feel responsible to others who make dance, because I'm well aware of the fact that I'm a well-funded choreographer.

This is a rare human being, a rare species, and therefore it is really important that I don't just accept that and just do nothing. I do support my administration in trying to find a broad programme of performances so that the subsidy is justified.

I know that I am very fortunate. I think it's also really important to think positively as an artist; it is an insidious poison to positive thinking if artists become completely bogged down with funding. One of the reasons we have all come here to this conference in Leeds is to celebrate the enormous amount of dance work in this country, the like of which is not to be found easily in other countries. It is amazing what happens in between all the gaps of the funding system; whatever is wrong about it, the right thing is that the work happens. I'm part of the same team as John Ashford at The Place, and I go to see all the young companies that he programmes and presents. There are other companies in the building, which is a huge support for me. It's tremendous, and it has made me feel much clearer about my own work. I don't believe that any artform will grow up until there really is a community that shares ideas and shares the excitement about the fact that this work exists and we're all doing the same thing.

Points raised in discussion:

- There tends to be a 'fashionable' set of artists who are regularly programmed on the circuit, whilst there are other equally interesting artists who do not receive the attention.

- It is difficult for young artists to be creative when they are constantly worrying about funding.

- Presenters are all very different, each with their own particular interests. John Ashford at The Place is interested in young choreographers who are starting out. Venues themselves can influence their programming through the structure of the space, which may be more appropriate to certain types of performance.

- A responsible presenter will sometimes have to programme work which does not appeal to his/her personal taste. There is a responsibility to be aware of the audience.

- The speakers agreed that certain companies of a particular scale should have a platform in London. Alistair Spalding said that it has been necessary to build a relationship with other presenters in the London area to ensure that a broad range of work is presented, and to provide 'a ladder of opportunity' for artists.

- Presenters often receive feedback on their work from within their own team. Richard Alston mentioned a very supportive team who assisted him when he was Director of Rambert Dance Company.

- People who have developed and matured as choreographers over several years, such as Richard Alston, still require feedback during the creative process.

Session 18

Nurturing Emerging Choreographers

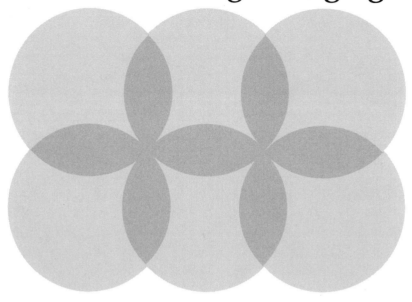

Keywords:

choreography   young choreographers   training   choreo-co-ordination project

Aimé de Lignière, Director of the Dance Department at Hogeschool Antwerpen describes his school and its aims, and gives examples of the ways in which help can be given to young choreographers in Belgium. In particular, and as Chair of the ELIA Dance Section, he shares aspects of the Choreo-Co-ordination project which took place in Lier, where 11 young dancers working with a choreo-co-ordinator, a composer and a video artist, completed a collaborative piece in just four weeks. Jo Butterworth, as Chairperson, introduced Aimé de Lignière.

Jo Butterworth

Aimé de *Lignière* is the Director of the High School for Dance in Lier near Antwerp. It is the only high school for dance in the whole of Belgium. He is going to tell us something about this school. Aimé is also chair of the ELIA Dance Section, ELIA standing for the European League of Institutes for the Arts. We as a Dance Section meet 4 times a year. We usually visit each others' institutions, and we also combine that with either, as in this case, a conference or some performances or seminars. We try to organise activities across Europe, not just for ourselves but also for our students. ELIA organises a major conference for the arts once every 2 years, and part of that deals with seminars for dance, but only part. So we made a plan in this last year that we should design something which was for the students of all the schools in Europe to come together in some way. Now obviously that would be very costly so we set up something where choices were made and one student from each institution was sent to this very special project. Aimé will be describing the choreo-co-ordination project which was run in Lier this summer (1998).

Aimé de Lignière

The Hogeschool Antwerpen

I have been a dancer for most of my life. It can be quite difficult for dancers to talk about their work, which is a big problem, and is one of the reasons why dance is not really taken seriously enough by people from the government and other important bodies. That is why we try to educate ourselves to talk about dance properly.

It has been said that classical ballet does not nourish modern and contemporary dance. I think this is a great mistake. There is a difference between classical ballet and classical dance, and classical dance is not dead. It is quite important and will grow more important in the new millenium. A lot of modern and contemporary companies are coming back to this classical trend. Classical training for a dancer gives many more opportunities in the way they dance. The National Ballet in Amsterdam is working towards finding new ways of working with classical material. Even in Belgium there is an association which protects classical dance and defends it. There are also courses where maybe we can find ways of being creative with classical dance.

It has been very difficult to run a school in Antwerp, because Antwerp in Belgium is a little like Leeds in England, where if you are not in London, nothing exists. If we were established in Brussels then the whole world would know about us. As we are in Antwerp, we are celebrating our 25th anniversary and hardly anyone knows that we are there, even though we have hundreds of teachers, around fifty dancers, and ten or fifteen choreographers who have graduated from the school and are based all over the world.

We are a very small school and we only take around 25 students a year. The Minister of Education said that there is little point in training 250 students every 10 years as dancers, because what are we going to do with them? So he gave us some money to try to expand our brief. Such money is never enough, but we have worked with it and tried to make the best of it. We have an enormous beautiful building, with six studios and our own theatre. We have a lot of things which even the big schools don't have. So now we train dancers, teachers and we are launching new choreographers, young choreographers. In Stockholm there is a school for choreographers, but they only take people from professional companies, which means that the students are anywhere between 25 and 40 years old. What do you call them? Emerging choreographers? Not a good name. New choreographers? They don't like that. Young choreographers? Certainly not because they are over 25 years old. I am a fossil, I know, but that is another story, but those who are trying to start a choreography career at 35 have problems because they are too old to be a young choreographer. So we get young students interested in choreography, we give them dancers, and space to rehearse and create. They don't have to make a product, we give them the opportunity to fail, which is very important. We pay for costume and designers and we organise initial performances in our theatre. If the work is successful then we may do more performances. We are our own bosses because we own the theatre.

Not all the students want to do improvisation and composition classes, and some become very frustrated because they want to be dancers, not creators. Maybe my school has to think about the possibility that those who don't want to do this shouldn't have to. It is something to think about. We know for sure that of the 30 students which we currently have only about 5 are actually interested in creating dances. Those 5 get all the support they need. Many dedicated people work to try to help young choreographers, and most of us know that choreographers have been creating dances for hundreds of years, whatever their style. Nobody taught them to choreograph, and still it happens the same way naturally. I think teaching choreography is something that happens in quite different ways in many schools. In Rotterdam, for instance, they have courses where they teach people to become choreographers. We work in a slightly different way. We advise them and help them, we give them opportunities and that's the way it works in our school. This opportunity is the most important thing; to do and also to be appreciated for what they are doing. Sometimes it is important to know that there are people behind you not only saying you have to do this, but also saying what you are doing is very interesting, please continue.

It is a wonderful situation to have dances created without pressure, but with the possibility for performances. The only thing is that we cannot get media interest. We cannot get through to them why they should write in the papers about young students who are trying to make dances. We do not have such a tradition as you in the UK do. Your country is known as the 'Dance Country', the biggest dance country in the world, bigger than America. A UK dance survey showed that there are seven million people working in dance here, from amateurs to professionals. I even heard that in a certain place in Scotland there are more people going to dance than going to the football, and that's amazing isn't it? So we all look to the UK for what is going to happen in the future with dance.

One of the strengths and also the weaknesses of dance is that although there is never enough money for the projects we have in mind and the things we would like to do, we always go on and do it anyway. Then the funders say why should we give them money when they are going to do it anyway? I think we need to become stronger politically. We need to get people dancing all over Europe, and this is what ELIA is trying to do. ELIA is trying to get us together and prove that we are worth listening to. I think that it will take another ten years if we are lucky before people start listening to us and accept us, but the Greenhouse Effect is one of the platforms where we can work now to prove ourselves.

The ELIA Dance Section Choreo-Co-ordination Project
Under the impulse of the ELIA Dance Section Committee, the idea of organising an international platform for young dancers working together to create a choreography became a reality. All member institutes of the ELIA Dance Section were invited to participate in this particular choreo-co-ordination project. Among them 13 institutes reacted in a positive way and selected one talented student who was willing to work intensively during the creation period that was organised at the Higher Institute for Dance of the Hogeschool Antwerpen during August 1998.

The project was a real challenge as right from the start the aims and objectives were very clear. This European work-platform for dance had to result in the creation of an original choreography to be presented and performed during the ELIA conference in Helsinki in November 1998. It was an opportunity for young dancers to work with other students and to experience the creation of a unique performance.

The choreo-co-ordination project basically started with a reduced budget. As planned the participants were in charge of the travel costs related to the creation period and the performance in Helsinki. If granted by the European Community, travel costs would be reimbursed. The Fontys Dance Academy from Tilburg and the Higher Institute for Dance from the Hogeschool Antwerpen took the responsibility for logistic and financial support, as well as the administration of fund applications. Without this partnership it would have been almost impossible to assure the organisation of this artistic project.

Overview of the aims and objectives – information on the working methods and the results. As the choreo-co-ordination project wanted to respect the input of all participating students by developing and supporting a creative process, it was of great importance to involve some professional artists in the project. First of all a choreo-co-ordinator, willing not to choreograph but to guide young people to select their own choreographic material, was an essential need. Marie De Corte, an experienced Belgian choreographer, accepted this challenge. Secondly it was of great importance to create possibilities for a multidisciplinary co-operation within the dance field. Therefore the composer, David Yoken, originally from the USA and representing Finland, was accompanying this experience. A special music composition was created together with the choreography, inspired by the movements of the dancers. In addition also the art of video was used in different ways. A Belgian videographer, Rik Van Meerbeeck was working on scenographic images as well as on the capture of the choreography and the making of a documentary on the working process.

In spite of the low budget the need for creating special costumes became inevitable. Sara Dykmans, costume designer and graduate student from the Art Academy of the Hogeschool Antwerpen, was chosen to design and make costumes. As we decided to organise a try-out performance at the end of the creation period we also worked on the lighting design created by one of the H.I.D. staff members, Francine de Frangh.

From August 3rd till August 28th a team of 11 (student) dancers and 5 professionals worked intensively to realise the creation of this original choreography which, after two weeks of improvisation and composition, was called *Skin-Friction*. Three of the dance students came from England (Bretton Hall, Chichester and Brighton). There was also one student each from Rotterdam, Holland, Helsinki, Finland, Italy, Greece and one from our own school in Lier. To get started the choreo-co-ordinator worked out a special concept with a large range of possibilities putting forward a general theme of Borders and Limits. Each participating student received information and was asked to take responsibilities to be able to work together as a team. Therefore the exploration of the participants' own borders and limits was sort of a departure point to start on.

From any point of view the creation period was very short, therefore the choreo-co-ordinator decided to work on a weekly schedule of six working days. To start in the morning, each day a different student was responsible for leading a warming up session, followed by a short break and a briefing from the choreo-co-ordinator. After the warming up there were basically two work-sessions and one round-up with video session programmed on a normal working day.

The working schedule was set up in different phases and in a way to allow for changes, if necessary.

Phase 1	(8 working days) - based on instructions with accent on improvisation
Phase 2	(8 working days) - the choreographic material from the students was selected by the choreo-co-ordinator
Phase 3	(6 working days) – stage setting and rehearsals

For the creation of the music composition, the composer was able to follow the dancers in their choreographic work. This close relationship inspired both dancers and composer to find the right atmosphere for *Skin-Friction*. David Yoken explored a number of instruments for their timbral possibilities. Lyrical and more percussive gestures, as well as the performers' personal voices and statements were included in the overall sound world of the choreography.

Alongside the movement there was a lot of talking, analysing and feedback in order to create a unity without losing the personality of each dancer. A strong physical condition, teamwork, communication, frankness and creativity were the basic ingredients for this project to succeed. The making of *Skin-Friction* was really an extraordinary achievement and a memorable experience for all participants.

Some reflections of Marie De Corte illustrate in a very strong way the unique atmosphere of the physical language such as emotion, strength and fragility that you can find in this choreography.

Skin-Friction...places the body into a tensioned field of power to show vulnerability.

Skin-Friction...is trying to see things through the skin.

Skin-Friction...a perpetual movement of borderlines is creating an ectoplasm in which 'nearness' and 'distance' dissolve into the universe.

Skin-Friction..an image of the present time in which individual steps are vanishing into immensity.

This choreo-co-ordination project was a choreographic experiment of great importance bringing together students with very different backgrounds and giving them the possibility to search for a common language in dance. Next to the students' and the ELIA Dance Section's enthusiasm, we also need to analyse, in an objective way, the differences between the aims and objectives of international dance educations in general. The choreo-co-ordination project revealed large differences between the participating dancers. It was shown in different areas, but always connected to the education systems. It is important to get a better knowledge of the European education systems by working all together in preserving and analysing quality to improve dance education.

Many thanks to all participating institutes from the UK, Italy, Holland, Finland, Portugal, Greece and Belgium.

Points raised in discussion:

- The issue of ownership of a choreo-co-ordinated work was raised.
  The choreo-co-ordinator had to deal with the structure of the piece for the most part, as it would be difficult for eleven students to all form the work together.
  The choreo-co-ordinator worked with the material created by the students but had to make the final forming decisions.

- The role of the choreo-co-ordinator was seen as one of encouragement and enthusiasm, and she helped the dancers to challenge themselves and their movement vocabularies with her comments.

Session 19

The Devising Process: A Framework for Collaboration

Keywords:

collaboration   process   collective   devising

Is it possible to make a performance piece without a designated director? What is the nature of the devising process when all aspects of the making of the work are decided collaboratively, and each member of the group feels equal ownership of the work? After platforming their practical research work last night, the group share their philosophy.The speakers from BPM were Roy Fears, Sandra Fisher, Jason Salvin, Sophie Smith, Tim Dickinson and Louise Bridges. The chairperson was Sue Doubell.

Sue Doubell

This presentation and discussion will focus on last night's presentation by Beats Per Minute. Firstly, I would like to establish how the collaboration came about, and in what context.

Roy Fears

We were asked to do this project as a model of good practice in the devising process. The initial idea was to use professional dancers, or student dancers, and make a straightforward contemporary dance piece. But we chose to integrate those things that are normally used as stimuli to choreography, i.e. music, light, dance. So we actually had a collective creative process and product. Instead of producing a piece of dance that then had lighting and sound attached to it, the nature of the group means that all elements within the piece are integral to the piece.

Sophie Smith

We all come from different specialisms, lighting design, music composition, acting, writing and dance.

Tim Dickinson

I found it interesting to become involved because I haven't done anything of this nature before. I thoroughly enjoyed working together in a team with all the different aspects of all the different specialisms we have.

Sandra Fisher

An important thing regarding the fact that we came from different disciplines is how, as different artists, we could mix our different interests and specialisms, and how that could come together and develop into something worthwhile. So we had to have some kind of common ground.

Sue Doubell

In general terms when you have a group such as this and you have no one leader, if you don't know each other, then you have to tread very warily as a human being let alone as an artist.

Roy Fears

That's actually an interesting point. We all know what we are capable of, we all know what we can do. I think an important point is that we are all comfortable with our disciplines. There is no need for a director to break it up or a choreographer to impose something here or something there. I think it is important, not necessarily to be friends, but to have a similar approach, a similar way of life. It's all about how comfortable you are with what you do, and how willing you are to embrace a variety of things, and have a wide vision as opposed to having blinkers on.

Sandra Fisher

And not be precious but to help shape a whole which is not necessarily yours.

Tim Dickinson

My contribution was the composition of the music with Sophie. I wanted to be modern without being too avant-. Working with the team gave me that opportunity to do that. I'd make something, we'd go away and listen to it and say which bits we liked and didn't like. It was a narrowing down process. I also worked in that respect with Sophie. I'd do a bit of music on my own, we'd get together and come up with the finished product. But we'd wait for everyone to be happy before we'd decided it was finished.

Sophie Smith

If you have different, very specific disciplines working together with each other, you have to work on an individual level to make a piece. In effect there were collaborations going on within the larger collaboration of the piece. I find it hard to say what I have brought to the project, because I feel that when you are doing a devising project people draw on what you've got to give. You never know what you'll be doing because you don't know what people are going to ask of you.

Sandra Fisher

I think that's true. It's very much a willingness to take on board other people's knowledge and expertise, and see how that can work with what you know as well. It's more of an open mind that you bring to the project. It's a complicated process and you have to have a common language and a way to communicate with people. You don't want to fight within a group because it will inhibit the creative process.

Sue Doubell

So what you're saying is that you need a certain amount of compatibility to allow the devising process to take place, to make it easier.

Tim Dickinson

Not necessarily easier, but you won't get as good a piece if you aren't close.

Roy Fears

Within the larger collaborative process, there were tiny collaborations going on but no one discipline imposed their work on the others. For example, Sandra, Louise and I would do a lot of character work, and at various stages in the process we would present this to the musicians and lighting designer. They then gave us light and music that was linked to that, or their interpretation of that. It was almost like a game of discipline tennis. They'd ace us, and then we'd ace them back, and things began to snowball. The end result was that all of the elements of the piece, built by those from the different disciplines, were inextricable from one another. Not one element of the piece we presented last night would have been the same if we had worked as separate entities under a director.

Sue Doubell

Did you find the process at times too complex? You talk about having great interaction with each other, and there are lots of different, very subtle layers within this collaboration. Did you find at any point that the process was too overpowering and you wanted a director to draw it all together?

Sophie Smith

We decided from the beginning of the project what we wanted the finished product to be. As a result we were all working towards the same thing. We decided on a structure, and even the atmosphere we wished to create for each section. The characters hadn't been developed, and the sound work hadn't been done, but we knew what each bit wanted to be like. Tim and I really pushed for a structure, because we wanted the music to flow and not just be individual pieces set to different parts of the piece. The devising of a basic structure and atmosphere allowed us to do that. The important word there is 'basic', because the structure was flexible and not set in stone.

Roy Fears

You have to have some sort of parameters because if we had total freedom we would have been going round in circles for years with nothing ever coming to fruition. There would have been some great bits, but there would have been no way to gel them together.

Sue Doubell

So, describe the process of this particular piece.

Sandra Fisher

The working process began with a sharing of ideas, working out a structure, a framework and some kind of common language. We set up a system called "show and tell" sessions. We would agree what each of us would work on, go away and do it, then come back and share that information. This was a way of keeping everyone up to date and making sure that not only everyone was feeding into the process, but that we were firmly on track. That happened at weekly intervals. This was to make sure that we could keep on top of the whole process, and make sure that it didn't run away from us.

Sophie Smith

Although the "show and tell" sessions were weekly, that didn't mean that that was the only time we worked on the piece. For example, I live with Sandra and I work with Tim. Roy works with Sandra and Jason, and lives with Louise. As a result, the project was talked about on a day to day basis and it almost developed without any of us realising. We decided that we were going to base the piece loosely on characters. We started by doing some writing work, and we all took part in that. Tim and I then took some of those ideas away and turned them into a song. The work we did with a certain character idea gelled with the work Roy and Sandra were doing because the atmosphere had already been decided on. That saved a lot of time. Otherwise we'd have been chasing our tails.

Roy Fears

There was a point in the choreographic process where I just felt "what on earth am I doing? I have these motifs and these things and they just mean absolutely nothing". An actor will always forget his lines unless you have a motive for them, unless you have done your late Stanislavisky actioning, units and objectives, super-objectives. If an actor doesn't know what he's doing with a line, he will forget that line, which is true for a dancer as well. I just didn't know why I was doing some of these moves. They were nonsense and meant nothing, they had to be contextualised. There was a point when we had to contextualise further. We had our atmosphere; our frameworks, our set sections, and we had episodes. But the episodes meant nothing. We had to create an environment; we had to give ourselves through lines, objectives and motives so we actually believed in what we were communicating. Unless you can make somebody believe you, why would you actually do it? I'm not a naturalism fan, but I do think you have to have motive, you have to have reason. I believe that you have to have environment, so we had to create that, we had to feed that in. Now that wasn't necessarily for the audience's sake, but there had to be those elements in there for us as performers.

Sue Doubell

I'd like to know the amount of time, perhaps the number of hours you devoted to the project.

Sandra Fisher

We're all holding down full or part time jobs as well as doing other things. So whenever we were all free we would work on the project.

Roy Fears

We'd like to say it was part time, but we would actually work through six till midnight, after each completing a full day at work. In total it was about six weeks.

Sue Doubell

Did the notion of pressure, i.e. you had to be ready for this particular event, get to you?

Roy Fears

I think that because of the sound and lighting, people thought that it was a finished piece of work. It was actually a snapshot of the work in progress.

Sophie Smith

Last week we had access to Powerhouse 1. Tim brought his whole studio down to Powerhouse and we set up to stage in the same way you saw it last night. By the time we went into Powerhouse we had the nugget of all the sections, however, we could finally bring all of the disciplines within the piece together.

Sue Doubell

So, if I can ask each of you individually how you thought the performance went yesterday.

Tim Dickinson

I thought it went very well. I had a lot of technical equipment running live, and there was a lot of pressure. If anything had happened, just a small power surge, or any variation in how it was set up, it would have all crashed and we'd have had to have waited half an hour for it all to be set up again. When I sat down and it worked, I think I knew from that point on it was going to be fine from my point of view

Jason Salvin

I think I'm the same as Tim. We brought all our own lighting. Four moving and two static lights. Because they were computer controlled you have to wire them up and get them plugged up the right way. You don't get a second chance. Once everything had completed the test cycle I knew it would be fine. If something were to happen at that point there would have been nothing we could have done.

Roy Fears

The thing to emphasise is that it was a live experience. Each member of the team was working live. We talk about computers and we talk about lighting desks, but it's not a case of pressing a button and off it all goes. The computer generated music and the lighting are both very sophisticated. There's a huge level of expertise involved in that sort of thing. It's not just about the performers, because all of us are responsible for the environment we create. Everybody on that stage last night had the same level of responsibility. Even though perhaps the conference was looking at dance, it was a collaborative affair, so it is what we would prefer to call performance.

Sue Doubell

Did it achieve what you felt you were going to achieve?

Sandra Fisher

I think it was a very creative experience, I think that's the best way to explain it. We did achieve a lot by working together, and something that was particularly choreographically creative because of the collaboration. I mean in all senses not just in movement terms, it was something creative that couldn't have been done without everybody else.

Roy Fears

We were feeding off each other's disciplines, using whatever we could to inform the characters, to inform the piece, to inform the environment. Every time we came to a creative block we had so much more to draw from.

Sophie Smith

What was nice as well is that nobody was precious about any of their work. I was working with a poem that Louise had written, and it was fantastic as a poem, but didn't work as lyrics for a song at all.

Roy Fears

Louise's poem, which was an absolute killer, never actually came to the stage in it's fullness. It was never there as a whole piece of work. It was there in the form of soundbites and particular stanzas became lyrics to a song.

Louise Bridges

As in every play you know you're never going to say everything you want to say to the audience. You hope with what you say and the honesty with which you say it that they will know that what's going on is more that just what they're hearing. Personally, I feel that's a good thing that we've done as a group. We've brought some honesty to what we've done, and it's so much more that just a piece of dance.

Roy Fears

In the dance world the whole idea of working without a choreographer or director is only embraced as an educational tool, or in community work. It isn't generally used as a choreographic tool. As we were doing something that was going to be a little controversial any way, we decided to take it a little further and collaborate not just with dancers, but with those who are usually the stimulus for choreography. Our society is a multimedia one, one in which people take in a vast amount of information in a moment, in a soundbite. The form of collaboration we participated in doesn't just talk about the environment on stage, but the environment that sweeps beyond the stage. It's an entertainment form that embraces part of that lifestyle but is still a theatrical experience.

Sophie Smith

After the performance last night, Kevin Finnan from Motionhouse Dance came to give us feedback. He said it was very obvious that what we had been drawing from was our lives, and that it really is a generational thing. It was created for us and people like us.

Roy Fears

And we don't apologise for that because the whole idea of this conference is about where dance is now, how are we getting new audiences in, and where are we going from here. If we're going to get people back into the theatre we have to talk about them and not us. We need to communicate to them in that multimedia level, in a level that they understand and accept. We need to talk about them, their experiences and their lives. We will not draw people into the theatre if they have no connection with what they are viewing.

Points raised in discussion:

- Collaboration supposes that the most important thing is the product, and all members of the team are as valuable as each other. Collaboration allows each of its participants to gain a greater appreciation of what the other does. This leads to a greater level of respect between all of those involved in a project.

- The ability of BPM to articulate their views and ideals in an intelligent fashion is something that all companies should be able to do.

- The work of BPM is designed to, and does reach those of the younger generations.

- BPM critise the dance establishment for only providing for a niche market. However, BPM's product may be as exclusive, just to a different group.

- One delegate expressed concern that all work showcased at the conference excluded far too many people. The greatest achievement for any company would be to stay true to their ideals, but enable anyone to get something from the work.

Session 20
European Promotion Practices: How do they nurture choreographers?

Keywords:

promotors/presenters   artists   independent choreographers
international

Speakers from Belgium, Portugal and the UK, Guy Cools, Maria de Assis and John Ashford,
discuss their experiences of promotion practices in Europe[1]. What strategies do they employ?
By what criteria do they choose work to present? How far does their influence extend?

---

[1]Due to a recording error John Ashford's contribution is not documented here

Guy Cools

'Everybody always wants to tackle the great themes, wants to connect metaphysically, wants to ask the essential questions, and for that purpose we paint with a broad brush. My experience in doing this is that you create only vagueness and abstraction. I try to tackle things by focusing upon their meaningful details.' (Arne Sierens)

The above statement by Ghent based playwright Arne Sierens about his own artistic practice is also relevant to the discussion about internationalization :

1. The formation of a strong, proper artistic identity, whether or not bound by a particular culture, prevails over any form of international expansion.

2. It is no use talking about the issue of international co-production or networking from a general or theoretical point of view. Every artistic project needs a specific an proper framework.

The Arts Centre Vooruit

When the Arts Centre Vooruit in Ghent started with an active production policy in the mid-eighties, priority was given to the development of a production infrastructure (consisting of studios, theatre spaces, offices and specialised staff) which could be used as flexibly as possible. With each (co)production, we consider anew the needs of the artists :

1. Free access to the studio and the performance spaces.

2. Technical equipment and the know-how of the staff (either technical, administrational, dramatic or press- and public relations) should be at the group's disposal.

3. In addition to this a financial contribution is given, which is often translated into a fee to commission part of the work: the music score, the choreography, the scenography, the text.

From the beginning all our work has been done in an international context. The artistic richness of the performing arts in Flanders since the beginning of the eighties could not have originated form an abundancy of funds or a particular clear vision on behalf of the government. An explanation should rather be sought in the fact that from the beginning the development of a proper artistic identity has been nurtured and compared with foreign examples and models which were presented by pioneering organisations such as the Kaaitheater festival in Brussels and the Klapstuk festival in Leuven.

Also Vooruit's production policy aims at stimulating an exchange between the local artistic community and the international arts community. As such Vooruit offers residencies to foreign artists and companies and participates in international co-productions and networks set up to develop and explore these collaborations on a permanent basis. A good example of the first is our contemporary music programme in which we on the one hand invite foreign composers to perform their work with local musicians and on the other hand commission work by Flemish composers for foreign ensembles. An example of the second is Dance Network Europe which joins The Place Theatre in London; CNDC L'Esquisse in Angers and Joint Adventures in Munich together with Vooruit in a constant effort to 'investigate different models of co-production by co commissioning and co-producing contemporary dance productions.'

In these international co-operations we have learned that in order to be successful the following conditions have to be fulfilled:

1. The collaboration should not involve too many partners and should be centred around a well-defined artistic project.

2. There should be artistic affinity between the different partners, i.e. a shared interest in the artists with whom we work.

3. There should be organizational equality (which does not mean they have to be identical) between the different partners.

The Relationship Between the Producer/Presenter and the Artist

'We (the producers/presenters) are led by the artists we choose to serve.' (John Ashford) The best definition of the producer-artist relationship was given by John Ashford at a conference in Barcelona in April 1998. We, the producers, have the power (negatively formulated); the responsibility (positively formulated) to make relevant choices but once we did, it is the artists who take over and guide us where they want to bring us.

How do you make 'relevant' choices ?

The question is often asked and there isn't a standard answer, since so much depends on how and when you meet an artist. But in general the choice is always a combination of a subjective, individual appreciation of the quality of an artist or a belief in his/her potential (you can't present artists whose work you don't like) and a strategic choice which in my case is always related to the development of a local dance scene. So for instance when the continental dance theatre tradition is already very much present in the local scene through our 'house company' Les Ballets C de la B (Alain Platel), then I deliberately engaged myself to choreographers such as Jonathan Burrows, and Filip Van Huffel and Sacha Lee of Retina Dance Company to introduce a more pure, movement based dance universe, since I think it is important for the development of any scene to show rather the diversity of the contemporary dance landscape instead of focusing on one style or aesthetics. And by inviting Retina we also brought in their experience with community based work which is completely lacking in the Flemish dance landscape.

How much do you interfere as a producer ?

Although I very much believe in the above dictum that the producer should follow the artist and not the other way around as for instance in film, I have become more conscious the last couple of years that artists appreciate your guidance as well. But this needs a long established relation and an open dialogue in which the producer can become the confident or dramaturg who helps the artist to make his choices and to 'deliver' (in the platonic sense) his ideas and visions. As such I have in recent years interfered in artistic processes forcing the artist to replace an artistic collaborator or even suggesting to cut part of a programme.

How conceptual can you be as a presenter ?

I think the visual arts have clearly shown the danger of curators or museum directors who became more conceptual than the artists themselves. Personally I think it is useful to have underlying concepts in your programme but I am always very hesitant to make them to explicit. On the other hand marketing more and more asks for concepts which can easily be translated in catchy headlines and themes in which they can pigeonhole the programme. As is so many of the above mentioned issues there is no right or wrong theoretical answer since everything depends so much of the how and when of the actual situation.

(the first half of this paper was originally published by the Magazine of Künstlerhaus Mousonturm. Issue 4)

Maria de Assis

ACARTE has been a main driving force in the development of contemporary arts in Portugal and took a decisive role in the emergence of New Portuguese Dance. It exists as one of the many departments of the Gulbenkian Foundation. Although private, this Foundation is a non-profit organisation acting as a public service in many areas, from health and education to science and culture. Its strategies have always been geared to complement or fill existing gaps in Portuguese Government policies and resources, thus providing a relevant contribution to the overall development of the country.

The decision to found ACARTE in 1984 with the mission to nurture contemporary performing arts has to do with the weaknesses found in this field at the time: it lacked money, information, presentation structures, artists and public.

To work in ACARTE may be considered as a privilege since it operates on an annual budget provided by the Gulbenkian Foundation. Box office returns are always an important contribution, but not in a restrictive way. The director is free to devise strategies and to set his own priorities in order to fulfil the broad guidelines of ACARTE's mission. These strategies and priorities have obviously changed over the years in order to respond to new contexts. As we all know there are no permanent formulas nor effective plans valid for ever and for everywhere.

Madalena Perdigão was the founder of ACARTE and its first director from 1984 to 1990. She designed a programme of activities that included presentation, production, training, research and debate. This programme has been kept ever since by the succeeding directors. Her first concern was to introduce into Portugal what was then considered the most innovative and experimental work being produced in Europe. This simple move had a tremendous impact both on audiences and on the artistic community. Her timing was perfect. Ten years had passed since the Portuguese Revolution put an end to 50 years of dictatorship and Portugal's isolation from the rest of the world. Portuguese artists and their audiences spent those ten years celebrating the culture as a democratic achievement. Most of the creative work produced and presented was Portuguese made and had more to do with the political and social situation than with aesthetic concerns. After that period, both artists and public were ready for something more, and ACARTE provided it.

If we concentrate on the dance scene - as dance is what concerns us here - it will be interesting to note that during the first 5 years, 90% of what was being presented by ACARTE came from abroad, mainly Europe and the United States. ACARTE encouraged then quite a few foreign young choreographers whose work had already caught the attention of specialised audiences, but were still outside the main international circuit. Portuguese independent choreographers were not included simply because what might be called an independent dance scene still didn't exist in our country. A few Portuguese dancers - very few - had already felt the need to develop their own creative work but they were still bound to the training, aesthetics and working conditions existing in Portugal.

The contact with the work of foreign independent choreographers strengthened the convictions of these few and influenced many more to venture into their own projects. This influence was so strong that it shaped the way Portuguese choreographers perceive dance to this day. This is because a lot of the work presented was multidisciplinary - either dance-theatre, physical theatre or multimedia. Subsequently, most Portuguese choreographers felt free to cross boundaries and explore the relationships between dance, music, theatre and the visual arts.

In order to reinforce the impact of these foreign companies on the dance community, Madalena Perdigão organised workshops, lecture demonstrations and informal meetings, enabling Portuguese dancers to experience new training techniques, exchange ideas and learn more about different creative processes.

Some promoters make it their responsibility to spot new talent, hoping to give an important contribution to artistic renewal. Doing so they restrict the number of artists they support to those whose work bears assumptions and aesthetic values which they share and believe. Madalena Perdigão, even though concerned with change and innovation, placed artists' needs ahead of aesthetic concerns. She combined this wave of innovative experimental work coming from abroad with support for the existing Portuguese companies, regardless of their style. The National Ballet Company with its classical ballet repertoire and the Lisbon Dance Company, which combined different styles of contemporary work, some quite conventional, were both invited to perform at ACARTE every year until 1989. It was clear to Madalena Perdigão that both these companies played an important role in the bleak panorama of Portuguese dance and that they would benefit from extra public exposure in a prestigious venue. In effect, it was only in 1989, 5 years after the foundation of ACARTE that Madalena Perdigão was able to organise the first showcase of Portuguese independent dance, presenting just 3 different groups. One of them was Rui Horta, who decided to leave the Lisbon Dance Company to pursue his own creative work taking some of the dancers with him.

When José Sasportes replaced Madalena Perdigão as the Director of ACARTE in 1990 there were enough changes to justify new options and widen the scope of ACARTE's policies. Some of them were directly concerned with nurturing dancers and choreographers. Firstly he increased the number of dance events. It was clear to him that dance needed extra support when compared to other art forms since it had remained the one with the least money, a weaker political voice, fewer performance opportunities and less international exposure. Training opportunities were extended, encompassing other dance traditions and techniques as well as specific creative projects which culminated in public presentations. These projects enabled young and inexperienced dancers to work with established choreographers, to take part in their creative processes and benefit from stage experience. There was an increase in dance debate. Conferences and seminars focused on the relevance of international networking and the need to place the work of Portuguese choreographers in the context of 20th century dance history. Relevant testimonies and discussions about what was then designated a New Portuguese Dance contributed to disseminate new concepts and make choreographers and dancers more aware of the meaning and extent of their common beliefs. Another important move had to do with the rapid artistic growth of the Portuguese independent dance scene. During the first years ACARTE had been nurturing Portuguese dancers and choreographers mainly by opening up their minds and bodies to new ideas. From 1990 José Sasportes invested strongly in producing and presenting their projects, from the young school graduates who were still attempting their first choreographic experiments, to the professional dancers and choreographers coming from repertoire companies but keen to develop their own creative work. ACARTE became their main source for project funding and presentation and remained so, supporting an increasing number of new choreographers, at least until the end of 1994.

José Sasportes left during that year and Yvette Centeno, the new Director of ACARTE, had to face important new challenges. Two major venues, The Belem Cultural Centre, state-run, and Culturgest, conceived and funded by the largest Portuguese bank, opened up to the public at the end of 1993. During the following year their influence was difficult to assess. The programme of Lisbon 94, as cultural capital of Europe, became the main artistic focus in the country, benefiting from joint efforts which involved these venues as well as ACARTE and the Gulbenkian Foundation. Since then both venues have been programming contemporary art work, including dance, on a regular basis. And this wasn't all. Big festivals originally restricted to theatre and music began including dance in their programmes. Furthermore, small dance platforms, showcases and festivals which came into existence at the beginning of the 90s grew in visibility and stability. As a result ACARTE lost its key role as the only venue nurturing dance and its artists. On the other hand, its aura of being the place to see unusual, experimental and stimulating work was radically altered by the healthy competition and the difficulty in meeting the high expectations of a public which had since become more sophisticated and demanding.

As I stated at the beginning, the Gulbenkian Foundation is always revising its strategies to channel its funds into the areas where they are most needed. Under these circumstances, it is easy to understand the recent decision to reduces ACARTE's annual budget. Education and Science are now considered priority areas instead of direct cultural promotion. Given this new context, Yvette

Centeno was forced to devise new priorities when she took over the direction of ACARTE in 1995. After assessing the weaknesses in the field of the performing arts and what was being done by the two other similar structures working in Lisbon, Yvette Centeno decided to invest in training and research projects to the detriment of merely presenting contemporary work. A fair percentage of what is presented is Portuguese made. This means ACARTE goes on supporting independent artists by producing and presenting their projects, including choreographers who are still striving for recognition. Nevertheless, since production costs are very high, it favours those who are able to bring in other co-producers. Training events are geared to alternative techniques and subsidiary disciplines still unavailable in dance schools. Some of these events are organised as multidisciplinary workshops. Their main objective is to provided dancers and choreographers with the chance to deepen their knowledge and experience in other artistic languages which are often present in their work but without the necessary skills. Research projects aim to provide choreographers with enough money, working space and technical conditions to think, experiment and do whatever they want without the obligation of presenting any concrete results. Since most artists are usually conditioned to produce new work, at least once a year, both to obtain financial support and respond to other promotersí commissions, this is a way of getting round deadlines dictated by market conditions rather than creative need.Another important priority is ACARTE's involvement in European projects which may help internationalise young Portuguese choreographers. For the past three years, ACARTE has been a partner in three international projects: the Rencontres Chorégraphiques Internationales de Seine-Saint-Denis, formerly known as Bagnolet, and the 'Rèpérages' project, both under French leadership, and Aerowaves, under British leadership. They are radically different from each other and this is why it makes sense, for ACARTE, to be involved in all three.

Bagnolet has to be regarded both in its international and national dimensions. Internationally there is no doubt it provides a lot of money, sound debate and wide media coverage to contemporary dance. This, in itself, is already an important achievement. The money is used to support new work and intensive touring to a number of dance companies. On the national level, it is unwise to concentrate all our expectations – and therefore the expectations of our choreographers – in the selection process which will determine the 15 or 16 lucky ones who will fully benefit from what Bagnolet has to offer. It is also unwise and untrue to think that these 15 or 16 were the best among all candidates. The selection is made by a group of people with different tastes and criteria and none of them has seen all the work presented on the many platforms organised around the world. We are simply aware that the selected work has generated a number of strong opinions.

Within this project and as organisers of a dance platform in our country we have to make sure we put enough thought and resources into it in order to make it an important event in itself, important enough to remain useful and worthwhile to the choreographers we present, regardless of their eventual selection to the final platform in France. This selection has to be regarded as an extra bonus. If we can use the international dimension of this project to raise more money, political impact, media interest and extra presentation opportunities to the choreographers involved, then yes, it is worthwhile remaining a partner in the project. This is what ACARTE has been able to do so far.

The Rèpérages project is less ambitious in scale but it achieves good results for both promoters and choreographers. It works because the seven partners from seven different countries respect and trust each other and 6therefore are willing to take the necessary risks. Actually the only risk resides in the obligation to include in our yearly programme one company from those who have been chosen by each of us to take part in the project. All these companies have the chance to present their work in Lille and they do so in good conditions, since only two companies share the same evening and are able to perform to a diverse audience. Indeed, unlike other international projects of a similar kind, Rèpérages doesn't use the format of a festival or a dance platform concentrating a great number of critics, promoters and agents from all over the world. Instead, the performances occur during the year (during three spaced weekends), which means the promoters involved are not under pressure. They have the time and freedom of mind to fully concentrate on each work. Promoters may choose any work for their own venues and their choices will depend on a number of different criteria – artistic taste, financial conditions, the piece's dimension or programme framing.

Another important aspect of this project is that it gives promoters and choreographers the time to meet and discuss many issues both about the work presented and about the project itself. These discussions are enriching and enable the project to keep growing. For example, realising, after the first edition, that the choreographers didn't have the chance to get to know each other, we took the decision to organise a summer residence. This means that apart from fiving the selected choreographers the opportunity to show their work in an international context with further touring opportunities, Répèrages is also offering them the chance of a summer residence, where they are able to meet, exchange ideas and explore common interests. These residencies have taken place in different countries. The first was in Lille, the second in Lisbon and the third in Montreal.

Subsequently, after the 4th edition, we decided to extend the number of promoters involved, not by adding more countries to the project, but by organising a second network with one extra promoter from each country. This way the project is kept on a small scale but enhances the touring opportunities for the companies involved.

Aerowaves is a more recent project and the one ACARTE has not been able to explore to its full potential. It is a very versatile project, concentrating on one annual meeting, lasting around 4 days, with a lot of people – I believe at the moment we are 23 European partners – and a lot of information about the independent dance scene in all 23 countries. Each partner is able to present and defend the work of a few choreographers from his country, those he considers more talented and promising yet still outside the main international touring circuit. This invaluable information, coming directly from the source, saves everyone a lot of money and time-consuming travelling. The fact that these 23 people come from different generations, have different tastes, programming criteria and professional backgrounds, works as an asset when discussing and evaluating the choreographic work presented on video. Each partner can thus balance his own artistic instinct, preferences and priorities within the general consensus and is free to use the information provided in any way he pleases.

Since ACARTE is inviting fewer foreign companies and concentrating their performances around its annual festival, it has been difficult, so far, to put this information to real use. It is vital to find the right context when presenting work that hasn't yet fully matured. We may stifle young artists rather than nurture them if we fail to frame their work correctly. This is particularly important if we present this kind of work within a big festival featuring well-established contemporary artists. So far ACARTE has been able to use Aerowaves to push forward a few young Portuguese choreographers, but hasn't yet found the right formula to nurture the other young talents, from all over Europe, discovered by this project.

In summary:
Promoters have to deal with a number of severe constraints: budget, presentation, spaces, technical conditions, human resources, artistic and social contexts. Therefore, before acting, we should make a rigorous diagnosis of the context in which we are involved. A good diagnosis will inform us, first, about how free we are to determine our own objectives, then it will help us to determine what to do and how to do it, in order to achieve those objectives. Implemented at the right time and in the right place, a simple move will always be more effective than an ambitious plan which disregards time and place. If our main objectives involve nurturing dancers and choreographers we mustn't convince ourselves that we know exactly what to do and how, in order to meet their needs. The dialogue between the promoter and the dance community is vital in order to devise the best strategies. When our planning seems to be running beautifully, we shouldn't relax and think that we have made it. Reality changes very fast, especially when our strategies are effective and therefore are actively contributing to that change. We must think ahead if we want to remain useful to the artistic community. And finally, more and more we need to rely on networking to extend our activities. By networking I mean all kinds of national and international collaborative projects which help exchange information, raise money and expand touring opportunities to the artists we support. But we shouldn't force ourselves to regulate these collaborations. They should remain as informal and flexible as possible, in order to escape mere repetition or even stagnation.

Session 21

Text, Context, Dance: In conversation with Shobana Jeyasingh

Keywords:

culture   cultural perception   choreography   dance vocabulary
classical/ contemporary

Shobana Jeyasingh trained in the classical Indian dance style Bharatha Natyam, but has spent the last decade experimenting with the idea of enriching this base in the dance language of her choreography. How is her work viewed, and how does she view her own work? Here she discusses issues of culture, dance making and contemporaneity with Sanjoy Roy.

Sanjoy Roy

(Sanjoy Roy introduced himself and Shobana Jeyasingh). Shobana set up her own company in 1988, and since then she has changed her style quite radically. Prior to setting up the company she was a performer for some time, and before that she read for an MA at Sussex. Her work is quite different in many ways from the work of her contemporaries. But Shobana started out doing postgraduate studies in Shakespeare.

Shobana Jeyasingh

At seventeen I chose to do a degree in English Literature because I had a vague ambition to write. But I discovered that this was not the right area for me, and I graduated dissatisfied and creatively unfulfilled. My decision to work in dance was not a sudden, huge one, but a series of very small decisions. When I left Sussex and came to London, I went to see some dance, and was quite surprised at how much Indian dance there was in London. I was intrigued by the first Indian dance performance I saw, which was at the South Bank. It made an extraordinary impression on me, and I think that this was the process by which I became interested in choreography.

Sanjoy Roy

You spent quite a long time as an Indian dancer before setting up your company. Perhaps you could tell us about the major transition between touring on the Indian dance circuit and where you are now in the contemporary dance genre?

Shobana Jeyasingh

I don't think I ever actually toured the Indian circuit really because my touring in Britain was mainly funded with subsidies from the regional arts councils, so the places I visited were really the venues of the small-scale touring circuit. Sometimes a small scale touring circuit also included some community venues, usually by accident, when performances had to be scheduled in school halls.

The transition from Indian dance performer to the current company was, again, not a huge decision made over-night. I think on the whole that I am a very, very slow learner! I knew I could never be a brilliant dancer physically. I knew that I would never achieve perfect turnout, although I did try fairly seriously. I was rehearsing by myself in a very small personal studio in London, spending whole days with only a tape recorder. I found myself thinking about the space and what I did in it. My interest in contemporary dance released me from being this rather isolated, less than-brilliant performer.

Sanjoy Roy

So was your background not specifically choreographic or artistic in dance?

Shobana Jeyasingh

No, not at all. When I was young I went to dance class, and I realised that I had an aptitude for dance. In my class of twenty I found that I was the one who could remember the sequence, and I didn't have too great a problem with co-ordination. But I think that always, when I was performing classical repertoire, I had a lot of questions within myself. Gradually I came to a point where I wanted to express myself as a person, and if I wanted to express myself in dance then I would have to shift my vocabulary from the confines of the classical language into something else.

When I first took on two dancers to form the company, I was not really thinking in terms of moving towards anywhere in particular. I was just thinking about how I was going to finish the piece. The biggest challenge of having, as I did, two other people waiting for you to tell them what to do is to find a way to communicate what you are thinking to them. That is the first lesson in being a choreographer. It is not enough to talk, and say this is what I want. I had to try to translate those intentions into another language. This first experiment in making dance for someone other than myself was in fact an idea which was mooted by John Ashford at The Place. His enthusiasm gave me the courage to sit down and think about it. It was programmed at the

Queen Elizabeth Hall alongside an Italian dancer, and I never really thought about whether I was in the contemporary world or not. I think the platform gave me a very different audience from those to which I had previously performed. So it was really outside influences determining my shift, rather than myself. I don't think I ever really delineated strictly between the terms classical and contemporary. This is the language which I have been taught, and which I have inherited, and I just use it to express myself.

Sanjoy Roy

So it was an unpremeditated shift. You said when you spoke previously that the transition from project-based funding to company funding was a great help. I think you spoke of having 23 part-time administrators over one year. Having a permanent administrator was a great improvement. You said that the whole period was a massive learning curve. Can you say something about the different pressures around that time of transition?

Shobana Jeyasingh

Choreography is a social activity. One cannot make it happen by sheer personal hard work. Writers, painters and composers can keep working away by themselves. Choreographers who have been students in Britain begin by enlisting all their friends who have studied with them and hiring a very cheap church hall. But I did not have that wonderful set of allies. When I had only project funding, it really meant that I had nothing. I used to teach English to help make the money to apply myself to choreography, buy costumes, make-up, record music. The problem with choreography is that whether you have funding or resources available or not makes an immense difference to what you can actually achieve; much more so than with any other art form. You cannot even begin unless you have the resources. So when I had a certain measure of continuity and security in my funding, it completely changed everything. The biggest difference was being invited to take a company-in-residence post, because I suddenly changed from being an orphan to being able to be part of a dance family, a dance community.

Sanjoy Roy

I would like to talk about other sources of funding now. There are particular funds to which you can apply for community projects, audience research projects and education projects, for example. It has been commented that there are monies available for the peripheral aspects rather than the central creative act of choreographing, rehearsing, and performing.

Shobana Jeyasingh

I do feel that in Britain generally there is a lack of faith in pure creative activity. People seem to find it easier financing what they think of as the worthy things, such as education and community dance, where they feel they can see a tangible and immediate result. The artist's activity is by its nature creating rewards which are much more long term. One's profit margins may have to be a little eccentric and may not always coincide with the commercial ideal.

Sanjoy Roy

You feel as if you are trying to measure some kind of semi-quantifiable element in the dark.

Shobana Jeyasingh

I think that at the heart of it there is a contradiction. On the one hand we want artists to be innovative, which actually implies taking risks based on a long-term view, and on the other hand we are told that calculations have been made as to how much each person who comes to see your company is subsidised, and how that relates to other companies. Innovation implies risk, excitement, but these do not necessarily add up to full houses and good box office returns.

The problem with fund-raising is that artists often do not wish to go through incredible contortions in order to adapt to the fundraisers' demands and make a profit. Art influences society in a very oblique manner, and it is a very complex process. There might be a performance in a very small hall somewhere and only three people might come to see it. But one of those three people might be completely altered by the experience and go on to other activities which might include six thousand people. But if you want every activity to be on a grand scale then you cannot really begin to develop the audiences.

Sanjoy Roy

We are going to talk a little now about the dancers and the music in Shobana's company. You currently have dancers from India, Trinidad, California and Glasgow, so that it is quite an international group. Why do you choose dancers from such a broad geographic area, and does it give you particular issues to deal with in terms of choreography, and in terms of running your company?

Shobana Jeyasingh

I look for dancers whose dance language could meet mine somewhere. Our starting points need to be similar, and we need also to wish to develop in roughly similar directions.

Every year I like to think that we refine our auditioning process. Basically I need lots of time with auditioning, and this year there will be a six week audition. Generally I find it easiest to communicate with dancers who have a hybrid cultural context like myself. They really belong to that new Indian-ness which is springing up in the States, in Canada, in Fiji, in Mauritius, because of all the immigration which happened after the Second World War. People who are interested in that context are the kind of person for whom we are looking.

Sanjoy Roy

Over the last ten years have there been any particular turning points or moments of insight which have affected your own work? I know you have mentioned Chandralehka as one particular inspiration.

Shobana Jeyasingh

Yes, I value her as someone who has the courage to question. She worked with my company in 1991, and I found her method of working interesting. I was surprised at the brutality with which she asked the dancers for what she wanted. She showed me that it is possible to ask classical dancers to break out of their traditional patterns of thinking. It is sometimes difficult when you have a room full of classical dancers who represent such confidence in belonging to a tradition. I am someone who values a strong sense of belonging anyway, so it is a case of having the courage to say "Well, actually this feeling of not belonging is just a different side of the feeling of belonging."

Sanjoy Roy

How have your dancers adapted over the years? Initially, certainly, they were all classically trained, and most of them have classical Indian dance training I believe.

Shobana Jeyasingh

It is always difficult if you are from a classical dance background, because for such a training you must be completely sure of everything you know. It is understandable because you spend many years of your life disciplining your body to be this particular entity. It requires an incredible amount of hard work, commitment and focus. Their training is also in terms of space. Classical dance is about a particular manner of relating to space, even if it is only studio space. Classical dance is about the centre of the space, centre stage. Classical dancers just gravitate to the centre as if by instinct. The first part of the learning process is to persuade them to understand that actually the centre isn't always the most desirable place to gravitate to. There are other interesting places by the doors, for example, or by the wall.

Sanjoy Roy

I think you have spoken about the creative process which has given you and the dancers some uncomfortable moments. The dancers sometimes have difficulty with their understanding, which have been informed by their classical training, of the correct position to take, or what is elegant or aesthetically pleasing in improvisation or performance.

Shobana Jeyasingh

Part of the company is about process. We are not in a perfect place where we can make perfect dances, and so we can only show the vulnerability and the excitement of trying.

Sanjoy Roy

To continue speaking of the dancers, they come from a variety of backgrounds. How do you try to integrate them into the group? What kinds of methods do you use?

Shobana Jeyasingh

I find martial arts very useful as a way of getting people together. Although martial arts are culturally based, they are not culturally based in the same way as classical or modern dance forms are. They have an element of the aesthetic, but I think that somehow aesthetics is part of the problem. The trademark of classically trained bodies is basically a tendency to find harmony and avoid tension. Martial arts are useful because they introduce the concept of tension and because the movements are there not to realise a specific ideal but in order to do something else, to reach a goal which is very different. Therefore they are quite useful in terms of questioning the ideal of the body.

When we tour we have regular classes. We also have a period of about six weeks for research and development just prior to choreographing, and then we have lots of different classes. We have ballet, and many other styles, including at the moment Capoeira classes. I haven't really found the perfect combination of techniques as yet.

Sanjoy Roy

That kind of mixture of backgrounds, and some of your questioning rather than answering is reflected in your choreography because it seems to be based on ideas of openness and different meanings. But that openness and ambiguity of identity can sometimes come into conflict with others' expectations. What kind of audience response do you find valuable and why? In audiences you can of course include critics.

Shobana Jeyasingh

For me it is a bonus if they talk about the dance as opposed to talking about culture. Something which I discovered very early was that if you are a migrant in a country, then you become invisible. For an artist it is not necessarily a bad thing, because when you are struggling with your own conflicts you are often a bit too visible. Then I realised that, perhaps, even though I am invisible in relation to what I was, I seemed to have developed another identity which is not of my own making. I realise that part of it has been built up over centuries with roots over which I obviously have no control. I have to spend a lot of time trying to understand where that identity comes from, how it has been manufactured. I experience everyday how this false identity takes people completely away from where I wanted to go with my work.

This is a very subtle cultural perception which is reinforced every time people talk about the non-European condition, and when they come to see a company like ours they subconsciously bring the whole myth of the 'Orient' with them. I think the myth of the Orient and the Oriental person has traditionally served a very particular purpose within the European culture, and as a person from the 'Orient' you realise that in fact you are supposed to fulfil certain expectations. It has become such an accepted thing that when you don't deliver what they expect, then that is where the problem starts.

Sanjoy Roy

I don't know if you want to read a typical review? I think one of the things which Shobana finds is the very entrenched idea that the contemporary is somehow Western and the traditional is almost invariably Indian. It comes up in audience responses as well as critics', does it not?

Shobana Jeyasingh

Yes, it does a lot. Here is a quote from one review: "a thoughtful synthesis of old Indian culture and trusting modern values of second generation British Asian." I find the suggested polarity between India and the West false, and not borne out certainly in my life or in the lives of other urban Indians. The critic then goes on to describe the dancers as "steeped in the temple dance form", whereas the biographies of the dancers make it quite clear that this is not the case. The critic regrets the loss of "gorgeous open palmed temple shapes" which have been replaced by "chainsaw arms". Now I've got a top notch Bharatha Natyam dancer sitting right in the audience. What do you understand by "gorgeous, open palmed, temple shapes", Stella?

Stella

Nothing! I don't agree with saying that Bharatha Natyam is a temple dance for a start!

Shobana Jeyasingh

Yes I know. Nobody dances in temples any more. What is wrong with chainsaws? I mean they are perfectly viable motivation for movements if you want to use them. The final comment is "The dance departs so far from the ethnic source as to be unrecognisable". I personally fail to see what the connection of movement to ethnic source has to do with choreographic practice.

Sanjoy Roy

It is ironic that your work becomes very much involved with outside issues somehow, even though the dances that you make are actually quite abstract and ambiguous. They are not issue-based at all, not about racism, and yet they are asked to represent cultural ideas by Indians, part Indians and English people.

Shobana Jeyasingh

I have noticed that our work is often seen as Indian, and for Indian read Orient. It is laziness rather than racism. I think it is ignorance, which is a kind of laziness because it is a refusal to go and learn. I think it is rather sad because it stops the eye from actually seeing what is there.

Points raised in discussion:

· Shobana Jeyasingh said that she has been accused of being naive to think that she could consider herself part of the mainstream of British dance because her main vocabulary was something alien to British culture. Her response to this criticism was that she could be compared to someone like Jonathan Burrows or William Forsythe who trained in the classical vocabulary and then shifted to somewhere else.

· It is purely a myth that people from the Western world learn contemporary dance because it is part of their culture, or that it is necessary to become an expert in Indian culture in order to learn Indian dance.

Session 22

The Black Choreographic Initiative : An Artist-Centred Approach to Professional Development

Keywords:

cultural identity   Black dance   choreography   training, development

This paper by Vivien Freakley describes the results of a two year programme which has taken an artist-centred approach to professional development. It gives glimpses of shared and individual journeys which have integrated personal, artistic and business development with the search for cultural identity and for new methodologies for professional training and development.

Introduction

The Black Choreographic Initiative is a courageous action research project. It has bucked the trend in so many ways. It is open-ended at a time of outcome-related objectives, focuses on individual artists rather than infrastructure, is initiated and driven by three collaborating regional arts boards, recognises the inter-relatedness of artistic and "business" practice, takes the artist's developmental needs as the starting point, provides ongoing individual support to artists and it eschews the high profile "brought in from outside to tell us how to do it" approach to development. It also supports the search for individually validated artistic/cultural identity in relation to the label "Black Dance".

This paper describes the origination of the Initiative and outlines the principles which underpinned the design of the programme. It gives an account of the training and development methods used and describes the infrastructural partnerships which evolved to facilitate the programme delivery. Finally it makes recommendations for the design of future professional development projects for choreographers. Above all it seeks to describe a journey in sketchily-mapped territory and offers some tentative signposts.

Origination

The Black Choreographic Initiative (BCI) was conceived by West Midlands Arts in 1994. It took two years to bring together the funding and the partners: Yorkshire and Humberside Arts, East Midlands Arts, the Arts Council of England, Yorkshire Dance, Dance 4 and Dance Xchange for a September 1996 start. The aim of the BCI was:

> To deliver a two year programme which offers on going support to Black dance practitioners through a range of training interventions in order to improve the quality of choreographic practice. 1

Its stated objectives were:

> To create an opportunity for Black British choreographers to experience a specifically targeted development programme, hitherto not available in the U.K. To enable black dancers to receive choreographic development under the guidance of internationally acclaimed choreographers, identified by the practitioners themselves. To create the opportunity for targeted training and development in the light of the lack of formal training available in Black dance. To support the articulation of a voice for the Black British experience through dance.[1]

All three regional arts board (RAB) dance officers articulated the need to address the lack of opportunity for regionally based Black dance artists to access genre and style specific choreographic training. Their primary concern was to invest in key regional dance artists who would then feed in to the development of regional Black dance activity. This priority informed the selection of the original six and subsequent eight participating choreographers and to some extent over-rode debates around inclusion on the basis of a specific Black dance form. The BCI choreographers represent Black dance in all its diversity: African forms, Caribbean forms, jazz-funk, Graham-influenced Western Contemporary, street and club styles and some fusions of these.

Plans were made to create the programme around a series of high profile international "Hothouses" to be delivered at the National Dance Agencies - building on the successful work by Peter Boneham at Birmingham's Dance Xchange. Choices of leaders for these Hothouses were to be based on the results of a previously commissioned survey, which identified the international Black choreographers with whom Black British dance artists most wanted to work.

The early history of the Initiative was characterised by a debate about the ethics of creating a project which excluded/included on the basis of ethnicity. For some this could only be justified by confining the project to the culturally-defined field of African Peoples' Dance.

Others argued that a range of dance forms had developed within Black British cultures which reflected different responses to Black British experiences but which could not be expressed within the traditional forms of African Peoples' Dance. There was however a strong consensus that Black artists did not have access to education and initial training which incorporated their cultural experiences. The need to redress this lack of opportunity provided the most compelling justification for the Initiative. The individual artists have wrestled with notions of artistic and cultural validity throughout the past two years. Their journeys towards self-validation are described elsewhere.[2]

A steering group was established in 1996, comprising the three RAB dance officers, an attached Arts Council dance officer and the NDA directors who then appointed the Initiative's co-ordinator in September 1996. Participating choreographers were recruited regionally through an application and interview process in the Midlands and a peer group proposal process in Yorkshire and Humberside.

Guiding Principles

There was a clear need to avoid any suggestion of "blueprinting" when working with professional artists. There is a craft of choreography, but no blueprint for creating a successful dance. Some areas of craft might be strengthened but artists depend on being recognised for their unique artistic qualities. The intention had to be to clarify and enhance the differences. A number of guiding principles emerged during the planning stages of the Initiative:

· The artist must be placed at the centre of the developmental process.

· The artist's developmental needs must be considered holistically - as an artist working in a specific context - at a specific career point - with particular aspirations.

· There must be an opportunity for setting individual development priorities and implementing personal development plans

· The developmental processes must focus on self-evaluation and encourage reflective practice and self-directed development.

· There should be a framework for self-assessment of progress.

· A common language and concepts of development must be encouraged through group activity.

· Self-validation should be nurtured.

· The BCI must be a safe space for experimentation - no judging but plenty of supportive critical feedback.

· The BCI should encourage artists to develop partnerships within their regional infrastructures in order to develop their own opportunities for work and also to grow the market for Black dance.

Programme Design

These principles presented some challenges for the design of the programme. Clearly, it would not be appropriate to think in terms of a "course" - the choreographers were at different points in their careers, working in different dance forms and with different aspirations - no one course programme could possibly be appropriate for all. It was agreed that the starting point in any learner-centred approach to professional development must be the identification of the learner's developmental needs and that once this had been accomplished, a programme of concurrent shared and individual activities could be devised.

Finding an appropriate methodology for the identification of the artists' needs was the first challenge. Training Needs Analysis (TNA) is an established practice in some employment sectors, especially in management training where the field of required knowledge and skills is well mapped. TNA techniques had been applied in the West Midlands within a number of arts organisations and also with freelance dance administrators working in the region.[3] The general approach seemed relevant to the BCI: map the skills and knowledge needed to "do the job" of choreographer, evaluate strengths and weaknesses against those requirements, locate the findings in the context of career and artistic aspirations and set developmental priorities. This approach was decided upon and applied in a Development Needs Analysis (DNA) weekend, described below.

The Initiative's programme was designed as follows:

· Development Needs Analysis designed to identify and agree the developmental priorities.

· The Personal Development Programmes designed to meet specific career development needs and drawing on a wide variety of training tools such as mentoring, shadowing, observation, placement, participation in workshops, hothouses and residencies.

· The Shared Programme of Hothouses, seminars, practical exploration and discussion; offering opportunities for working together on common areas of developmental need under the guidance of lead artists and opportunities for guided reflection and critical discourse.

Development Needs Analysis

The development needs analysis was carried out in four stages:

1. A menu of choreographic knowledge and skills was sent to each choreographer and they were asked to answer questions about themselves in relation to it.

2. The choreographers then attended a weekend of structured presentation, self evaluation and diagnostic activities based on building a shared understanding of the developmental concepts and identifying strengths and weaknesses.

3. Individual interviews guided the choreographer to the identification of development priorities.

4. Follow up interviews clarified the priorities and devised the personal development programme for the year.

The process took four months to complete on average but it was not a tidy process. Some choreographers identified their priorities very quickly and stayed with them for the year, others found them quickly but changed them over time, others took almost a year to decide on their priorities. At times this was frustrating, since it meant that the individual programmes could not progress and funding could not always be spent in the designated financial year. Nevertheless the process itself was a valuable one - prompting the "Reflecting-in-practice"[4] necessary for the growth and development of the practitioner.

The menu of choreographic knowledge and skills listed:

Articulating your vision
Knowing your language
Communicating with dancers
Crafting your work
Being your own critic
Presenting your work (production)
Working collaboratively

Choreographers were asked to comment about themselves against each category in advance of the weekend. Following diagnostic exercises during the weekend, they graded themselves against each category.

The tasks and activities of the weekend included:

·   Presentations about work and vision to the group.

·   SWOT analysis.

·   Choreographic exercises to draw out devising methods, communication issues (musicians and dancers), structuring techniques, language/technique issues.

·   Self evaluation exercises.

Most of the choreographers were able to complete individual interviews before the end of the weekend and identified some broad development areas for further reflection. Everything was documented by the co-ordinator and used as the basis for follow up interviews when further clarification towards the personal development plans was possible.

It is interesting that by the end of the weekend the menu had been significantly enlarged to include the philosophy and practice of community choreography, project management skills, fundraising skills, the use of new technology and advocacy skills.

As the development priorities began to emerge they proved to be diverse.
This is a small sample:
Devising strategies
Structuring material
Communicating with dancers
Characterisation in dance
Community choreographic practice
Integration of styles
Collaborative working with design
Business set-up skills

This diversity reflects the career pathways and working practices that currently characterise dance employment. Hierarchical/linear models of career progression no longer apply because there are too few permanent dance companies for dancers to be able to progress from performer to rehearsal director to choreographer to artistic director. Dancers tend to work across the range of performing, teaching and choreography.[5] With reduction in revenue funded companies and growth in community/dance development work.[6] they also need to be able to apply project development/management, partnership and profile raising skills.

Personal Development Programmes
The diversity and range of the developmental priorities led naturally into diverse personal development programmes. The choreographers were made aware of the types of activity they might want to engage in and were free to add others, as long as they would lead to meeting the priorities. The suggested activities were:
Attending workshops, short courses or classes.
Observation of others.
Mentoring.
Studio-based R & D
Research
Surgeries
Studio-based choreographic labs

Each had a budget of £900 p.a. to spend on fees, mentor expenses, travel, accommodation, studio hire, or other expenses associated with the activity.

It is not proposed to give an account of the personal development programmes in detail here. Elements of three of the journeys were described by the choreographers during the Greenhouse Effect Conference. A brief resume of these accounts gives an indication of how the training activities were incorporated.

Villmore James described how he developed his new role as a community choreographer. In year one his development priorities were focused on building his understanding of community choreographic practices. He identified his chosen mentor as Royston Muldoon. Observation, shadowing, discussion and guided practice were chosen as the most appropriate activities. Villmore was able to undertake these activities on two of Royston's projects, one of which was in Ethiopia. In year two Villmore's employment situation had developed and he was managing the community programme at the Northern School of Contemporary Dance as well as teaching and choreographing in a wide variety of school and community settings. His second year priorities focused on managing this workload and building a sustainable and satisfying portfolio of work. Surgeries with Gwen van Spijk, an experienced freelance arts manager, are helping him to develop an appropriate business plan to this end.

Gail Parmel described and demonstrated a journey towards integrating her artistic and cultural influences. She began the BCI as artistic director of a new West Midlands based company: African Cultural Exchange. Her year one priorities focused on finding out more about African and Caribbean forms and finding new ways to develop ideas into dance form. She attended workshops with Koffi Koko, L'Antoinette Stines, Germaine Acogny, Werewere Liking, David Rousseve and Emlyn Claid. She chose Koffi Koko as her mentor and he spent two days in the studio in the final stages of the rehearsal of African Cultural Exchange's first programme: *The Path*. In this programme she was exploring ways in which Western Contemporary choreographic techniques could be used to devise and structure African/Caribbean dance language. Her artistic priorities focused down in year two onto her search for characterisation in dance which she carried out through studio-based R&D, attending more workshops with Koffi Koko and through the Janice Garrett Hothouse (described below). At the same time Gail had other priorities related to the establishment of her new company: building the business plan, fundraising, developing her skills as artistic director. Surgeries with Gwen van Spijk and observation of (and discussion with) other artistic directors were chosen as appropriate activities.

Sharon Donaldson described and demonstrated her journey towards finding the expressive truth of movement - away from a dependence on a technique-derived language of "steps". Finding Sharon's priorities proved to be challenging. At the start year one of the BCI she was a highly experienced performer and choreographer seeking to develop her artistic identity from within the Phoenix Dance Company. She had worked with many choreographers, attended the Gulbenkian Choreographic Summer School and had generally been exposed to the working methods of a wide variety of different choreographers. Sharon's year one priorities focused on developing her own artistic voice and building her project management skills in preparation for a career as an independent artist. BCI funded studio-based R & D work and this was used diagnostically in dicussion with the co-ordinator. It became clear that Sharon had an extraordinary facility for the generation of articulate, highly-detailed and technically-complex movement but was keen to develop her structuring techniques. However she was frustrated by the results of her work. She needed highly experienced performers to realise the subtlety and complexity of her material. Setting up an opportunity to work with more experienced dancers became a priority and she applied for a number of funding schemes with the help of Gwen van Spijk and the BCI co-ordinator but was unsuccessful. In the second year of the BCI, Sharon took on a new appointment as a lecturer at the Northern School of Contemporary Dance. Initially, this left her little time to develop artistically but during this time she made a number of different versions of the same duet, working alternately with Stephen Derrick and Warren Adams, who were both dancing with Phoenix Dance Company. Her new approach to making work has begun to develop through this process as was demonstrated at the Greenhouse Effect Conference. Other BCI choreographers have undertaken research in India, attended workshops in Austria, spent intensive research periods in London (especially at the Video Place), worked with dancers on studio-based R & D, been supported to create business and project plans, attended IT short courses and researched design opportunities.

The Shared Programme

The shared programme was designed to meet the common needs of the choreographers in terms of devising and structuring techniques, learning new languages, integrating forms, developing understanding of working with design and learning about project management. It also offered opportunities for critical debate, the sharing of ideas/experiences and the development of presentational skills. The following activities were programmed over a two year period:

- September 1996: Development Needs Analysis Weekend led by the co-ordinator and Robert Edwards at the Birmingham Royal Ballet Studios and Dance Xchange.

- February 1997: Choreographic Craft Week led by Germaine Acogny and Emlyn Claid at Dance 4, incorporating seminars by Gwen Van Spijk on project management and funding and Craig Givens on design for dance.

- September 1997: Development Needs Analysis (DNA) Weekend at Dance Xchange

- July 1997: Hothouse led by Werewere Liking at Yorkshire Dance

- May 1997: Hothouse led by David Rousseve, in partnership with Dance Xchange

- October 1997: Hothouse led by L'Antoinette Stines in partnership with Dance Xchange

- March1998: Crossing Borders, a West Midlands showcase of participating choreographers' work and promoters seminar in partnership with Dance Xchange

- April/May1998: Hothouse and Sharing in partnership with Dance 4 in Nottingham led by Janice Garrett

- September 1998: Hothouse in partnership with Yorkshire Dance and the International Workshop Festival (IWF) led by Germaine Acogny and Abdelaziz Sarrokh

Lead artists/tutors were chosen from across the African diaspora or because they had particular areas of knowledge to contribute. Many were suggested by the participating choreographers and all were agreed by them. The early Hothouses tended to focus on a specific part of the choreographic process from the lead artist's perspective. Information about the purpose of the event and the lead artist was sent out in advance as preparation. Discussion and debate was guided throughout the event by the co-ordinator and a follow up report was sent out to the participants after the event. The intention was to encourage the participants to interpret and contextualise the experience within their own development. At each event, participating choreographers were encouraged to talk to the rest of the group about their progress towards their developmental goals.

Evaluation at the end of the first year of the Initiative showed that the participating choreographers wanted to engage in a more individually-focused and facilitated developmental process within the Hothouses. They wanted to be supported to work more critically on their own choreography. The Janice Garrett Hothouse was developed to allow this to take place.

The Janice Garrett Hothouse formed part of the NottDance'98 Festival. In this event it was possible to take a different approach. Janice is an experienced facilitator with the expertise and interest needed to focus on releasing the creativity of others. The BCI co-ordinator worked with each choreographer to help them to identify a particular choreographic "problem" that they needed to solve. Janice was given these "problems" in advance and they were discussed with the co-ordinator in a pre-Hothouse meeting. Throughout four days, Janice was able to work with each individual through a series of questioning techniques to help them to find a way forward. The choreographers and the co-ordinator found this the most valuable of the shared experiences provided by the BCI over the two year period.

The individual objectives were diverse:

- To work on a partially-choreographed duet to clarify intentions and make firmer connections with the ideas needing to be communicated.

- To recreate and rework an existing duet on more experienced dancers and gain a clearer understanding of how to draw out more detailed and complex interpretative qualities; to gain a clearer understanding of how to use modern classical music with dance language.

- To find ways to begin choreographing a solo work in response to a poem, translating complex ideas and feelings into physical form.

- To expand the repertoire of choreographic and teaching strategies for working with large numbers in community/school contexts.

- To develop strategies for planning a choreographic project and communicating choreographic tasks to dancers. To find ways to closely connect feeling and form; to find ways to create movement organically; to work on process rather than product.

- To rework ideas for an existing section of a dance using character as a starting point. To escape from own well-trodden choreographic pathways.

Janice stressed 'the need to listen to ourselves to find our own voice', 'the authority of our own expression'. She made the following points:

"The process of how you work comes out of what you want to say – it emanates from your own intention. Turn the amorphous response into clarity, something which can be used.

Translate real events/experiences/feelings into the body. Ask lots of questions of yourself and others - to find clarity.

Emotions are our ally – we must allow ourselves to feel to make potent dance. We must turn emotion into motion". [7]

Her approach is best illustrated through the development of the solo work from poem to initial phrases: The choreographer brought the poem on tape for the group to hear and gave them key lines from the poem written on pieces of paper. Janice suggested that the group ask questions to help to clarify what it was about the poem that the choreographer wanted to express in dance. The sort of questions asked at this stage were:

What did the poem mean to you when you first heard it in the late 70s?
How do you respond to the qualities of the music?
Which words are most important?
How do you feel about the poem now?
Why does it remind you of a preacher?
What does the preacher mean?

This questioning method is similar to an Action Learning Set, but applied to a creative process. Action Learning Sets were developed by Reg Revans in the 1940s for National Coal Board managers. He describes them as " a social exchange in which managers learn with and from one another during the diagnosis and treatment of real problems" [8].

The poem evoked complex and powerful emotions in the choreographer and almost had too much potential – too many directions for choreography. It was difficult for him to find the central motivating ideas for the piece and then see how to use them to create movement. Questions were then asked which externalised the feeling into the physical body, space and dynamics eg:

Do you feel the pain in a particular part of the body?
How do you imagine the preacher moving - fast/slow, tense/relaxed?
Do you have a sense of where the preacher is located on the stage?
Does the preacher move freely about the space?
Do you see your dance as a solo or a group piece?

Following the questioning, the choreographer was able to describe some features of the movement he wanted to create for the solo: A solo, in a confined space, using slow tense movement, feeling pain all over the body but especially in the head. From this he was able to define choreographic tasks to generate material. Four dancers worked on short solo phrases using these tasks. They were recorded on video and used by the choreographer to develop material for himself on the following day.

Developing the Regional Infrastructure

One of the important lessons learned through the BCI is how much can be achieved when different parts of the dance infrastructure work together in partnership. Scarce resources can be used to maximise effectiveness, shared understanding and new practice can be developed, individual artists and companies can be supported and the market for dance can be expanded. The primary objective of each RAB dance officer has been to strengthen the practice of Black dance within her own region by investing in the development of (regionally) key individuals. They have worked strategically to try to support their regionally based choreographers with advice, guidance and project funding. At the start, the National Dance Agencies were open in expressing their reservations about the BCI. Some NDA directors were concerned that the proactive lead taken by the RABs could undermine their programming autonomy and were doubtful about including/excluding choreographers on culturally-defined grounds. None of this should be surprising given the lack of resources in the NDAs, the unusual and open-ended nature of the project, the lack of experience of this kind of professional development support and most important of all, the lack of high profile, audience-pulling programming opportunities. It is to their credit that the NDA directors and representatives were able to suspend their disbelief long enough to engage with the Initiative and then be convinced of its value over time.

The BCI has been at its most effective where the priorities of the different partners have coincided and "synergised" and so made a strategic impact on the region. There are two quite different examples of this:
-    Gail Parmel and her company African Cultural Exchange were supported by WMA with project grants and management training opportunities, offered free rehearsal space at DX in exchange for teaching classes and premiering work. Through the BCI, Gail made use of Koffi Koko to oversee the final rehearsal stages of the new work. The results were an exciting new production, a platform opportunity for a new company which generated tour bookings made by a new administrator, African - Caribbean classes for young people and new audiences for DX.
-    Pam Johnson and Villmore Jones were supported by the Yorkshire and Humberside Arts dance officer in a series of meetings designed to generate opportunities for growing the dance market in Yorkshire and Humberside. Villmore was instrumental in building the beginnings of a relationship with the local Training and Enterprise Council which could lead to accredited training for community dance teachers and Pam has confirmed relationships with professional football clubs in the region.

As the BCI moves into its third and final year, it will seek to build on the partnerships forged with regional infrastructure organisations, so that the programme of Black dance development activities can continue to grow. The RABs have made pump-priming funds available and Dance 4 is already planning a second Janice Garrett Hothouse. Dance Xchange and Warwick Arts Centre are collaborating on a programme of showcase/hothouse events.

Conclusions and recommendations

The Black Choreographic Initiative has achieved a significant measure of success in reaching its objectives although not perhaps through the methods envisaged by its originators. The participating choreographers are articulate in expressing the benefits they feel they have gained, the Regional Arts Board dance officers are vocal in their advocacy of the Initiative and keen to offer ongoing support and the National Dance Agencies/regional venues are willing to build Black dance development into their programming. The co-ordinator has been able to work on developing the methodology for the nurturing of artists and has begun to identify some guiding principles and appropriate learning strategies. But it is only the beginning. The ideas need to be developed further and applied in other contexts. An already over-stretched infrastructure needs to take on board the additional responsibility of effective support for artists' development. The BCI has certainly proved that where artists are unable to locate themselves in a coherent and co-ordinated regional infrastructure (whether as project workers, employees or freelancers) no training intervention can be fully effective. In a way all dance artists have the same needs:

- **To develop artistically**

- **To develop an appropriate working context in which to create, perform, teach, and/or produce dance**

- **To develop the professional partnerships and relationships needed to work effectively**

- **To develop the skills needed to thrive in their working environment.**

Projects such as the BCI can help to develop the artist's ability to do all these things but if the regional infrastructural organisations are prepared to participate and enhance working opportunities then the benefit to the artist is greater and the funding system's investment in that artist is safeguarded. There is still work to be done to develop the ecology of the regional dance infrastructures. There is even more work to be done to build the infrastructural organisation's understanding of methodologies for the support and development of artists.

References
1. *Black Choreographic Initiative Evaluation Report 1996-7 p5*
2. *The Realisation of Who I am p 14-16 Animated, Autumn 1998*
3. *Training Needs Analysis for Administrators in Dance Projects in the West Midlands :*
West Midlands Arts unpublished report.
4. *Technical Rationality to Reflection-in-Action Schon p.26. Boundaries of Adult Learning*
ed Edwards, Hanson & Raggatt pub. Open University 1996.
5. *Careers and Training in Dance and Drama Jackson, Honey, Hillage and Stock IMS*
Report 268. Brighton 1994.
6. *Fitness for Purpose Report. Dance, Drama and Stage Management Training: an*
examination of industry needs and the relationship with the current provision of training.
Birch, Jackson and Towse. Arts Council of England unpublished report 1998
7. *Black Choreographic Initiative Evaluation Report 1997-8 Appendix A3*
8. *Action Learning unpublished paper by Ruth Cook for the AMTF Conference,*
Birmingham 24th & 25th October 1997.

Participating Choreographers

West Midlands
Patrick Acogny, Artistic Director of Kokuma Dance Theatre (years1 2 & 3)
Gail Parmel, Artistic Director of African Cultural Exchange (years 1 2 & 3)

East Midlands
Leonard Jackson, community dance choreographer at Derby Dance Development Agency (years 2 & 3)
Kwesi (Carl) Johnson, Artistic Director of Kompani Malakhi (years 1 & 2)
Joey Thomas, Asheber Dance Company (year1)
Louise Katerega, Artistic Director, Kantikoy Dance Company (year 3)

Yorkshire & Humberside
Chantal (Sharon) Donaldson, ex. Phoenix Dance Company now dance lecturer at the Northern School of Contemporary Dance (years, 1 2 & 3)
Donald Edwards, dancer/choreographer RJC
Villmore James, community dance choreographer, Leeds
Pam Johnson, ex. Phoenix Dance Company now Education Director of Kokuma Dance Company

Lead Artists/Tutors
Germaine Acogny - Director of the Dance School of the Third World, Senegal
Robert Edwards - Freelance trainer/facilitator
Barry Ganberg - Independent composer and musician
Janice Garrett - ex Associate Director Dan Wagoner Dance Company
Craig Givens - Theatre and Dance Designer
Werewere Liking - Director of the Compagnie Ki-yi, Ivory Coast
David Rousseve - Director David Rousseve Dance Company
Abdelaziz Sarrokh - Director Hush, Hush, Hush, Belgium
Gwen van Spijk - Freelance arts manager.
L'Antoinette Stines - Director Kingston Dance Company, Jamaica

Session 23

The Manager-Choreographer Relationship

Keywords:

arts administrator   artist   communication   roles   commitment

For some people involved in dance, there exist clearly defined roles separating the manager or administrator of a company on the one hand, with the choreographer or artistic director on the other. One stays in the office writing applications and selling tours, and the other makes new work in the dance studio. But in reality this scenario is rarely the case. Four managers with different perspectives talk about their roles and understandings, their relationships with particular choreographers and their contribution to the art form and its development. The speakers at this session were Julia Carruthers, Leonie Gombrich, Gwen van Spijk and Suzanne Walker.

The session was introduced by Julia Carruthers, Manager of Jonathan Burrows Group and Russell Maliphant Company. She explained that although management and administration workers tend to be invisible, they are still key elements. Artists make the work, but the managers and administrators find the venues and organise the financial side so that the artists and performers can make a living. Most of the small- and middle-scale dance company administrators in England are female. The two largest companies, The Royal Ballet and Birmingham Royal Ballet, both have administrators paid over £45,000 per year, and both are male.

Julia wanted to note four general points. All these managers felt that what was precious and valuable was having the closest relationship with the artists and the artistic process. This exclusive privilege is often overlooked by others working in the field who simply see company administration as a low status job. The work can take place at anytime, from 8.30am on a Sunday morning to midnight. All administrators have opinions and ideas about artistic work that are often either overlooked or subsumed without acknowledgement. Finally, artists can make work without the managers but they can rarely get work without them!

Leonie Gombrich

I have been working with DV8 for four years and I worked with Michael Clark for a year previously. Before that I did not work in dance, although I have worked in various fields to do with arts management. By the time I joined DV8 in 1994, the company had already been in existence for 8 years. The company had a firmly established recognisable identity, and was at a phase of its career where people had certain expectations of it. I believe that my role is primarily facilitating what the artist wants, and I work well with Lloyd Newson. However, I think that at the point at which I arrived, DV8 and Lloyd needed an excuse to break from some of the ways in which they had previously been operating. Lloyd and I discussed how administrators often provide a sort of smokescreen between the artist and the rest of the world, to allow the artist to make difficult decisions. Sometimes the artist needs to move on, and to grow away from people who have been incredibly useful and important mentors and supporters earlier in their careers, but who are no longer working in the same direction as the artist.

One very striking point is that people never assume that you represent the artist's point of view. Promoters like to talk about their close liaison with the artist. When I am in a difficult discussion with a promoter, I often think they feel that if they could just get to the artist directly, and avoid this irritating woman, they would be able to get what they wanted. It is a very important service to provide for any artist, to allow them to maintain a degree of freedom, even when they have reached a certain level of being established.

Suzanne Walker

I joined V-TOL just 9 months after they had started. I come from a creative background, with a degree in Music/Drama/Dance, so I have some experience of the practical side of the work, and the artist's point of view. Joining V-TOL at this stage in its development meant that there was a chance for me to play a key role in how the company was shaped and developed. This is an unusual position in which to be. I was lucky in that the artistic director, Mark Murphy, and I were a similar age and at similar stages in our careers. The whole company concept was new to us, so there was a chance for us to learn, develop, and grow together in that process. I see the manager/choreographer relationship as a creative partnership. I have a creative role in the company and I think that is important to recognise. We did not have any inherited structures that might be restrictive for us, and I could see from all the companies that were around us what I would like to try to avoid in the development of the company.

My challenge was to reflect an approach which was appropriate to Mark's personality and way of working in the management and administrative structure of the company. It was about building a team, with a democratic approach in which he could communicate with dancers and administrators. So I set about creating a good support structure for myself, including a Board of people to whom I could turn. I felt that it was also important for Mark, who was a young developing artist, to have access to more experienced people around him. The whole process of the dialogue I think is very important. These are a few ingredients which I think are key to making a successful relationship between manager and choreographer:

- Finding the right match, so that skills are complemented in each other

- An honest and open relationship, with mutual respect and understanding of each other's perspectives and roles in the work

- Good communication at all times; it is the responsibility of both parties to maintain that

- Compatible personalities; so much of this work is about personalities, and it is important to have a sense of humour. It is difficult working in arts administration, and it is helpful if you can have a little fun at the same time.

- Commitment and belief in the work, whilst still being able to challenge, question and inspire each other

Arts administration is not about placing the artist in a protective bubble, where s/he is only concerned with creating the artistic dream. Artists need to be in touch with the basic realities and responsibilities of what running a balanced budget really means. If the artist requires a marvellous set with three film screens in it, then the consequences are that we might have to have one less dancer. I feel that it is very important that Mark has a shared responsibility in making those very difficult decisions.

As an arts administrator, you have a responsibility to represent someone else's vision, someone else's opinions and values. They are not always your own, and that can be very difficult at times but it is your responsibility to translate them into the company's operation, be that the marketing copy, policies about education, how many students you can work with, and at what age levels.

I feel that the company has really succeeded and we have come to a landmark point. It has not been Mark alone who has achieved that, but also the dancers, his long- term collaborators with the company, and people like myself. I have been very lucky to be with an artistic director who has really valued my opinion artistically, who has wanted me to be involved in auditions for dancers and who invites me into the creative process with the dancers. I think it is really important for the administrators not to be too office-bound and to maintain contact with the artistic work. That is what gives me the strength and the energy to deal with the difficult times in the office.

Gwen Van Spijk

I work with three companies on an ongoing basis, and then alongside that I work with companies on specific projects. Projects range from one-to-one training to consultancies about the running or development of an organisation.

I work with each of the three companies for one day a week, and try to do everything in that time that Suzanne and Leonie would do over the course of a week. The companies are obviously small scale and with perhaps a lesser level of activity, but nevertheless the roles which I fulfil are the same as those which Suzanne and Leonie and Julia fulfil as well. I will just talk a little bit about the relationships that I have with my artistic directors/choreographers. They are all very different relationships, but underpinning them all there has to be trust and an absolute commitment to communication between myself and the artistic director because I am not actually based in the towns where the companies are. Communication generally takes place via the telephone or a fax machine or e-mail, and we rely on these mechanisms heavily because there is no company office to be the hub of activity. So important factors are trust, communication, and respect for each other's roles and responsibilities. The artistic director has to appreciate what the breadth of my work is and I obviously have to appreciate what the company is doing too. The driving force must be a shared dream, because without it, the limited resources of working in this fashion would mean that nothing would be achieved.

The ways in which I work, on such a restricted basis, means that I have had to learn to draw the line. When I worked for one company full-time it took all my time, 7 days a week. Now I cannot afford to give that much commitment in terms of time, although emotionally I give as much as I can. Working freelance has taught me to be assertive about what I am or am not able to do. It is too easy to commit oneself too much and spread oneself too thinly, be it for one company or several.

Julia Carruthers

I am going to focus more on the work I do for Jonathan Burrows Group, as Russell is short of money to pay for administration so I tend to fit that in where required. When I took on the Jonathan Burrows Group it had severed ties with The Royal Ballet. Jonathan had cut his teeth on the first administrator and had a reputation for being difficult. The company had rather strange tours with slightly illogical dates in unusual places in the UK, but there were some very important glimpses of European interest and the first bits of European co-production money were coming in. Certain very important things happened in my first year of working with the company. The first was that we got the Prudential Award, a sponsorship prize of £25,000. We were the least favoured option amongst the nominees because we were the smallest company, but £25,000 meant an enormous amount to us. There was also the Spring Collection, which is a showcase where about 300 promoters from around the world come and watch British dance companies in London for one weekend. Jonathan and the dancer, Henry Montes, showed part of the first section of Jonathan's *The Stop Quartet* in this Showcase, and we got a terrific response. Some very important bookings came out of that event and some useful European and American contacts.

Jonathan and I discovered that we worked very well together and respected each other's skills and opinions. For example, he is better at writing press releases than I am, and occasionally I say important things about his work which nudges it in a particular direction. It is really necessary that you believe in each other, and that you are both disciplined and reliable. I know that if I tell Jonathan or Russell that they need to be somewhere by 9am, then they will be there by 8.55am, and I don't have to telephone them at home to ask if they are awake.

The Jonathan Burrows Group is in an unusual situation in that we are feted abroad, but neglected at home in the UK. We might have 700 people watching us in Estonia, but I cannot get a date in Oxford or Cambridge. Part of the problem is the lack of suitable theatres in England. The small ones have tiny stages, and the larger venues are concerned about finding a big enough audience for this slightly difficult work. This means that the company is under enormous pressure to get performances and earn income abroad. We have excellent relationships in Europe, but it can become very tiring with all the travelling involved. Also there is not enough money for me to tour with the company, so much of the management rebounds on to Jonathan and the dancers.

I know that I am very reliant on the goodwill and efficiency of the dancers in Jonathan's company, with whom I have a very close and friendly relationship. It is particularly difficult as I actually only work two days a week. It is often the case that when I get into the office, there are 23 messages on the answer phone and fax paper is curling up the wall. It can be very pressured and very stressful.

Points raised in discussion:

· In Belgium there are a lack of management training courses at university level, which means that most arts administrators are self-educated.

· Arts administrators see their role as covering the dancers also, in terms of providing them with information and listening to their comments and needs. Companies tend to be very close-knit communities.

· One of the problems with working as a promoter or venue manager in arts management is that you tend to lose the intimate contact with the work and the creative process. The four speakers all felt that they did not want this to happen to them. They felt that they could grow within the structure of their current work.

Session 24

Choreographic Experiments in Safe Havens

Keywords:

National Dance Agencies   Associate Artist schemes   support   choreographers

How does a relationship between a choreographer and a particular organisation come about? What is the nature and function of the artistic partnership, and what are the most obvious and more covert needs from either side? What kinds of opportunity can be offered to choreographers, and what benefits accrue for the organisation? Three choreographers in conversation with a representative from their respective partner organisation give some exemplars of this model. The session was chaired by Richard Alston and presented by Jane Mooney (Suffolk Dance, UK) and Paula Hampson, Emma Gladstone (The Place, UK) and Carol Brown, Mairead Turner (Yorkshire Dance, UK) and Charlotte Vincent.

Richard Alston

We're going to talk about three different projects which have happened in various parts of the UK, setting up what have been described as "safe havens" for choreographers. We have three partnerships represented here. They are Mairead Turner and Charlotte Vincent (Charlotte has a 'safe haven' relationship as a 'Yorkshire Dance Partner'); Emma Gladstone from the Place Theatre and Carol Brown (Carol was an Associate at the Place last year and will be Choreographer in Residence next year); and Jane Mooney is going to talk with Paula Hampson about her relationship with Suffolk Dance.

Firstly I would like to ask the people who set up the havens if they can tell us about the nuts and bolts of how they started and what the havens were intended for.

Jane Mooney

I expect that most of you will know that a National Dance Agency (NDA) is responsible for a wide range of activity, including promoting, producing, commissioning, research and development, community development and so on. As an NDA, Suffolk Dance regards its work with choreographers as one of its most important activities. A hallmark of all the work we do with choreographers is that in each and every project we have to enter into the unknown together. We have to try and do something that we have not done before, and it takes both of us to a new space. When you look at that notion, and then look at the title of this session Creating Choreographic Safe Havens, you might think that there is a little bit of a contradiction. How can something that is about taking risks, about trying to break new ground, be safe? I would like to share with you how we respond to that dilemma and how we define 'safe' as not just the removal of obstacles; 'safe' is also not necessary the same as 'comfortable'.

A number of months ago we piloted our Associate Artist Scheme. We wanted to create something for artists who are just at that point of development, ready for touring, wanting to begin national relationships. We wanted it to be a sustained relationship, an interactive one, not one where we implanted artists into Suffolk but one in which we could build an identity between the artist and the area. In this scheme the agency makes a number of commitments to the artist and it is a contracted relationship. It involves things like commissioning, mentoring money for anything that the artist might need to use it for, and I mean that in its broadest sense. It could be choreographic work, it might be business management, it might be marketing, a photographic bursary, pre-rehearsal space, hospitality, accommodation support, a range of services that we have made a commitment to provide for that artist. This pilot project has three companies; I D Dance, Retina Dance Company and Paula Hampson.

I suppose the question we have to ask ourselves is - what's this creative safe haven, and what is safety without risk and challenge? I think we have identified three elements that we think are important in building a safe haven. One is that a choreographer is very much an individual and it is not right for us to assume what the needs of that individual are, what the best working practices are. The choreographer has to make that choice, and this requires understanding of their personal interests, their aims, their ambitions and constraints. These are the motivating factors for an artist. We as an agency also have motivating factors, so there has to be a two-way relationship. The uniqueness of our relationship is that it is a commitment to the artist, not a commitment to invent a product; it is a commitment to a relationship and it is developmental. Within all the restrictions and demands of an agency that requires us to be very fluid and to find ways of maintaining that fluidity so that we can be responsive. We need to develop foresight so that we can create an environment in which the agency and the artist are adapted to each other.

Secondly we've provided practical help, nice warm studio, fresh coffee in the morning, a welcoming smile, all these are nurturing things for the artist. But we believe there is a relationship with the artist that is more important, which is about providing opportunity, challenge and stimulation. We have been looking at ways of introducing artists to other artists to form collaborations or to experiment with different working practices, and to find ways in which the artist can receive feedback in the most appropriate way. The final decision, however, must be with the artist as to how he or she chooses that stimulus. We provided Paula with an opportunity for a dance and video commission within a particular environment. The outcome of that commission was much more that we could ever have anticipated as the artists took that environment much further than the agency could have asked. They have to take that initiative and the agency has to let it go.

Thirdly, Paula works under the terminology of Associate Artist. It's very easy for artists to have an attachment to an agency, but it is difficult for them to have an identity within it. That's what we are trying to achieve, so that the artists belong to the family which is made up of the staff, other dance professionals, the community environment and the audiences that belong to that area. Another of our aims is to create a dialogue between the artists on this scheme which can result in enrichment for them, but also give advice to me on ways in which the agency can continually feed and support artists at a particular stage of development.

A safe haven has practical elements, money, space, time. It nurtures the artists, helping them to feel that they can belong, but also it has to provide some challenges for the artist because we share a responsibility not just for their well being but also for their growth. The safe haven must have the ability to manage that unpredictable element so that it continues to give assurance and builds the confidence of the artist.

Paula Hampson

My involvement with Suffolk Dance Agency over the last five years, through a number of projects, has enabled time for our relationship to develop, trust being a valuable ingredient. The organisation and Jane in particular have created an environment which encourages, guides and supports. I am able to talk about my work and discuss any problems or future aspirations openly. They have a genuine interest in the individual needs and concerns of the artists.

The scheme has enabled many new collaborations, through both my own initiative and those suggested and guided by Jane. One suggestion, which I enthusiastically welcomed, was the opportunity to make a short dance film in collaboration with film maker Martyn Hollingsworth. Our challenge was to make the film in one day as part of the Cross Currents Conference. I performed two improvisations, both with a back drop of video projected images. Martyn filmed each improvisation from a different view point. The movement recorded was edited with the back projected images to create our film. This was then shown at the end of the day.

I believe that the success of this initiative was due to the fact that Jane had offered a simple framework which we could tailor to our own needs and inspirations. This new collaboration took place within a supportive environment. It allowed us the time, space and the facilities to play and to explore the potential of a new working relationship. This safe haven project has provided the inspiration for further collaboration.

Richard Alston

From what you both say, it was really the months of knowing each other before this project started that enabled it to happen so effectively.

Perhaps Emma could tell us a little bit about what she has been offering Carol Brown in The Place Theatre.

Emma Gladstone

Carol is currently an Associate Artist and will be a Choreographer in Residence, crucially different from a resident Choreographer, from next month. There have been Choreographers in Residence at The Place since 1987 and there have been Associate Artists since 1995. It's changing constantly; sometimes it has involved money as a self-help scheme, and at other times it has not involved money but has involved help with administration. The Lottery has helped us change it again, and now it depends mainly on the personalities of the people involved.

There seem to be three constant things about it which were echoed in what Jane said, and I'm sure that all three of the schemes will have similarities. The first thing is that it is a personal and enduring relationship which is built between the organisation, of whatever shape or form, and the artist. Secondly , it is a crucial point in that artist's development, where it can make a genuine difference to how they develop, but being involved in the development of that work does not involve an ownership of it. Thirdly, the fact that it is contracted in some sense gives it a professional edge which I think can be quite liberating. It has the clarity of time about it which is different from, for example, in an academic institution where you could have an open-ended connection.

I have divided up what we offer at present between hardware and software. The hardware is the studio space, theatre time, administration. All the Associate Artists and the Choreographers in Residence have time in Choreodrome, which is the research and development project that takes place over July and August and involves all the facilities, technical and otherwise, at The Place. The software is the psychological aspect of it, the belief that support can be given, and the courage to make the work. The invitation to come into an organisation and its acceptance imply a level of respect on both sides which can allow for constructive feedback between both parties. The artist knows that s/he has been invited there out of respect for the work that s/he is making and it can give a personal but professional level of exchange between the people involved.

I met Carol while I was teaching at Surrey University and was very impressed by her work and the mixture of text and politics which she involved in it. We kept in contact partly through Surrey and John Ashford. Carol had done Resolution as well. I first started working at The Place last year and we were talking about who we might invite to come in and see if they were interested in joining us. Carol's name came up and that was the beginning of it all.

Carol Brown

I had just come to the end of a period of extended research at Surrey University into choreographic practices and was really trying to get out of that context and work in a more freelance capacity. The Place provided an address and a base for that work, which was a huge benefit.

While I was working at Surrey, by the nature of my environment, I was very often working on my own. Since I moved to The Place I have worked more with other people. At The Place not only are better resources obviously available, but there is a community of people around you. You are linked into a network, so there is more opportunity to try working in a different way. It has been exciting to branch out into this different scale of work and to build a resource in terms of dancers with whom I am interested in working. The shift from Associate Artist to Choreographer in Residence has given a sense of continuity.

Richard Alston

Mairead, can I ask you to tell us a little bit about the situation at Yorkshire Dance?

Mairead Turner

I would like to talk about what we call a Partnership between Yorkshire Dance and Charlotte Vincent as the Yorkshire Dance Partner. Simon Dove originally saw Charlotte as she performed a piece in one of our choreographic platforms, which is an informal showing of work at Yorkshire Dance. Simon was impressed by Charlotte's work and decided then that he would offer her continued support over three years. There are lots of similarities with the other safe havens in what we've offered Charlotte over those three years; space, administrative support, financial support. I worked out the other day that we've given Charlotte £15,000 over those three years, which I think has been a secure form of support, although it may seem controversial to some. What Simon really wanted to put in place was continuous support for Charlotte so that she would receive more money for each project through those three years. I think it's great that she's had that security.

Charlotte Vincent

I've also tapped into the human resources at Yorkshire Dance which is probably one of the most important things in that there is a communication which is constant and holistic, and like a sort of marriage between me and the team.

Mairead Turner

It feels almost like an emotional support mechanism as well. There's that belief in Charlotte which I hope that we've given to her as an artist.

The other thing that's been very useful over the three years is to have critical feedback on the work. It has been mentioned earlier that it's a sort of exchange. It's not just giving the artist the support, but it works the other way as well. We wanted Charlotte to add to our organisation as well as adding to hers and I think that it's very good to have that artistic vision in an office.

Charlotte Vincent

It's educational for me as well, because I learn from the office environment and from how a building runs and what's going on. I get an opportunity to engage with the international workshops or other workshops that are going on. I run classes when I am in residence, I go to classes when I'm not. It's about an exchange and I think that's the strength of it in a way.

The only other thing that we haven't mentioned is that there's also been a sustained effort to present the work as well, because in the last three years Yorkshire Dance's main studio has got seats and black-out and lighting. Since I first started engaging with Yorkshire Dance there's been a slightly more professional outlook to how we present 'work in progress'. Being able to present work in progress in a safe haven is very important because then you can open up a dialogue with the audience. Generally there isn't enough opportunity across the country to do that, so I think National Dance Agencies have a really important role in providing that platform and critical feedback.

Richard Alston

The idea of a safe haven for an artist is probably about facilitating something which they might not be able to do at all in a risky situation, something which might involve process rather than product.

Charlotte Vincent

In the last few days a lot of people have been expressing the need not to fail but to take risks. The system in which we work is not really set up to allow for risk-taking. My relationship with Yorkshire Dance is a bit like unconditional love, whereby I can play with new ideas: there's an understanding that it is part of the continuation of my artistic process and progress, and there is dialogue about processes, rather than just being judged on the product.

Mairead Turner

I think the safe haven is giving the artist the choice to decide if they want to show their work or not. We react to what Charlotte wants to do, so if Charlotte wanted to spend a year in research and development, with no finished product that would be absolutely fine.

Richard Alston

An accent on process, support and lack of isolation is something that all the National Dance Agencies can offer. There is a very real possibility, and one to be cherished, that as a result dance will be enriched, and therefore the audience will see richer work. So whether they know about the process or not, they will benefit from it.

Points raised in discussion:

- Relationships between artists and National Dance Agencies are mutual investments.

- Externally there is great concern over the selection process of artists for these schemes. There are no formal application processes or set of formal criteria. People felt entitled to apply for the opportunity to take part.

- There seems to be a lack of transparency surrounding appointments that could be diminished.

- The criteria for how an artist can help a National Dance Agency, and how a National Dance Agency can help an artist and the timing of the artist's career were seen as perhaps overly loose and informal.

- Jane Mooney responded that each of the Agencies has a distinct artistic policy and strategic aims appropriate to their context. In addition, within all NDA's equal opportunities policies, selection has to be transparent, clearly made and accounted for to ACE and the RABs.

- Many schemes run by NDAs are one-off experiments and money is often received for a pilot scheme only.

- The artist-NDA relationship is a contracted relationship with clear objectives set out for either party.

Session 25
'Ruthless and Rigorous': Editing the Dance

Keywords:

communication   rehearsal process   choreographic feedback

Val Bourne, the Artistic Director of Dance Umbrella, has been instrumental in the development of contemporary dance in the UK since the first festival in 1978. Here she is in conversation with David and Ain Gordon from New York, who are currently running a choreographic development project in London called 'The Outside Eye'. The course is based on the premise that choreographers need to be more reflective, more critical and more rigorous in their choreographic processes. Many of us remember David Gordon from his contribution to the Judson Dance Theater and his choreographic work in Britain. Now, with his son Ain, he offers the benefit of his experiences to both choreographers and teachers.

Val Bourne

The workshop which David and Ain are leading in London is called The Outside Eye. It started last year when I read about an interview with Stephen Sondheim. He was talking about workshops that he and Cameron MacIntosh had set up for writers of music theatre. It was interesting because if you substituted the word 'choreographer' for 'writer', many of the points he was making still applied; 'am I seeing what you wanted me to see', 'do you know what effect that image has on people'. Basically it was to do with self-analysis and editing. Then David started talking to me about workshops that he had been leading, and many of the same points came up. We started talking about Robert Dunn and Judson Church and the principles of criticising one's own work and the work of one's peer group. The Outside Eye was born from that. If you work in the theatre or film there are always other people through which the work filters before it is presented on stage or screen. Often the choreographer is all those things for him/herself. We are halfway through the course now, with one more week to go and there are only seven people on it of which five are dancers, but it is very interesting.

David Gordon

When I moved into the theatre world I had to begin to deal with the various people who wanted to be partners in the working process. At first I found it very frightening that so many people were going to be looking at what I was doing before I was done, and were possibly going to be offering opinions. I found the way in which the process was conducted strange as well. When you have a commission for a dance, you go into the studio with dancers, and it takes six weeks if you have a six week rehearsal period or four weeks if you have a four week rehearsal period. At the end of that time you are doing technical and dress rehearsals and the piece moves on to the stage. In the theatre, my experience is that you have a workshop and then you re-write the script, and then you think about it all and then you talk again, then you work with some new actors, the actors ask questions, the producer comes, the dramaturg comes... The process is much longer. At first I thought that this was awful, and then I began to realise that the product was actually becoming more interesting, and I was having time to develop something which I hadn't understood existed. The next phase came about when the work finally went on the stage. There was something called the 'previews' and during that period of time I could watch the work every night in the audience and I could work with the actors and dancers next day. I could make cuts, I could make additions, I could change things, based not on some idea that I was going to eventually make everybody in the house happy, but on the idea that I was making myself happier, relative to what I was seeing in this situation called the audience. So the piece did not finally open until more work had been done on it in the theatre itself.

In the dance world we had initiated periods of time at the end of the rehearsal period, when the making process was generally over, when we invited each other to our final rehearsals to give notes. It was unofficial and we invited people whom we trusted. The theatre situation was not necessarily about people I trusted, in fact it was about people who had no interest in me and were only interested in what they were seeing on the stage and had paid for. I was hearing reactions and seeing points where people were confused by what I was doing, or were understanding what I was doing. It all informed the working process in a way I had not experienced as a choreographer in my own studio with my own dancers. That process began to change from the very first time I worked with a theatre company. I brought nine dancers along to deal with nine actors at the Guthrie Theatre in America, with the intention that my dancers would teach those actors how we moved, and those actors would teach my dancers how they spoke. Everybody did all of that, except the other thing that happened was that the actors asked questions. The dancers never asked questions. The actors asked so many questions that I had to go home every evening and try to figure out what I was going to say to them the next day to illuminate the process, so that they and the dancers could begin to experience together something which would make a new thing happen for us all. This then re-informed my own process when I got back into the studio with my own dancers alone. I began to think about what I needed to tell people which was an entirely different approach to that which I had used before. Ain had been doing some of this all on his own prior my discoveries and prior to our working together officially on anything.

Ain Gordon

Of course there are producers who are better at talking to you, and dramaturgs who are better at talking to you, and I have been a better and worse listener at various times. I now have a rule that I don't talk for the first half hour of dramaturgs talking to me because at first I tend to be more defensive. Instead I just try to stay calm and hear what they are saying. If they are good at it, what they are talking about is in the context of what I was trying to do. I am not interested when somebody starts telling me that we all wore red shirts and they like blue. At some point you begin to know who to trust because that person is talking about what they believe you were trying to do, and how successful you were with what you were trying to do. Then a whole conversation can happen which is not personal and not about likes and dislikes, but about the goal of this piece of work that is happening now.

David Gordon

I begin to have a clearer understanding of the goal of my piece when I try to explain it to somebody else. It was perfectly possible in the way I was working previously to walk into the studio on the first day of choreographing a new work and not know what my goal was very clearly. I often did not determine in advance what I was going to do with the dancers. I would literally arrive on the first day with human beings, time and space and say 'let's all go and stand over there'. That was how I loved to work. The first time I couldn't do that was when I received a commission from a large ballet company, who wanted to know how many dancers, how many corps members, how many principals, how many soloists and what music they should be finding the clearance for and be beginning to orchestrate. I had to make decisions before I even walked into the studio. I was terrified!

Working and writing together with Ain, I had to figure out how to talk to this other human being with whom I shared an intimate life. We had to learn how to say 'I like that idea, I don't like that idea, I still like you!'. When working with someone else you have to be able to begin to formulate your ideas; you could change it fifty times but something has to come out and you have to pass it along and ricochet it back and have something to deal with - and that's the same game you have to play with these producers. They also are not frightened if you change your mind fifty times - well they are, but you can get them to like it if you know how to charm them. But you keep stamping the word 'Draft' with a big rubber stamp. We stamp it on everything, until the last day. Sometimes we get embarrassed when it says draft number eight so we stop counting and just use the date. But once I started getting used to having to try to explain what I was thinking about and not being horrified at how foolish it sounded when it first came out of my mouth and not being horrified by the look in the eyes of these total strangers, I worked faster and more specifically. It became clearer what was appropriate, or what was an interesting idea but not for this play, or what was garbage.

So what does this have to do with dancing and what does it have to do with choreographing and what does it have to do with abstraction as opposed to narrative or fragmented narrative as opposed to linear narrative or any devices, any intentions? One of the things we're trying to do in The Outside Eye workshop is to begin to find some way to discuss one's own work - to be able to communicate it to a dancer and also to be able to communicate it to another artist, to be able to see how another artist works, makes decisions. We are looking for the way in which we can talk to each other which says 'do you intend to do this in your work?' rather than loading the question with 'when you do this, I feel this, do you mean it?' That alters the way we respond because we already know your opinion of what we did, and now we have to either defend what we did, change our mind, or apologise to you for having put you through it. There must surely be a way to talk about art as if it exists and has a life of its own, in the same way that we might discuss the dinner you prepared in which the chicken fell on the floor, and we can talk about it as if it's chicken and not the worst thing you ever did.

Ain Gordon

We should have those means between us as artists, as people who support artists, as people who write about artists. There should be ways to discuss the art as if it has an existence, as if we can objectively examine it and help to support it and make it better. So we think that some of what we have heard at this conference about nurturing artists seems to us must include a process which begins to critically support work as well as economically support it.

David Gordon

The problem with having your friends, your acquaintances, or other artists who know you talking about your work is that it is very hard to not talk about it in relation to what they know you are, or who you are, or what you want. In the course that we've been doing, we've been using a system invented by Liz Lerman called critical response, which helps to create a language which makes your friends into strangers. You can make a language to talk to each other about the work that isn't personal and isn't conveying with every question exactly what you really thought. When I see a piece I already know what I thought, I don't need to know it again. What I'm interested in finding out is did I see what the artist thinks they did? So this language helps me to ask them in such a way that is open enough to allow them to tell me what they thought they were doing. Then at some point, if I want to be critical, I can talk about the fact that what they are talking about didn't happen to me, or didn't happen to me all the time. My response to what they were looking for - whether or not I liked what they were looking for - is just an attempt to help them do it. And understanding their lapses in being able to achieve what they wanted helps me to go back and make my own work.

Points raised in discussion:

· Critical language is written about by Liz Lerman who practises in Washington, D.C. It is a system whereby the artist gathers information to inform their work; it is not a didactic instruction to the artist. It is a good foundation on which dance practitioners can build.

· Questions can be succinct and to the point – every time the speaker comes to an 'and' or a 'but' or a breath, that's it. That's the question. Aim to cut out unnecessary and superfluous language.

· Dancers imply questions with their physical experimentation and actors tend to be more cerebral; but this is not 'natural'. Communication is taught and learned like turn-out or pirouettes! Dance practitioners must practise speaking to each other as often as they practise dancing.

· This method of critical response complements both narrative and abstract methods of presentation. The questions are in relation to the artist's intention.

Session 26

The Plenary Session, chaired by Gregory Nash

During the Conference, three or four presentations were scheduled concurrently, and the two plenary sessions were designed to give delegates some insights into issues that had been raised in other fora. Here, for purposes of clarity in the publication, the two sessions have been synthesised. The Chair was supported by notes provided by the three conference monitors, Fleur Darkin, Louise Katerega and Claire Nicholson.

Gregory Nash

The conference had an excellent beginning in Bob Cohan's testimony. As an artist who represents both our past and our present it was fantastic to hear his recollections and also his thoughts about the future. Bob was followed by three important choreographers, and I want to share with you some of the things that they said.

Session 1. Can Choreography be Taught? An artist's response.

Kate Flatt described 'crossing the border' from art to education. She talked about her own journey as a choreographer, and the need, when she emerged from college as a dancer, to create space for her ideas and to make herself a choreographer. She asked a question: do choreographers have the responsibility to educate?

Janet Smith also asked a question: if tastes emerge or if rules emerge, is it a choreographer's responsibility or tendency to always break them down and start again? For her, choreography in teaching is something that feels 'other'. She asked: do you need to trick yourself into playing to recognise excitements and is there the danger of disengagement from the play in the creative process?

Rosemary Butcher made a statement of four very succinct points:

Yes to the importance of creative environment.
No to expectancy.
No to a predetermined language.
No to outdated choreographic practices.

Also arising in this session was the suggestion that students should be allowed to find their own choreographic methods and process, to be true to the self rather than be restricted by rules; and that teachers of choreography need to act as mentors, to offer support to students and individual choreographic development.

This tied into another question: is this actually possible to achieve within the modular structure where emphasis is placed on assessment, grades and reaching set targets?

Session 2. Dance Festivals: Can they nurture the emerging choreographer?

Estrella Casero Garcia spoke in her paper about the role and function of five Spanish dance festivals in terms of the diversity of approaches, and the different attitudes towards the making and performing of dance. The choreographers come via national competitions, and the festival seems to function as a dance "market" where choreographers show their work and promoters "buy".

Victoria Marangopoulou talked about the Kalamata Festival that she directs. Key to its success has been a holistic approach. The festival is in some way helping to create a community of artists and choreographers by looking at dance in Greek history and looking at the potential for the development into the future. I wondered if it might have been equally useful to contrast this example with some from countries that have more established festivals, dance cultures and infrastructures. This way we could see if there's space for choreographic development or even if it is appropriate to place such activity within the context of a festival.

We talk about festivals as ways of representing nationality and belonging. I wonder if a festival is international and you are presenting work which you perceive to be of international standard, what do you do then with the emerging work that you are nurturing which may not be at that stage yet?

Session 3. The National Dance Agencies: their role in the infrastructure of choreographic development in Britain.

This session raised the question of the National Dance Agencies' autonomy in the selection of artists within their programmes. John Ashford stated that 'We are led by the artists we choose to serve'. This autonomy has a flip side - accountability to major funders - and there can be a struggle of juggling multiple agendas according to funders' interests and regional variations. After the session it became apparent that each director had her or his own personal direction. Sometimes in dance we are very critical of the idea of curatorship. One of the points that came up was that for artistic directors of theatres like the West Yorkshire Playhouse and other repertory theatres, nobody questions that right.

One of the perceived problems may be that most artistic directors of repertory theatres are practising stage directors, while the directors of our national dance agencies have come sometimes from other areas of the profession but not necessarily having been a choreographer. So there is possibly a difference in status in the way that the two groups are perceived. National Dance Agencies exist within small communities, there are family tensions, and they exist in mixed economies and so there can be a sense of being pulled in different directions.

Session 4. The Creative Voice:
Reflections on the Independent Dance Review consultation.

Somebody described artists who are 'not in the system'. I didn't ask the question then but I would like to ask now, when we say 'the system' do we mean the funding system, or are we talking about 'the community' of choreographers or 'the community of dance artists'? Are we talking about people who are not within that community for geographical reasons or reasons of status? Or are we talking about people who are invisible because they are not in the state funding system? People talked about 'making it' as a choreographer. I don't know what that means. How do you know if you've 'made it' as a choreographer?

In the process of researching the Independent Dance Review, Gill Clark and Rachel Gibson identified the 'raw materials' needed to create work as space, time, people and support. Most of all, there is a need for flexibility. The process requires money, but sometimes money isn't the only answer. There needs to be a fluidity of artistic roles. Often dance artists, and I mean both dancers and choreographers, are able to work as dancers, choreographers, and administrators; there is multi-skilling. Funding tends to be focussed on the individual, but it should also support continuity for experienced choreographers. In a real sense there has been isolation and fragmentation of dance artists caused by inflexible funding structures.

Session 5. Your Brain is a Muscle - Flex it!
Towards a new approach to training in dance.

Even choreographers at a professional level are struggling to find effective verbal languages in which to express themselves in the studio. On a course of 25 professionals, almost all had great difficulty in perceiving that there might be an audience reaction to their work, and/or what that reaction might be. Enhanced linguistic skill, enhanced perception of self, other and situations, results in much time saved in the studio and happier dancers who contribute usefully to the work without taking over the choreographer's role.

It is important that artists understand their needs in terms of their own individual self, i.e. person, personality, personal development. Many attend courses simply to make their CVs look better and not generally to develop themselves. The notion of genius can be demystified by looking at who does things well and why and how and dance artists tend to look within at the physical landscape of their own discipline. They need to realise that there are external systems, semiotics, hermeneutics, from other disciplines that can provide a language with which to appreciate dance.

Looking at the first point it occurs to me that if choreographers at professional level are struggling to find a verbal language, then it's going to be even more difficult to communicate that outside of our own community. However, I would say that the presentations we have heard from choreographers at this conference would go a long way to contradict that.

Session 6. Promoting Choreographers: What does the promoter bring to the table?

First question: What do artists have to do to get to the table? Answer: You have to be invited. And, it was suggested, with limited resources and limited scope for presentation, the people who are in the position to invite have, inevitably, to be selective about who they bring. There's a difference between 'presenting' and 'producing' theatres. It was strongly felt that dance needs to embrace a theatrical way of producing with the Arts Councils paying promoters to produce and select work.

This debate has also been ongoing in the context of the Independent Dance Review: should money be given to artists to make work or be given to promoters/producers to develop work with artists in the context of audiences? Is there room for both? Is the role of the producer solely as an income-generating engine? Perhaps a venue or a festival, as a subsidised agency is in the best position to help an artist to make a project happen? Is there work that presenters feel they should present? I wonder if this means 'have' to present? It was felt this could be 'seasonal', it could be to do with targeting a particular area of your community.

Ron McAllister talked about bringing about excitement as essential to a community, and I think he was talking about a geographic community, but perhaps that could be broader? Is one of the jobs of a producer to bring about excitement?

Producing venues change with seasons or with trends, and one of the things that keeps coming up in all of the sessions that I've been in is that there is clearly a difference between the way that decisions are made in other art forms, and I refer to the whole process by which work is made. We make these comparisons and we discover the differences. There may be lessons to be learnt but it may also be that making dance is a radically different route.

Session 7. Vocational Training: Current practices and future needs

Three years is not long enough for art to be taught in schools and we need to consider the importance of continuing education. There is a need to increase the number of excellent teachers and one of the ways to make that happen is probably through a designated training course for dance teachers. There is a need for a balance in training, and a consideration of the body, the soul and the spirit of young dancers. We need to get rid of negative attitudes in dance training; and to think more carefully about the development of dancer as performer - good choreography and its demands can inspire and move you forward.

Expression in creativity needs to be part of training and can happen through improvisatory tasks and composition classes, introducing knowledge of the craft of choreography. Finally, the Government needs to be persuaded to fund realistically and the time to do it is now, through advocacy and lobbying.

Session 8. Artists Programme Artists: The Finnish model

This session examined a Finnish dance organisation called Zodiak. I think our closest equivalent in England is the Chisenhale Dance Space.

Zodiak is a centre for dance based at an old cable factory with a 100-seat theatre and rehearsal space. Its management is a board and an artistic committee made up of ten dance artists, who make decisions about 150 performances a year in several venues. Every premier has ten performances. Every company takes responsibility for it's own promotion. This model works because the attitude at Zodiak is that more can be achieved collectively; 'joined together' you are a greater force. Can this work in the UK?

There is such generosity of spirit between artists in the UK; do we assume that artists cannot make objective decisions? I remember years ago when I was working as an artist in Scotland I asked why there were no practising dance artists on the existing dance panel of the Scottish Arts Council. I was told that artists couldn't be expected to be impartial. Are there ethical questions about being an artist and being confronted with making choices? Is it good for artists to make selections themselves?

Session 9. Craft, Skill and Application: The Higher Education Sector

Speakers outlined their own institutions' programmes of development for young choreographers; there was consensus that all students of dance should study composition skills for a minimum of two years, and then specialise in the third year. Chris Bannerman emphasised interaction, communication and self-awareness; Karen Greenhough spoke of seeking to balance rigour with free expression of a personal voice; Evelyn Jamieson advocated a very structured but varied way of teaching and assessing which allowed students to test themselves in a variety of choreographic situations, and Valerie Preston-Dunlop encouraged an approach which developed thinkers as well as movement generators, interested in total theatre not just dance. Questions concerned the function of these courses - is the HE institution supposed to provide enough for a career choreographer or just a taste for the all round dance professional?

Session 10. Funding Dancemaking: International Perspectives.

Sue Hoyle, Nancy Duncan and Jerril Rechter each gave snapshots of the situation in England and France, the United States and Australia. It was fascinating how different the three systems were. France is quite politically driven, and the US system is driven by the need to generate lots of private and trust funding because there is very little state support.

Sue came up with an interesting comparison: to the British everything looks greener in France because there's money, whereas the French think that our tendency to present work in a number of venues in one city is unusual, because in Paris there are just one or two people programming the venues. The conclusion was that there is quite a lot to be learned, but that not all models can be transferred as they are obviously culturally specific.

Nancy was very envious of the whole National Dance Agency system. She feels that although the United States is a much bigger country, with different needs, that 6 to 8 dance centres in the United States could take care not only of the artistic process but also of the welfare of dancers and choreographers. Nancy worries about dancers; indeed, several people have said, 'we worry about dancers in this whole process'.

Jerril, coming from Australia, said that she just wanted to work in a more cultural environment, where audiences might have more hunger for dance. She wanted to work in more philanthropic environments, with more resources for exploration.

Sue would like more self-esteem and confidence among dance artists, and audiences who were hungry for danger. In England we have half of one per cent government spending on the Arts. Local authorities should pull out the stops. We need research and information, investment and flexibility, encouraging collaborations and removing of national boundaries.

Session 11. Mentor Models

Is mentor an over-used term? Is it simply a repackaging of something that has always happened? Artists have always learned from their more experienced elders and maybe with the demise of the repertory system here in the '70s and '80s we removed lots of possibilities for doing that. One of the things that came up in the previous session is that youth dance companies also provide a very important opportunity for lots of people. I can probably name about 6 or 7 choreographers that I know who began their careers by performing in works by choreographers in youth dance settings.

There are many mentoring models:

·   The workshop model where one choreographer leads and supports other artists.
·   The one to one - where one choreographer works with another as mentor.
·   An open forum - groups of artists, platforms, sharing of works.

I remember thinking, when mentoring first began happening and people were being allocated mentors, that surely a mentor is somebody who you respect and admire and want to work with in this way.

Session 12. Choreographers Interviewed: The choreographic debate

An opportunity to listen to four choreographers speaking about their processes, and reflecting on the contexts, intentions and structures of the works viewed at the conference gala.

Session 13. Urban Culture and Dance Making

There is a concern that hip-hop and street dance are simply 'flavour of the month', and are not respected as a technique like other contemporary techniques. In fusing street and contemporary dance, there are barriers to be surmounted between the various experiences of the individual dancers. Street dance can have an overbearing aesthetic of cool which restricts the vulnerability that is necessary for good theatre.

We need to question our misconception of African dance - which is a Western construct - that homogenises a diverse range of techniques from over 44 countries. African dance is a great diversity of difficult time consuming-techniques that take years to perfect. There can be implicit racism in the negating of technical skills and prowess in African dance. It is assumed that African dance is learned by a genetic code and is a natural, as opposed to a learnt, technique. There is a huge danger of exoticism when dealing with African dance which must be addressed.

There is also a question of anatomical difference, of developing another language to evolve a new technique, and the notion of respect for the non-Western dancer. A fusion of styles means that dancers must adapt techniques to their own body and take the principles with them into their own body. African contemporary dance is whatever is being done today by African dancers.

Session 14. Can Choreography Be Taught? European Examples (Part 2)

A Swedish model was described where there is a small intake of students, a maximum of 5 per year and these tend to be mature: 25-35 years old. Here there is an emphasis on individual movement language and collaboration with other art forms. There is also development of verbal articulation and the discussion of work and learning of dance related skills, administration, stage craft etc. The University College in Sweden employs professional dancers to work with the student choreographers and the college offers support after completion of the course in the form of free rehearsal space.

A similar Dutch model was described with the same number of students and an emphasis on flexibility. Flexibility is a word that keeps coming up this week. Flexibility and the response to individual needs.

Does the university sector stifle creativity, and is it restricted by bureaucracy? Could the British system learn from these models? With a rigorous audition process resulting in committed students, could we still run these courses in the UK if we didn't make the required numbers? Perhaps a change of language is needed. Artists don't want to go back to into education for MA courses; they should be reconsidered as professional choreographic developments.

Session 15. Visual Arts as a stimulus for Choreography: An Independent process.

A synthesis of theory and practice; a welcome opportunity for some delegates to get into the studio and respond to Ana Macara's ideas.

Session 16. Learning to Choreograph: A Conversation with Rui Horta

Learning to choreograph happens by a number of processes and from a number of resources. Rui described his experience of these as:

· a deep personal reflection and self development in dance and all related art forms.
· a deep study of the work of others he admired in related fields.
· luck, preparation, meeting, opportunity
· being asked to work within commissioning guidelines, which can facilitate learning in fields otherwise not engaged in.

- resources, other artists to work with and ideas
- informed promoters, enthusiastic teams of people in fully equipped venues
- live-in accommodation and a wage for a few years
- mature, 30+ creative dancers with whom relationships have been built up over
- a number of years
- having only to create, not also to organise and promote.

There was a discussion of the definitions of the choreographer and choreography. Rui felt that choreography can be taught but choreographers are born and realise their potential.

He described his own methods and how he first felt it was important to develop them alone, and afterwards his hunger to pass them on. He talked about ownership of the work; for example he gave a duet to two of his dancers because it was they who made it in the first place.

Session 17. The Artist and Presenter: A positive artistic partnership

The main point that came out, is that sometimes it is not the space, the physical space of the theatre and how suitable it is that matters, but the person in charge of that space. People are the key as well as human resources, physical resources and money. Richard Alston spoke about how much he appreciated it. He was asked who he would choose for a mentor and again this raised the subject of fragile egos. Richard talked about the very trusted friends and colleagues that he invites into the end of the rehearsal process, and the point that emerged was that sometimes reassurance and harsh criticism need to come in the same package. The discussion was very London based, predominantly about good relationships between artists and presenters in London. Blitz! emerged as a model, with its open rehearsals where anybody can walk in.

Session 18. Nurturing Emerging Choreographers

This session described an interesting project organised by ELIA Dance section called a choreo-co-ordination project, which allowed 12 young students from institutions all over Europe to come together to create a collective choreography under the guidance of a practicing choreographer. Questions were raised about forms of training, and the value attached to such a process. However, should we insist on teaching improvisation and composition to young dancers in training who are basically disinterested?

Session 19. The Devising Process: a framework for collaboration.

This session was based on the final piece of the first night platform showings. It was suggested that this piece had been created through 'total' collaboration, with all elements of dance, music, design and text working together, equally importantly, so that the process and product were inextricably linked. Clear aims were needed and identified at the start of the creative process. The company worked together and gave each other feedback, and in this way they were constantly challenged and supported by each other. They developed skills in their own discipline and that of others. Essentially the work was a group collaboration, but is it possible to make art in this way?

Session 20. European Promotion Practices: How do they nurture choreographers?

Again promotion was the theme, with John Ashford's statement, made at a conference in Barcelona, that we are led by the artists we choose to serve. I asked him if some artists were led by the taste of the promoter they most wanted to impress. He denied it!

The comment was made that a promoter's success is dependent on an artist's success. This raised the question: why then do most promoters have salaries and most artists not? Both Guy Cools and John Ashford talked about the promoter as an invisible frame builder, and there was concern about the imbalance between salaried promoters and non-salaried artists.

One artist in the audience talked about having a tender ego which suggested that good promotion and good relationships are a balance of the personal and the strategic.

Rui Horta suggested that good promotion is simple help at the right moment. John Ashford felt that the whole point of Pan European promotional schemes is the opportunities for artists to reassess their work and their approaches by presenting their work in the context of different cultures.

Session 21. Text, context, dance: a conversation with Shobana Jeyasingh.

Shobana felt that there was a lack of faith in pure creative activity. Funds tend to go to education and there is a philistine element at the heart of British culture. There is a contradiction between the funding system - which requires quantifiable results - and the demands of risk taking. The importance of a choreographer having a home, a work base, belonging is as great as having money. A wide cultural agenda tends to be played out in response to Shobana's work, one that is not intended by the choreographer.

Shobana sees choreography as a consultative process with the dancers, with the role of the choreographer as a theatre director, somebody who has to make up the script, inventing an invisible text. The skill of the choreographer is to make visible the text.

Session 22. The Black Choreographic Initiative:
An artist centred approach to professional development

The Black Choreographic Initiative was an initiative that came from the Regional Arts Boards rather than central government or the Arts Council. Referring back to creative managers, the individuals in these arts boards recognised a need, and created a pot of money and a system to fulfil that need.

The other point that was made was that perhaps artists should be given some credit for knowing what they want. Much has been said about packages of teaching and systems of teaching. The Black Choreographic Initiative begins with an individual development skills analysis and that is the foundation of everything that happens next. So the individual identifies what they need and then Vivien, as co-ordinator, looks at this with the choreographers and determines what they each need as individuals. The scheme addresses the needs of the practitioners to be somehow more than just artists, but to have business skills and communication skills. One participant had taken an information technology course as part of their required development. So it was about developing a holistic individual programme and one that fits the outside world, not just the world within the studio.

Session 23. The Manager/Choreographer Relationship.

Julia Carruthers, who chaired this session, began with some very good statistics, the gist of which were that most British dance companies - with the exception of the two Royal Ballet companies - are run by women or gay men.

What I perceived from this session, was that none of the managers on the panel felt that they were in any way in a secondary position to the choreographers or artistic directors they worked with. In the case of the two that were on salaries, they had pay parity with the artistic directors of the company and my perspective is that most of them are regarded as teams. They talked about why they do what they do, the fact that there is inspiration and excitement in the work, and they had the desire to provide a bedrock of support.

Leonie Gombrich talked about some of the frustrations she found when she first joined DV8. People wanted to get to Lloyd Newson direct, and not have to 'circumnavigate this annoying woman'!

Suzanne Walker from V-TOL came up with a list of values and definitions about the relationship between the manager and artist:
·   this relationship must be honest and open;
·   it must have mutual respect and good communication.
·   there has to be commitment and belief, a questioning, inspiring and a shared responsibility in decision making;
·   that boards are a support structure for both administrators and artists.

Session 24. Choreographic Experiments in Safe Havens.

Safe haven means a supportive environment psychologically as well as practically for emerging dance artists. Money, space and time are equally important as belief and commitment to an artist. There are a number of mutual benefits to the scheme of Associate Artists and Choreographers-in-Residence.

Concern was expressed from the audience over the selection of artists and the criteria for selection. There seems to be a certain amount of mystery regarding the artistic choice of a director to select one artist over another, and a deep feeling that the criteria for such selection needed to be more open, otherwise there is a danger that equal opportunities are not respected and this may be a real problem. Members of the audience felt strongly that such opportunities must be made public and accountable.

On behalf of the NDA's, Jane Mooney spoke about the need for clear aims, and transparent policies; all directors are required to be accountable to ACE and the RABs. Safe havens are not just for emerging choreographers but also to support mature choreographers. And what happens to the artists after their safe haven experience? This reminds me of a comment that two people have made to me, which is that we must remember that some of the artists that are here today will still be choreographers when they are 50, 60 and 70, and that there will still be more generations coming up behind them. Safe havens afford the opportunity for artists to infiltrate the managerial system of arts and have a role in shaping the dance world.

Each member of the panel talked about how their relationship was more than personal, the relationship was between the artist and the organisation. It might have begun with the artistic director but it is more than that. Jane Mooney, Director of Suffolk Dance, made a very interesting comment: she said people just have to call her up, and that basically anyone who has ever called her with a good idea has ended up working in her building.

Session 25. Ruthless and Rigorous: Editing the dance

Many interesting points that came up in this session; David and Ain Gordon were clear, articulate and self-confident. They advocated clarity and consideration in all dealings as a choreographer; how to be clear about your questions, how to phrase your questions and how this impacts not only on making and mentoring processes but also in the devising process, on the process of how we make funding decisions, and how we make artistic choices. Nurturing must include "critical" as well as economic approaches, shifting from trust to exposure. It must be possible to judge the work with out judging the individual; i.e. "I don't like the idea but I still like you".

The critical debate is lacking in dance; dancers and choreographers should learn to place dance in the context of the world 'community', and to consider the relationship between the dance work and the audience.

Are we still looking to America after all these years?

Session 27

New Opportunities in Classical Ballet

Keywords:

training   programming strategies   building community relationships
audiences

David Bintley became Artistic Director of the Birmingham Royal Ballet in 1995. His ballets are in the repertoires of companies all over the world. His former career with the Sadler's Wells Royal Ballet and the Royal Ballet place him in an invaluable position from which to reflect on the future of choreography from a classical ballet perspective. What changes does he perceive in the development of choreography in the UK and Europe?

Jo Butterworth

I'd like to introduce you to David Bintley, who is Artistic Director of Birmingham Royal Ballet. David has already raised the question of the lack of numbers from the ballet world present at this conference. I think it is fair to say that obviously invitations did go out, but the Lottery award was not notified to us until November 1997, and by the time that we had a team in place to start formal planning, many people already had other commitments. The question of lead time is something we have to consider for the future if we want to continue with these kinds of conferences. But perhaps David, there are other reasons for it?

David Bintley

I think there are. There seems to me to be a whole network of dancers in the regions who have not been part of a national gathering for a long, long time. I think that obviously the experience that we have as dancers and as choreographers, at the level and money on which we operate, is something which leaves us with not a great deal in common, but I think that clearly that is a situation which has to change. I'm not sure what the classical world believes the benefits of being at this kind of conference would be, but sadly, to stay away from it is going to be of no benefit.

I'm kind of pleased that I am the sole representative as I feel slightly less guilty! I never come to an occasion like this without the knowledge that I am going to be attacked from some quarter, because BRB can spend the whole of Ireland's annual dance budget on one single production. Of course, there is somebody else with a camera and a film crew spending five hundred times that over in America, making something that is going to go straight to video, so cost is all relative. It does seem to me that the old attitudes we have about classical dance and modern dance are so often based on a purely financial consideration and an artistic consideration that is very much bound in with that. When I became Director of BRB, it wouldn't have bothered me if I had never put on *Swan Lake* or *Sleeping Beauty* or *Giselle* or *Nutcracker* ever again. I have spent my whole life juggling how much of that stuff I have to do in order to pay for the work that is really interesting. I can't say that this is true of every artistic director - it isn't. And some of them believe they have to only do the classicals to pay their fees. But as I say, it is a juggling act. I think the only thing that keeps us going, that keeps us able to employ sixty dancers and forty musicians, is the infrastructure that will pay £80,000 for a big production of one of those classicals. While they have their own artistic integrity, I can understand that people see us spending a quarter of a million pounds on *Swan Lake* and then look at their own situation and the way they have to fight for money, and feel resentment towards the situation. So we have that double-edged situation; we're seen as extremely wealthy, which we're not (we have our own fights for money all the time) and extremely unadventurous artistically - but we are not really! At least not in Birmingham!

Jo Butterworth

I think that that is another interesting development from Birmingham, which I would like to return to later. This conference is about the making of dances, so I wanted to start by asking you what makes you a dance maker - who nurtured you, how did you learn choreography?

David Bintley

I was choreographing before I heard the word, I think, as a number of choreographers do I was just making pieces in order to dance in them, to give myself the best role. However, I'm very pleased to say that I have never choreographed for myself professionally, because I took a long, hard look at myself in the mirror and I was never the dancer that I wanted to be. But that's how I started. I remember making one of my first pieces which was comprised wholly of pictures from all my ballet books. I thought this particular pose looked nice so I put it in there, I just went from one picture to the next. It only really became apparent to me when I got to the Royal Ballet School, and quickly realised that I was never going to be the dancer that I wanted to be. Therefore I had to make roles for myself because nobody else would, and actually it was far more interesting. I have always been much more interested in making work than doing it.

Jo Butterworth

What did you put in between the one picture and the next? How did you link them up?

David Bintley

With the odd step, a few classroom steps!

Jo Butterworth

What about music?

David Bintley

I had a musical background because both my parents were musicians and they taught me piano when I was very young, which was a bad idea. I'm always amazed at ballet families - we have a young Australian choreographer working with us at the moment. His parents were both dancers in the Australian Ballet and I am always amazed at people who do what their parents do, because my immediate reaction was to run away. I remember being made to eat a kipper for two days - this kipper kept reappearing because I wouldn't do my piano practice. It was either the piano practice or the kipper! Then I started dancing and gave up piano because I was too busy dancing. Maybe that's why I took to dance - just to avoid the piano and the kipper!

Jo Butterworth

Were there any people with whom you were involved in the early days who really pushed you, supported you, nurtured you in the direction in which you eventually went?

David Bintley

I think undoubtedly so, and I always consider myself the luckiest person alive in this respect. I really wasn't having a very good time because - well - I was nearly thrown out. I just didn't fit the mould at all, but suddenly de Valois saw me in a studio and took an interest in me and that was my salvation. Then Ashton again saw some early things that I did when I was eighteen, which was like starting to play the piano and Beethoven notices you. To have those people interested in you as a teenager was awesome. Then Peter Wright left a deep impression upon me as a director who gave me the chance to work professionally (very bravely), and the kind of trust and the kind of risk that he took with me.

Jo Butterworth

So was one of the things perhaps observing Ashton and de Valois and learning the craft from observation?

David Bintley

That was the only way. There was a little prize they gave at the School but there was no set choreographic course at all, and I think there was also a feeling at that time that they didn't want anybody else choreographing. The Royal Ballet had been through a period where there was a lot of talent around with Ashton, de Valois and MacMillan. There wasn't the space, and I think there was a feeling at that time that there were a number of people who were given chances but they were small chances, and they were kept down. I think I was just fortunate in that they suddenly thought 'Oooh we'd better do something about this' because there was no-one new around. I was the first of a lot of people including Michael Corder, Jonathan Burrows, Suzy Crowe and Jenny Jackson. A lot of us got a chance at that time. That was largely up to Peter Wright, who took that chance.

Jo Butterworth

And what was the nature of that chance?

David Bintley

The chance was that you had the stage for a period of time. Not long after I had left the School, they did begin a choreographic course if you like, or a workshop, which I think was beneficial. But again it was sort of sink or swim as far as you were concerned with the Company. Then you get the added problem that you are trying to break in as a very youthful, inexperienced person into a programme of work where, if you are in a triple bill, you are normally placed beside two great and popular works. So you are not only being judged as a choreographer of that piece, but you are next to master works of the twentieth century, which is not always the best way to do things to impress!

Jo Butterworth

As Birmingham's ballet director, what responsibilities do you now perceive towards nurturing others?

David Bintley

As I've said, it's my responsibility which I almost can't meet because I have to balance it against the programme and the work that more people want to see. My biggest mission at the moment is to persuade audiences back in to see new classically-based choreography, or even non- classically-based choreography but on a classical programme. For the best part of fifteen years now, I would say that many companies have just been heading up the primrose path giving audiences what they think they like, which is just a steady diet of nineteenth century works. This is absurd given that we are two years away from the next millenium; it leads our branch of the art form absolutely nowhere. So my mission really is to persuade them that new work can be entertaining. Again, I think that a lot of the stuff that was produced in the 70's and 80's, where people just picked a piece of music and hopped around to it, was deadly dull. There are very few people that can do that well! So I think you have got to persuade them that just going in for something new, to be there at the launch of something new, is exciting. Hence the programme that we do once a year which is a sink or swim event, where I have about 11 or 12 aspiring choreographers within the company who present a work which they choreograph on a big stage. We have a paying audience and I'm thrilled to say that the last time we did it we completely sold out in about nine days, which even *Swan Lake* doesn't. We also charged only £10 for tickets, which is an important factor.

Jo Butterworth

Another special initiative seems to be the education work in the company and the degree to which the dancers can be involved. Can you tell us a little bit more about that?

David Bintley

We've had an education department since we moved to Birmingham, as it was a large part of the mandate that we had from Birmingham City Council. I remember when we operated it at Sadler's Wells and we had one person doing things; it was a terrible, amateurish thing. Everybody hated doing it because they used this awful place with an audience of three people and a dog. But I think that has completely changed now and it is extraordinary the number of dancers who voluntarily choose this kind of work. Again, because I have a lot to do with them, I go to nearly all the shows and it is tremendously rewarding. What started off as a sort of politically correct thing to do has become not only important but I wouldsay in some respects the most important thing we do.

We recently did a tour of South Africa. I went to South Africa four years ago and I loved the place, I loved the people and they are a dancing nation. When I went to the BRB Company I said 'Let's go and be the first large scale Western company in there.' So we did that and it was very exciting. Of course, a lot of the interviews which I did whilst in Africa and before we arrived there included the question 'Is this political? Have you done this to get funding and credibility?' - and I could quite honestly say, no, we do this work all the time in England. So we sent the education department out a week before we arrived so they were already working there. Then the rest of the company arrived, and I have to tell you that despite the fact that we had a really very good two weeks, without a doubt the most impressive thing, the most enjoyable and most moving thing, the most significant part of the work we did down there was what our education department did. In the end we had to provide coaches to take the dancers out to witness thes eevents because they were so exciting. Hopefully from that we will be instituting some kind of exchange programme so that we can bring some of those young people over to do arts management courses, and to work with our education department. Also, in practical terms a lot of the kids there don't have the very close relationship of working in a local dance school.

When I left London, three years ago, I had my foot down to the floor because I couldn't get out of there quickly enough. The Royal Ballet had an education department but it impinged so little on the main Company's attitude or work. In actual fact, the Royal Ballet is like an island in the middle of London - it doesn't have those links which we can have in Birmingham. Not only do we have links with the Birmingham Symphony Orchestra and with the Birmingham Repertory Theatre, with DanceXchange, with all the local schools, but also with the politicians, with the people. We talk about public art, and it's tremendous when a ballet company - not a modern dance company which tends to be more into the people and the location - but when a ballet company can actually become a part of the very real fabric of the city. It's a tremendous feeling, and we work very hard trying to find as many links as we possibly can with as many areas of city life, because that's so much more rewarding than just knocking out a few ballets and doing your three performances a week in an opera house.

Jo Butterworth

The relationship you have created for example with certain people, with South Africa, how are you going to maintain that, to sustain it if you like, and continue it? What further benefits can you give?

David Bintley

As I say, we're talking about further touring, which would also entail taking the education department there. We're trying to help in a way by actually sending them some things that they need. Just materially we send as much stuff as we can in terms of videos to them. We're hoping to have some kind of fundraising gala for a brilliant programme that this man runs in Cape Town which is called Dance For All. He runs it in a township called Klatch and he has 200 kids to whom he teaches ballet and dance, amongst the most extreme deprivation you might see. But at the moment that is what we are actually asking: 'What can we do? How can we help?' I couldn't live with the guilt if we did all that, we promised all that and then we just left. And that's what these people were saying - please don't leave us - please don't forget us.

Jo Butterworth

How much autonomy do you have making those kinds of decisions?

David Bintley

Again, I think I'm finding that out. I've only been three years in this job and I am still finding what kind of autonomy I have in every direction. If I say 'no' does everybody listen to me? Everything that I have done so far has been OK. I have a wonderful administrative director who was a dancer as well, and he doesn't want to sit and watch *Swan Lake* all the time, so we are of a like mind. And we have a very good Board which is very much Birmingham-based, and very broad in its background. I really have got a wonderful job.

Jo Butterworth

I would like to ask you a little bit about your new Lottery application and the opportunities it might present?

David Bintley

Yes, it's very exciting not least because the Hippodrome at the moment is in a pretty poor area of Birmingham. We've had lots of people mugged, and it's a rough area. But the Lottery money will regenerate that entire area I think. It was an enormously strong bid, and one of the partners in the bid is the Royal Ballet School, which isn't mentioned and I don't mention that much because I'm told not to, which I still find astonishing. There will be facilities for a division of the Royal Ballet School; as though there was some kind of shame in teaching kids to dance... But it's this whole thing about privilege these days. When the bid was initially put in, it was submitted as one of the most successful commercial ventures in the country; for the DanceXchange, which does fantastic work in the region, for the Company which has obviously been a big success story in Birmingham, and also for the School, because again I'm trying to decentralise the School.

I think it is very important as well that people have an alternative place to send their children. Some people who live in Leeds don't want to send their kids at 11 down to some park in London (White Lodge in Richmond Park). We have one of the biggest thriving junior associate centres in Birmingham and they all work with the Company, they're part of the Company family. Then they hit 11 and they have to wave bye bye and go down to the Park. And they don't want to - and they all say 'I wish there was a school near so we can stay close'. They're very keen that any company of any standing that has its own profile, which Birmingham Royal Ballet is acquiring now, has a school, that it can influence not just in the work that it does, but in the people that they have. There has been an awful lot of publicity now about perceived problems from the Royal Ballet School about a year ago, and so there is some complete tosh about - well most of it was complete tosh. But there is still underneath it all a better way of treating children who after all are going into an extremely rigorous dance training. There's no two ways about it - there's a big fall out, a big casualty rate, not many jobs at the end of it, but you don't have to treat them like little robots from 11 in order to get them to be that thing.

Jo Butterworth

What do you believe needs changing in terms of training?

David Bintley

I just think that somehow there's got to be a point where there is a better demarcation between that kind of discipline and what can be perceived as bullying. And as somebody who has kids, I always think that the debate about punishment is interesting, because you can't really reason with a three-year-old not to eat sweets ten minutes before dinner. They scream and they howl and you can't reason with them. And some people say that if you give them a wallop - but I mean that's why the whole issue about the Royal Ballet School came about, because you are talking about something that is very physical. It's a fine line and I think that needs addressing in the teaching of young kids.

In classical dance a lot of children start at a very young age and many of them don't have a lot of outside experience of real life. There are people in their mid thirties who started when they went to school at eight or nine, and went to that one institution right through. They're not complete idiots, they're not children, but they certainly have had a degree of shielding from the real world. Whereas a lot of people who go into modern dance go through college and university and start their training at that time, and they have a life outside. And I personally didn't go to the Royal Ballet School until I was 17 and I'm glad.

Jo Butterworth

So, if you were given carte blanche, what opportunities would you like to see made available in this country to ensure the health of the art form generally? A wish list!

David Bintley

I want things for us to be cheap, I want tickets to be cheap; I wish that more of the funding that we do get would simply go to making tickets cheaper so people would come more. Because the more people that come, the more people know about dancing, the more they value dancing.

Also I really would dearly like to break down all of the barriers between everything, that many people seem to like to keep in place. I think that critics and people who write about us like to keep those barriers there. 90% of the people who write about dance never take the young classical choreographer seriously because he is a classical choreographer. Simply because he works with toe shoes... He's trying to acquire 200 years of knowledge before he rejects it all, yet it's almost impossible to acquire all those skills and practise them, because the only way you acquire them is by doing them. In a sense it is more difficult than in modern dance because you can't acquire 16 ballet dancers at the end of a day to practise, but classical choreographers have got to acquire those skills or classical companies will become redundant. Having those numbers there just to perform a nineteenth century work is irrelevant and a waste of money.

Points raised in discussion:

- The issue of how classically trained dancers adapted to work by choreographers with a modern or eclectic training was raised. David Bintley was of the opinion that classic training in fact gives dancers the versatility to cope with other styles of dance, and that the BRB dancers were always willing to engage with new styles and challenges. He felt that it is the choreographer's responsibility to communicate effectively with dancers in the studio to help them engage with his/her style.

- Comparisons were made with other ballet companies in mainland Europe. Bintley questioned whether there was a connection between the fact that the Paris Opera Ballet had not produced a choreographer of note for over a generation and its insistence on keeping to an established, rigid, hierarchical, 'factory-like' system of managing its dancers. BRB consciously includes choreographic opportunities for dancers within the scope of their employment.

- Bintley has a vision of very direct contact between BRB and the branch of the Royal Ballet School in Birmingham. He would like Company professionals to input directly into aspects such as pas-de-deux, make-up and music. Young artists will be encouraged to access their imaginations alongside the development of their classical technique.

- Bintley spoke about the value of teaching and choreographing in the educational context for the dancers in the Company. It has made dancers feel less a 'part of the machine' and given them vital insights into the working of their own company and art form. Significantly it has helped a number of dancers who were concerned about feeling isolated outside London to feel part of their new home city and to become aware that it is not the cultural desert which they had feared.

Session 28
Looking Forward

Keywords:

the future   choreography   promoters   funding   nurturing
culture   new media

Jonathan Burrows, Guy Cools and Rui Horta, from London, Belgium and Germany respectively, contribute to an interchange and debate about creative processes between artists, producers, funders and the academies. They chart possible future directions for choreographic development and make suggestions for how we might implement them in our respective situations. The session was chaired by Assis Carreiro from the Bockenheimer Depot in Frankfurt.

Assis Carreiro

There have been some very inspiring personal revelations during the Conference from artists, promoters, managers, teachers, about models which do work, which do allow us to flourish and which do avoid the paper chase. These models put responsibility and trust in artists. But we still have a long way to go, and whilst we are looking forwards, we need to move forwards. I want to share with you a quote from an aboriginal relating to western culture: an aboriginal said to a westerner, "It seems business has become a hazard to you. Your businesses were started so people could get better items collectively than they could get for themselves and as a method to express individual talent and become part of your money system, but now the goal of business is to stay in business."

Rui Horta

Choreographic culture

The first topic I wish to speak of is our own choreographic culture. Dance is at the crossroads of several art forms, which offers many opportunities, but it is also very demanding for the choreographer. We can make our choices about music, sets, lighting, conceptual goals, but with this emancipation comes a responsibility, too. It means that one has to have at least a grounding knowledge and good taste on which to base those decisions.

Lately, some of the most innovative dance events have not been directed by choreographers, but by very creative and skilful artists who have used dance to communicate their goals. I believe it is time to learn from these experiences and to understand that a choreographer is someone who uses the movement language to create strong theatrical events impossible to dissociate from other art forms. If I think about the challenges of the future in the choreographic creation I would mention this one: knowing how to use these arts forms in an intelligent aesthetic way, without being lost in the gimmicks of exciting tools, and keeping the body in movement as the key protagonist of our research.

I do believe that the best way to develop interesting choreographers is to develop really good dancers. This means people involved in the creative process, interpreters that are implicated with their generosity, physicality and often with their ideas. Therefore we should think of a sophisticated educational system based as much as possible in scientific knowledge, experience, and a respect for the individual as a whole, never dissociated from the cultural environment.

In the performing arts circuit we need promoters and organisers standing on the side of the choreographers, sand actively involved with the struggle of the creation, and not people exercising power for power's sake. We need professionals who help the profession as fund raisers, curators and organisers, spotting talent and nurturing the future of our art form, but leaving the initiative to the artists, and never losing the perspective of serving the culture we share.

I would also like to consider journalists and critics as belonging to our profession and not as outsiders. I believe that the press that writes about art is interested in art and, therefore, has an overall supportive role. With all the respect for freedom of speech, I would just say that one should think carefully before saying 'no', and how to say 'no'. Our's is a very fragile scene.

Choreography and social development

My second topic is that I believe that choreography cannot be isolated from social development. We are part of a society of services. More and more people are doing jobs not connected with the production or transformation of essential goods. Seventy or eighty percent of our work force is involved in administrative work (this is often the case in the performing arts, where we see heavier and heavier structures. Sometimes it takes 600 people to facilitate 150 artists to work... and usually the dance company is in the basement...).

We are mainly reorganising and administrating – this is not a judgement, it is a reality from which we can not escape. This causes major alterations in our values and in the way we relate to each other. Most of us are living in urban spaces and urban spaces means that we often are displaced from our dreams, dealing with very complex systems. There is a schizophrenic distance between the mind and the body, so the body is lost. I came here in a taxi; there are hardly any trees in the centre of the city, and the only part of nature which I could see was my own flesh. The body becomes a refuge, the last place where we can store our emotions. And the theatre is where we put bodies, like a museum. You go to the theatre and you say, 'Oh, look, a body !' In thirty years it is going to be like that.

We are specialists of the moving body, so I think we have something to say in a society that is isolating itself from the body, and that is loosing a solid, archaic relation with that same body. Theatres are one of the last ritual places of our times, places where we come together to sit, talk and think. So we should think about what we do on stage. We have to ask ourselves with a certain amount of humility 'where do we come from ?' and 'who are we serving in the first place?' or 'can we produce something with a positive social effect?'. A good culture follows up what a good education started, but can also help to adjust what a bad education missed.

The growing choreographer

This conference focused intensely on the idea 'how to form a choreographer'. Again, I would like to stress the importance of the relationship dancer/dance maker. Becoming a choreographer is a very personal enterprise and each of us had his/her way to find it. Still, I do believe that if a dancer has a strong creative potential and is able to express it during his performing years, he has a much better chance to surface as an interesting choreographer. Part of the solution belongs to us choreographers (we should stop complaining), and we must take responsibility for the stimulation of dancers to develop their creativity and, if possible, give them chances to choreograph also. We should not be afraid of bringing competition into our own houses. It is a beautiful thing to pass on knowledge.

At this point the role of the dance promoter is vital, since they are often aware of the emerging talent and can provide the next qualitative step. In her paper, Maria de Assis referred very wisely that subsidies can be given in a sensitive way, and sometimes, even if you give less money but you give it at the right time, you are really doing the right thing.

About the question 'can choreography be taught?' I don't think we can find easy answers. Surely the basic ideas of composition as well as comprehensive knowledge about aesthetics and related art fields can be part of a curriculum. And I do believe that one can be given the chance of trying one's first pieces inside the walls of the institution. But the real stuff happens after that education, in the real world, like most of the jobs. The case of the Portuguese scene is clear: we all left to look for something else, and we came back to do own pieces and find our personal language. Besides that, we knew each other, we worked with each other and with varied degrees of complicity, we collaborated (and disagreed) with each other. The simple fact that choreographers were talking to choreographers made a real big difference. So, I can imagine that supporting a 'local scene' to develop and exchange ideas, is also a long term way of 'forming' a choreographer.

Composition is a very complex building, almost like trying to make sense of a chaotic universe (and often a very chaotic soul) and recycling it into a dance piece. It is not only about administrating dance steps: it is about combining theatrical elements, it is about ideas, it is about life. And in this process we are in a very solitary journey. There is no such thing as a ready made choreographer. Like a good doctor, he studies all his/her life. Choreography is about constant researching to develop to your full potential, so it cannot be a case of 'look, we found a choreographer'. The problem is that the marketing system uses a choreographic talent for instance success, like any other product. If in one way the promoter is vital in discovering and nurturing young talents, on the other he should resist the quick trends of the scene, developing complicities that last for longer periods and create a sense of stability in order to develop a sense of risk taking from the artist and not just immediate success.

My experience as a choreographer is actually an interesting (and atypical) one. I started my choreographic experiences in Portugal during the eighties away from the scrutiny of the mainstream European scene. I could do my mistakes (and I did a lot of them) and, although they were never 'forgiven' at home, no one outside got to see them... Would it be the same, if I had developed in a more cosmopolitan environment? I don't think so... Later, when I came to Frankfurt, I got from the Mousonturm and Dieter Buroch, the right help in the right moment in time: I had behind me a structure that enabled me to really concentrate on my creative work, and besides that, the result of many years of tryouts (and mistakes) was suddenly seen in a very unexpected way, creating a lot of interest. Now, in what I would call a third phase, and after seven years in Frankfurt, I realized I needed a break to rethink my creative work. Stepping aside was my decision and luckily this was a 'luxury' I could afford.

If I mention my experience, it is because it is a microuniverse of ideal development for a creator: In a first phase allowing mistakes, later being supported a steady creative environment and finally allowing a creative break to gather new energies. We have to find ways which enable choreographers to grow steadily. If we want something to grow up, we have to give it a broad basis, allow time and create structures to sustain development. Otherwise we will be sending the wrong message, meaning that the 'dream' of any talented young choreographer will be to join the established scene as soon as he can, looking for a steady job...

Looking ahead

Most of us choreographers, even in my generation, had tremendously repressive and conservative dance educations which tend to be passed on to others also. For years, dance has been taught in a highly systematic and stereotyped way, which prevented communication. We spoke with our bodies, so we were told 'shut up and dance'. The whole system encouraged a sense of competition, and a fear of communication and collaboration. We have to change this system, but the system is very conservative and it perpetuates itself. You suffered, so when the next generation comes in, they suffer again. Someone has to stop this and I trust that a new generation which already experienced a different kind of education will do it. Even if we have differences, we should try to overcome them and get down to practical things. That means engaging in a positive discussion, accepting our differences and learning to listen to each other. We need to resolve our differences so that we can present a united front to the outside when problems arise, and then we can lobby for the good of dance.

In times of crisis, when there is less and less money for culture, the focus becomes fund raising and most of our energy goes into surviving. The artistic views in the debate are often lost at these times. I see a lot of people who were talking about art a few years ago, and now they are exhausted managers trying to make their structures survive. There is a huge obsession with money. You go to someone with an idea and the person says immediately, 'how much does it cost?' If only at first he/she said 'come and sit with me, let's dream first. Let's see if we can do it after, but let's engage in an aesthetic discussion'.

My final comment goes to something that we often forget and that is at the centre of our work : the audience. Dance is often considered as the last art form: for me it is the first. Can we bring the audience to believe in it, too ? We should try to enlarge the basis of our public while keeping the quality of our research. We should reach for new audiences, in schools or in working places and we should keep our own working spaces transparent and accessible.

I think that when we will look back to the cultural history of this century we will be amazed with the 'triumph' of modernism and the recognition of abstract forms in all arts, etc... But without any doubt, the real mass culture, the one that captured our young souls was the pop/rock culture. Putting our snobbishness and elitism aside, couldn't we reach for these people, couldn't we try to\ amaze them with our art form?

The non-verbal nature of dance itself is very close to the non-verbal approach of music, making them connected art forms and available to a wide audience of different cultures. As choreographers we have also experienced this, since our cultural market is very wide and creates the possibilities of exiting tours and very rich exchanges, beyond political borders. Ours is a very beautiful profession. So let us take good care of it.

Jonathan Burrows

I would like to take this opportunity to speak from an artist's point of view to the people who are working with artists. Recently I was lucky enough to be asked by Alistair Spalding to programme an evening at the South Bank, so for the first time I was the promoter and it was very interesting. I was very humbled by that experience. I realised how pressurised a promoter feels, how vulnerable a promoter feels, and I realised that even though you bend over backwards to help the artist, there is still somebody who complains to you, so I say all these things with that knowledge. I think that we have to resist the temptation to mistrust artists, to think that what artists do always has to be mediated by a professional. For instance, maybe it is time that the artists got to fly round the world meeting each other. I think the good manager or the good promoter understands the absolute value of unshaped periods of time as a very fertile place for new ideas. By unshaped periods of time, I don't mean research and development, or any other schemes in which you have to jump through hoops to describe what you want to do and justify it. Then by the time you come to do it, you are so bound up with pressure that you can't do it anyway.

Promoting and Mentoring

Yesterday in Julia's session on management I took the opportunity to say why I like the relationship which I have with her as my manager. I said that something which she does, and which promoters can also do, is on the one hand to protect my sense of freedom, and on the other hand to open doors and then stand quietly back. I might not go through the door or I might not go through it straightaway, but it is there. There is often more than one door open at the same time and she never pushes me. The subject of mentoring has come up a lot. I have been asked many times to do mentoring jobs. I agreed once, and I found that the biggest problem was that since I was being paid, I felt that I had to do something. I must say that I made a complete mess of it, because actually what I should have been doing was nothing. I think this is something which we need to think about. I have worked with a composer called Matteo Fargion as my mentor. If I have a problem with my work, I telephone Matteo and he comes round to my house. We watch the video, and he never says a word but I know immediately what is wrong. Payment can sometimes twist the priorities. Always remember that however vulnerable you might feel as a promoter, when the artist is making something, or just before or just after a performance, they are in a place where they feel as if they have opened themselves up. It is a frightening place and it needs very careful handling. I think that something which helps everybody is for us all to remember that our mistakes are as great an asset as our successes, and that often we learn more from those mistakes.

David Gordon said yesterday, "One should be able to say, I like this idea, I don't like that idea, but I like you". We are separate from our work and you can accept us as people even if you hate what we do. There is whole network of promoters here in Britain and across Europe, and I enjoy travelling around Europe and performing in different festivals. All this did not exist until recently and we should celebrate it. At the same time we could all work towards it being a little less of a meat market. What is the relationship between manager and artist, between promoter and artist? I think it is a relationship of collaboration. Kevin Volans, the composer, said to me, "The point of collaboration is the point when you ask the right person to work with you and after that you take the responsibility. You are as responsible for how they mess up as they are, because you asked them. and you just have to trust them." That is true on both sides of the coin, for the artists and for the managers and for the promoters. Before you get into this relationship, ask yourself very clearly, "What do you want? What are you expecting? Is it there, or not?" Don't do it for the wrong reasons. People are always asking me, "What is dance? Is it theatre?" I don't think there is any other art form which is so good at splitting itself up into classifications; theatre, abstract, classical, contemporary. For me, dance is performance. The notion that performance equals theatre is a very Western notion and I think performance can be performance.

The Meadow Effect

I will sum up by mentioning the Greenhouse Effect. To me a greenhouse is something you put things in to grow bigger, but I think that prioritising growth in that way builds hierarchies and I am not sure whether hierarchies are useful. I want to suggest that what we're really looking for is something which I might call the Meadow Effect. You have grasses and really delicate blue flowers and you also have some trees. But you want them all and the promoter's job is to let the public in and nature will take its course. The strong things will grow and the weak things won't grow, or they'll grow into something else. In cases of absolute passion the promoter might look out for a few of the more delicate plants. We often speak about 'the minority art form' in which we are all involved. I recently took part in the last two nights of the Hamburg Summer Festival which was a huge dance event with hundreds of people doing various things. There was a sell-out audience of 1000 people for 2 nights and they sat there until one o'clock in the morning watching new work. I think we should all stop apologising for what we do.

Guy Cools

New media and dance

A conference is currently being held in Frankfurt under the title: 'Vision Zukunft 2', which among other things focuses on the future of the performing arts in the next century. I attended the first edition one and a half years ago, which dealt with the use of new media and new technologies in the performing arts. I myself have always been rather sceptical about this. For one thing, I have never in my entire professional career seen a performance which really benefited from the use of new media. Either they are just an effect or gimmick of the scenography or they render the three-dimensional live aspect indirectly into a two-dimensional experience. To boot it is ironical to notice that the biggest investments made in the industry of new media (e.g. computer games and film animation) are, of all things, made to try to make the illusion of the live aspect of three-dimensionality as perfect as possible. So I attended the conference with some reserve. Fortunately, with the exception of the first speaker who gave a very naive and simplified 'vision' of how new media could be applied in the theatre, most other speakers didn't project their ideas about the future, but rather spoke about the past. Futurology can only be developed out of analogies with past experiences.

My first thesis is that the future of dance or the performing arts in general lies not in the imitation or integration of new media in the theatre. To put it more bluntly, I am convinced that they shouldn't be applied at all, or at least not as part of the conceptual element. They may always be useful as a technique or means, but only to support the way in which dance adheres to its fundamental anthropological origin, i.e. the live performance of one human being in the presence of another.

The essential qualities of live performance

The more new media and new communication technologies invade everyday public life, and as such replace direct 'eye-to-eye' contact, the more people will look for compensation to experience the live element in the private space of the theatre. As such, I think there is a danger in the way the performing arts are sometimes produced and presented by structures which try to imitate the state of perfection and control you can reach, e.g. in film. The main quality of the live performance lies in its necessarily unsuccessful striving for perfection.

Here are two examples to illustrate this. A couple of years ago, I was the privileged witness of an intimate dialogue between Steve Paxton and Yvonne Rainer at a colloquium in Montpellier, France. At a certain point in the conversation Yvonne confessed to Steve that she had left dance in order to produce films because she was a control freak and couldn't stand the imperfections of her medium any longer. Paxton, however, cultivated them in his improvisations. I need not explain to a professional dance audience that high quality improvisations aren't anything-is-possible events but highly organised performances in which an underlying, preconceived structure creates a frame and as such allows the freedom of the actual 'hic et nunc' improvisation.

In a similar way, the production structures and rehearsal periods of dance should be organised in such a way that they allow unforeseen 'accidents' to happen without threatening the final result. Here are two examples of this out of my own practice as a producer. Last May within one week we had both the premiers of new creations by Alain Platel *(Iets op Bach)* and Jonathan Burrows *(Things I don't know)*. In both cases we had to adapt the programme at the last minute because something went wrong. In *Iets op Bach* a dancer seriously injured her elbow. The premiere had to be postponed for two days. Her role was rewritten and she performed it wearing a plaster cast. Burrows' *Things I don't know* could be performed as intended, but the other part of the programme *Quintet* had to be replaced because one of the dancers in it also got injured. We replaced it with a live version of *Hands* and the percussion piece *Donna Che Beve* by Matteo Fargion, which fitted the new piece so well that since then it has continued to be part of the programme. It is my conviction that in both cases the quality of the work depends on or lies in the way these last minute changes can be integrated and in certain cases may even improve the final result. One of my favourite books illustrates this. It is called *Use your Defects* by Grace Jones. Organisation and preparation are not there to fix a result but to keep it as open as possible, ideally until the last minute of the actual performance.

My second thesis is therefore that the future of dance lies in the celebration of its, by definition, unsuccessful effort to achieve perfection. The tension and the energy of the live performance, which are two of its major constituent elements, are derived from the friction between this striving for perfection and the way in which it is more or less successful.

Multidisciplinarity and dance

A third thesis is related to the concept of multidisciplinarity. I think we all too often have a superficial, not to say wrong concept of this basic art principle. It is not because you place together or even mix different art forms that your work will become more multidisciplinary. To me multidisciplinarity relates to the actual process of renewal in which a particular art form uses some concepts of another art form as a source, translates these (cf. R. Jakobson's concept of transmutation) towards its own discipline and as such adds new possibilities to its own range of means of expression. As such dance is one of the most, if not the most, multidisciplinary art form because in its ranks you find artists who use the whole range of other art forms (music, theatre, literature, visual arts, film, etc.) as a source for its own renewal.

My third thesis thus is that dance should celebrate its basic quality of multidisciplinarity and continue to use the whole range of other art forms as a source for its own renewal.

Until now I have expressed a fundamentally optimistic view on the future of dance, as long as it sticks to some of its basic artistic and conceptual qualities, such as the live aspect, imperfection and multidisciplinarity. There are, of course, also some negative signs, especially with regard to the political and economic structures which are supposed to support dance. From time to time I, too, have serious doubts about the future.

For one thing dance remains too dependent on the production and presentation practices of the more dominant theatre or music theatre. As such its development is slowed down, more for economic than artistic reasons. In my contribution to the book *Creative People: Current Issues and Future Strategies for Dance Management*, which will appear later in the year with MacMillan Press, I tried to describe some of the strategies which might be helpful in combating this.

In my more recent thinking, however, I am convinced that dance should not only invade the theatres more but also other public spaces such as museums, art galleries, concert halls and even the street. The dance policy here in Britain in this particular case, is a forerunner and an example for continental Europe.

Also with the latter you have to be careful, because popularising the art form doesn't necessarily mean improving its quality and its social position. At the launch of the new theatre season we had a public debate about the 'arts mountain'. The question was raised as to whether too much art was perhaps being produced. I was asked by *De Standaard*, one of our national newspapers, to express my point of view on the issue. Although I didn't know at that time that I would attend this conference, I started my contribution with the question of whether the profusion of art might be responsible for the greenhouse effect, and I argued that this is an absurd question because there can never be enough art, there can never be enough quality.

Democracy and the arts

Do allow me to expand on this point of view. Although I am myself a product of the democratisation of higher education, I think it wise to be wary of a democracy without value hierarchies, since this yields states of confusion such as the one in which our society is currently living. In my opinion this is best described in Kazuo Ishiguro's novel *The Unconsoled*. In this novel Ishiguro draws a surrealistic portrait of a European middle-sized town, where everybody has lost his direction and where all hopes are pinned on some 'guidelines' from a famous foreign musician and 'director'. The timetable of the foreign artist is constantly messed up, though, and instead of being able to prepare himself properly for his concert/talk, he is constantly being led astray and wasting time on trivial matters.

Not by coincidence, the second edition of the colloquium in Frankfurt deals with democracy and the arts. In the same way that the first edition concluded that to save the future we have to celebrate the past qualities, this time they might well conclude that in order to guarantee the pluralism of our society and of the arts in particular, we have to find less 'democratic' ways to organise it.

For one thing, both the production and reception of our access to art have never been democratic and never will be. Simply compare the production budgets and the ticket prices of opera with those of contemporary dance. More fundamentally, also with regard to the underlying conceptual and aesthetic principles, we should make clearer distinctions between a mature artist who really masters the principles of his art form and may even have added some of his own invention and a younger or less talented artist who is just being a good pupil or craftsman. In a pluralistic and diverse landscape they all deserve a place, but these should be better defined and not intertwined. I am not pleading for the restoration of a traditional vertical hierarchy based on power, but rather for a horizontal hierarchy of well-defined positions – for creative art, education, community based work, etc. - based on competence in a diverse landscape with flexible structures which allow people to change position when they are up to it.

Concrete Utopia

I know this may sound highly idealistic and utopian, especially with respect to the existing political and economic structures, but we are here together to dream aloud, aren't we? I myself am an adept of the German philosopher Ernst Bloch, who introduced the concept of concrete utopia. If you believe in your ideals, you have to try to change reality step by step in the direction of this ideal but at the same time your ideal has to be redefined in the direction of reality too otherwise it will become dogmatic. I have seen this model being applied successfully in micro- and meso-contexts, so why not be ambitious and try to apply it to a more major macro-context?

I therefore think it is good for the evolution of dance that some of our major artists not only concentrate on their own artistic creation, but also take responsibility for their whole community. I am referring to Anna Teresa De Keersmaeker, who with PARTS created a greenhouse for the next generation; to William Forsythe, who is taking artistic responsibility for TAT in Frankfurt or to some of the mentoring projects which have been discussed during this conference, like the International Course for Professional Choreographers and Composers, organised by Gale Law here at Bretton Hall.

Biographies of Presenters

Germaine Acogny, Choreographer & Dancer, Senegal/France

Germaine has emerged as one of the world's most pivotal figures in modern African dance. She grew up as a member of the Yoruba tribe. Following studies in Paris, she began an exhaustive study of the different forms of African dance and then developed a structured system whereby it could be taught as a technique. In 1977, Germaine joined forces with Maurice Bejart to found the Pan African dance school Mudra Afrique in Senegal. The school attracted dancers from all over Africa and the West, and combined teaching in both African and contemporary dance. Today, she runs her own centre in Toulouse and is soon to open an international centre for African Dance near Dakar in Senegal. Her performance and masterclass at London's South Bank met with an overwhelming response and won her the 1991 Dance Umbrella/Time Out for outstanding achievement. Germaine's work has provided inspiration to dancers from all backgrounds for the past twenty five years.

Richard Alston, Artistic Director, Richard Alston Dance Company, London, England

Richard Alston trained at the London Contemporary Dance School where he made his first work. He went on to choreograph for London Contemporary Dance Theatre before forming Strider in 1972. In 1980 he was appointed Resident Choreographer with Ballet Rambert becoming the Company's Artistic Director in 1986. In 1993 he took up the position of Artist-in-Residence with the Contemporary Dance Trust and in 1994 was appointed the Trust's Artistic Director, with forming his own company an important part of his brief. Richard Alston Dance Company was launched in November 1994. This year he celebrated 30 years of choreography as well as his 50th birthday.

Janet Archer, Director, Dance City, Newcastle upon Tyne, England

Janet originally trained at the Welsh College of Music and Drama in Cardiff followed by time at the London School of Contemporary Dance and the Rambert Academy after winning the Cosmopolitan Dance Award in 1981. After three years as a freelance dancer and choreographer during which she worked with Diversions Dance Theatre, HTV Wales and S4C she was appointed as a community dance co-ordinator in Bridgend, South Wales. That was her lead to a similar position in Welwyn Hatfield, Hertfordshire where she eventually became Arts Manager. In 1996 Janet created Nexus Dance - a repertory company which toured throughout the UK and internationally. Janet took up the post of Artistic Director at Dance City in 1991. Janet is a board member for Phoenix Dance Company, the Dancers Resettlement Trust, and the Association of National Dance Agencies, and represents the NDAs as an observer on Dance UK's Executive. In the past she has sat on the boards of Diversions and the Foundation for Community Dance.

John Ashford, The Place Theatre Director, London, England

John Ashford has been Theatre Director at The Place in London since 1987, initiating the annually repeated dance seasons Spring Loaded, Resolution!, The Turning World and Re:Orient, the choreographic research project Choreodrome, and the international showcase for British dance Spring Collection. The Place Theatre now presents 32 weeks of independent dance each year, and leads London's National Dance Agency with its Resident Companies, Choreographer-in-Residence, Associate Artists and Dance Services including the Video Place. He was previously Director of the ICA Theatre, and founding Theatre Editor of Time Out, the London listing magazine, championing Fringe Theatre and performance work.

Maria de Assis, Festival, Encontros Acarte, Lisbon, Portugal

Maria studied dance and music, and graduated in history. She pursued further studies in Arts Business and Administration. She worked as professional journalist and dance critic for several Portuguese newspapers and dance magazines, and was the author and presenter of cultural programmes for radio and television. She is the author of a book entitled *Movimentos*, interviewing 19 independent Portuguese choreographers published by Canças na Cidade festival. She also co-authored the book *Dançaram em Lisboa* (survey of dance in Lisbon, 1890-1994), published by Lisbon 94 and *Present Movement - Aspects of Independent Dance in Portugal* published by Livros Cotovia and Danças na Cidade. Currently Assistant to the Director of ACARTE/Calouste Gulbenkian Foundation and Programming Advisor at CAEV-Centre for the Performing Arts in Viseu.

Professor Christopher Bannerman, Chair, Dance Academic Group, Middlesex University, London, England

Christopher Bannerman has had a long career in the dance profession. As a member of London Contemporary Dance Theatre, he danced numerous principal roles and choreographed many works; he also choreographed for numerous professional companies both in Britain and internationally. In 1989 he became Head of School of Dance at Middlesex University and was awarded the title of Professor of Dance. He is Chair of the National Dance Co-ordinating Committee and Chair of Dance UK, who work to improve the profile of dance and to voice the concerns of the dance profession, from dancers' health to housing for dance.

Thea Barnes, Artistic Director, Phoenix Dance Company, Leeds, England

Thea Nerissa Barnes has been the Artistic Director for Phoenix Dance Company since January, 1997. She performed with Alvin Ailey Dance Company, Martha Graham Dance Company, on Broadway and on television in work by Alvin Ailey and Martha Graham, as well as appearing in the Arts Council of England's educational documentary entitled *Not Just a Somersault*. Having taught choreography and technique in community and academic situations in the USA, Britain and Europe, Thea's experience crosses a range of jazz and contemporary dance expressions and management. She is pursuing her Ph.D

Ken Bartlett, Director, Foundation for Community Dance, Leicester, England

Before becoming Director of the Foundation for Community Dance, Ken was Head of Arts and Cultural Sevices for Walsall MBC, with overall responsibility for the development of arts policies and strategies across council services, reporting directly to elected members on planning, delivery, evaluation and finance of arts services. The key to the arts policy he developed was that it should be centred on the needs and aspirations of local people. He was advisor to West Midlands Arts and raised substantial funding for capital and revenue projects from the EU, Arts Council of England as well as from the private and charity sectors. As a member of the Schools' Inspectorate for Walsall he had responsibility for Arts Education and in-service training for teachers, youth and community education workers. Prior to that he has variously been an actor and teacher/lecturer in drama, dance and cultural policy across the spectrum of age, ability and background in this country and abroad.

Theresa Beattie, Director, The Place Dance Services, London, England

Theresa worked at Sadler's Wells for five years initiating and developing the theatre's community and education programme and then moved to the South Bank Centre for a further five years to develop the dance programme and administer international festivals. She subsequently worked freelance with clients including Dance Umbrella and London Arts Board. Currently she is Director of The Place Dance Services; an information, support and professional development initiative for the independent dance profession based at The Place.

David Bintley, Artistic Director, Birmingham Royal Ballet, Birmingham, England

David Bintley succeeded Sir Peter Wright as Director of Birmingham Royal Ballet in 1995. His many ballets for both the Royal Ballet companies include: *Consort Lessons, Still Life at the Penguin Café, Hobson's Choice, Tombeaux, Carmina Burana, The Nutcracker Sweeties, The Protecting Veil* and *Far From the Madding Crowd*. His work is in the repertory of companies in America, Canada, Germany, Hong Kong and South Africa. He has had particularly fruitful collaborations with San Francisco Ballet for whom he has created several original works including the full length ballet *Edward ll*.

Louise Bridges

After graduating from Bretton Hall in 1994, Louise returned to her greatest passion, writing. She has had poems published in The North and Anchor Books. She is currently an Equities Dealer in Leeds.

Val Bourne, Artistic Director, Dance Umbrella, London, England

Val Bourne trained at the Royal Ballet School, London, and performed, briefly, with the Royal Ballet Company and then with Sadler's Wells Opera Ballet for three years. In 1968 she became Press and Marketing Officer for London Festival Ballet and a year later moved to do the same job for Ballet Rambert, where she remained for 8 years. After a year in the Dance Department at the Arts Council, Val was appointed the first Dance Officer for Greater London Arts. Whilst still at GLA, she organised the first two Dance Umbrella Festivals with Ruth Glick, in 1978 and 1980. Dance Umbrella is now established as an annual festival in London and has also initiated three other regional festivals, in Leicester, Newcastle and, most recently, Woking. In 1985, Val was awarded a 'Bessie' a.k.a. New York Dance and Performance Award and in 1989 she received the first Digital Dance Premier Award in recognition of her outstanding contribution to British Dance. The prize money accompanying the Award went towards the funding of Lloyd Newson's production of 'Dead Dreams of Monochrome Men' for DV8. In March 1990 Val received the International Theatre Institute's award in recognition of her achievements in international dance. In the summer of 1991, under the Queen's Birthday Honours List, she was awarded/received an OBE and in 1992, Dance Umbrella won the prestigious Prudential Awards for Dance and for the Arts. In 1994, Dance Umbrella was again awarded the Prudential Award for Dance. In 1996, Val became a Chevalier dans l'Ordre des Arts et Lettres.

Carol Brown, Choreographer, Carol Brown Dances, London, England

Choreographer in Residence at The Place Theatre, London, Carol Brown originally trained in Central European dance in New Zealand, Australia and Europe, where she has performed with Dunedin Dance Theatre, Dance=Arts and Bronwyn Judge. She has degrees in dance and history, and in 1995, Carol completed one of the first doctorates in practical choreographic research at the University of Surrey. Since 1995, Carol has worked as a freelance choreographer, performer, lecturer and Artistic Director of her own company, Carol Brown Dances. Carol has most recently been shortlisted for the Jerwood Award and been awarded a commission to complete a live art collaboration with Esther Rowlinson for a tour of galleries in the South East region. Her new choreographic work, entitled *Like a House on Fire*, will premiere in Spring '99.

Jonathan Burrows, Artistic Director, Jonathan Burrows Group, London, England

Jonathon Burrows danced in The Royal Ballet from 1979 - 1991. From 1979 - 1983 he choreographed a number of commissioned pieces, and showed work independently. The Jonathan Burrows Group was formed in 1988 and is one of Britain's leading dance companies and much in demand throughout Europe. Between 1997 and 1998 the Group has shown seven of his works: *Hymns, dull morning, Stoics, Very, Our, The Stop Quartet* and *Quintet*. In 1995 Burrows choreographed two films: a 'Dance for the Camera' piece *Hands* and *blue yellow* for Sylvie Guillem. His piece for Frankfurt Ballet, *Walking/music*, premiered in 1997. His latest work, *Things I Don't Know* is touring in 1998. He is Choreographer in Residence at the South Bank Centre in 1998/1999.

Rosemary Butcher, Choreographer in Residence, Laban Centre, London

Rosemary Butcher is one of the most important and influential choreographic artists working in Britain today. With over thirty works to her credit, she has had a radical effect on dance in the UK, and a prestigious group of choreographers and dancers have emerged from her company over the last twenty years. She firmly established the concept of movement as a cerebral form of expression and has developed a unique dance vocabulary that is pure, minimal and performed with minute attention to detail. Rosemary Butcher is renowned for her teaching of improvisation techniques. She spent a number of years as an advisory teacher in dance in London, followed by a lectureship in Dance Studies at the University of Surrey. She recently joined the dance faculty of the Laban Centre London.

Jo Butterworth, Head of Centre for Dance and Theatre Studies, University College Bretton Hall, Wakefield, England

Jo trained at the Laban Art of Movement Studio in Addlestone and Goldsmith's College, University of London, and received an MA in Performance Studies from New York University. She introduced the BA Hons Dance degree at Bretton in 1988, and the MA Contemporary Performing Arts (Dance) in 1994. A board member of Motionhouse Dance Theatre, Jo is also a committee member of the ELIA (European League of Institutes for the Arts) Dance Section. She is Conference Director of The Greenhouse Effect.

Assis Carreiro, Artistic Director, TAT, Bockenheimer Depot, Frankfurt, Germany

Born in Portugal and raised in Canada, Assis holds a BA Honours in Dance History and Criticism from York University, Toronto, Canada and MA (distinction) in Dance Studies from Surrey University, Guildford, England. She worked for The National Ballet of Canada in various capacities, culminating in her appointment as the Company's first Director of Education and Community Outreach. Assis was founding Executive Director of the DanceXchange, a National Dance Agency in Birmingham, England. She is Vice Chair of Dance UK; is on the Board of the Jonathan Burrows Group; has acted as an advisor for the Arts Council of England's Arts for Everyone programme, the London Arts Board, the Ontario Arts Council and Canada Council. Most recently, she was Executive for The Place Theatre, and General Manager of London's Peacock Theatre. In September 1998 she joined William Forsythe as Artistic Director of TAT, Bockenheimer Depot in Frankfurt, Germany.

Julia Carruthers, Manager, Jonathan Burrows Group & Russell Maliphant Company, London, England

After a degree in English & German Literature at the University of York, Julia worked as John Drummond's secretary at the Edinburgh International Festival and then with David Gothard at Riverside Studios as Programme Co-ordinator and as the first administrator for the Michael Clark Company. She was Festival Co-ordinator for Dance Umbrella and ran the Independent Dance Programme of masterclasses with Miranda Tufnell. She was Dance Officer at the Arts Council of England before moving to freelance work with Jonathan Burrows Group, Russell Maliphant and other consultancies.

Hilary Carty, Director of Dance, Arts Council of England, London, England

Hilary has been Arts Council Director of Dance since 1994, with responsibility for the development, dissemination and implementation of the dance policy; a varied and diverse role, involving liaison with government, dance artists, supporters/advisers and the national/international arts community. Prior to the Arts Council, Hilary was General Manager of Adzido Pan African Dance ensemble, Arts Officer at East Midland Arts, Community Arts Worker and Development Officer for key Midland-based organisations as well as fulfilling a career as a freelance tutor. Qualifications include a BA Hons in Performing Arts, Certificate in Dance Education and Master of Business Administration. Hilary Carty has a keen interest in the arts, sports and international cultural development.

Gill Clarke, Independent Dance Artist, London, England

A founder member of the Siobhan Davies Dance Company and previously dancer with Janet Smith, Gill works as a freelance performer and choreographer including ongoing projects with Rosemary Butcher and the Gandini Juggling Project. She teaches extensively in the UK and abroad for students, professionals and companies. Gill is Director of the Choreographers and Composers Exchange 1995 and frequent 'mentor' to emerging choreographers. Chair of the Thursday Group, a regular discussion forum for dance artists, and closely involved with Chisenhale Dance Space - an artist driven experimental space – Gill is a member of the executive of Dance UK and the British Association of Choreographers. Recently she and Rachel Gibson co-authored the 'Independent Dance Review' for the Arts Council of England.

Robert Cohan, Choreographer, Gard, France

Robert Cohan trained at the Martha Graham School, moving rapidly into her Company and performing throughout the world as a regular partner of Graham herself. His association with London Contemporary Dance Theatre (LCDT) began in 1967, when he was invited by Robin Howard to become the founder Artistic Director of Contemporary Dance Trust, the body which controlled the Company, London Contemporary Dance School and The Place Theatre. Cohan's influence on the development of modern dance in Britain has been considerable. Having pioneered the introduction of American contemporary dance technique in Britain, he has been instrumental in the development of a vast following, not only for the repertoire of LCDT, but also for the many other British companies and artists which have grown up in the last 20 years. Robert Cohan has been continually in demand as a director of choreographic courses, notably at the International Course for Professional Choreographers and Composers. In 1988 he was awarded an honorary CBE in recognition of his outstanding contribution to dance in the UK. He has since taken British nationality. In 1989, Cohan officially retired from Contemporary Dance Trust, but returned in 1992 as Artistic Advisor.

Guy Cools, Dance Director, Kunstencentrum Vooruit, Ghent, Belgium

After studying German philology and theatre science, Guy combined teaching with freelance criticism and several jobs in the performing arts sector (as a dramaturg and copywriter). Since 1990 he has been working full-time in the Arts Centre Vooruit in Gent, being responsible for the theatre (until 1995) and dance programme (until present). More recently he has also been curating dance projects in Frankfurt (1997) and Venice (1998). His interest in cultural policy resulted in a government mandate as Deputy-Chairman of the Council for Dance, the advisory board for the Minister of Culture of the Flemish Government (since 1993)

Tim Dickinson

Tim has a varied musical background including engineering at Matrix Recording Studios, London for musicians such as Bjork, The Orb and Bryan Ferry and at 'Fon and Axis' in Sheffield for The Spice Girls and 808 State. Tim is currently director of 'Alternative Action Productions', an audio production company creating music for commercials and computer software, managed from the company's 'Silver Studio'. Alternative Action Productions have also produced music for both dance and theatre events for a range of venues.

Hilke Diemer, Co-ordinator of Choreographic Studies, Rotterdamse Dansacademie, Rotterdam, The Netherlands

Hilke Diemer (b.1951, Eindhoven) is a choreographer and teacher of modern dance, teaching methods and improvisation/composition at the Rotterdamse Dansacademie and guest teaching/choreographing with national and international companies and schools. As a result of her experience as a freelance choreographer and teacher, her years on advisory boards, in management and academia, she was the right person to investigate the possibilities of, and develop and co-ordinate the first Choreography Programme in the Netherlands. The first group of five students from the Choreography Programme at the Rotterdamse Dansacademie graduated in June 1998.

Sharon Donaldson, Lecturer in Contemporary Dance, Leeds, England

Sharon (Chantal) Donaldson BA was a pupil at Harehills School before training at the London School of Contemporary Dance. She was a respected performer and choreographer with Phoenix Dance Company from 1989 to 1998 and has danced and taught dance throughout Britain and overseas. She is now a lecturer at the Northern School of Contemporary Dance, where she is planning to develop a professional performance project for touring in the early Summer of 1999.

Sue Doubell, Deputy Head Faculty of Arts, Bretton Hall, Wakefield, England

Complementary to her lecturing duties at Bretton Hall, specialising in Textile Design, Print and CAD, with close industrial links, Sue Doubell has been active in research based project work for the last five years, working on such initiatives as 'TEED - Developing Students' Subject Area Knowledge and Skills in the Workplace', 'A Network in Art & Design' and currently 'A Higher Education Business Partnership for the Clothing and Textile Sectors'. Her current academic role as Deputy Head of Faculty of Arts, encompasses the development of European Funding Initiatives, overall supervision of current Faculty projects and Income Generation alongside supporting duties to the Head of Faculty.

Nancy Duncan, Director/New Initiatives, Pentacle, New York, USA

Nancy Duncan joined Pentacle in 1993 and now serves as Director/New Initiatives. She produced Dancing in the Isles: British Invasion '97, a four-week dance festival in New York City. Duncan founded CoDance Co, a company established to nurture contemporary dance artists. From 1982 - 1990 she commissioned over 50 works supporting 38 choreographers and composers. This earned her a 1991 New York Dance and Performance Award (Bessie). Duncan served as Artistic Director of London Contemporary Dance Theatre (1991 - 1992), was awarded a 1992 National Endowment for the Arts fellowship from the Presenting and Commissioning program, and currently is a Dance program panellist for New Jersey State Council of the Arts.

Roy Fears

Roy Fears trained at Bretton Hall in Theatre Arts. After obtaining his honours degree in 1996 he began touring with Frantic Assembly (Klub), a collaboration that is always re-surfacing. He has worked extensively in Italy on other physical/dance theatre projects, and currently manages Powerhouse 1 Showcase Theatre in Wakefield. Here he promotes productions with an emphasis on 'performance', as well as creating shows in house.

Kevin Finnan, Co-Artistic Director, Motionhouse Dance Theatre, Leamington Spa, England

Kevin Finnan co-founded Motionhouse Dance Theatre with Louise Richards in 1988. Committed to cross art collaboration and new directions in devised dance theatre, he has created all of Motionhouse's productions and also undertakes solo commissions and projects for other companies. Kevin is also director of Fierce, an occasional company created to bring together teams of artists to make new strides in theatre. Fierce are to be commissioned by the Tramway in 2000 to produce *True*, a new work written by A. I. Kennedy, in collaboration with Spanish installation artist Rosa Sanchez. Kevin has a BA (Hons) in Theatre from Dartington College of Arts and an MA (distinction) in Contemporary Performing Arts from Leeds University.

Sandra Fisher

Since 1995 Sandra has worked as a freelance choreographer and co-director of Assault Event, a music/dance/performance management company. Her choreographic work focuses on the production of live art into popular culture. Working closely with experimental musicians, freestyle breakdancers, in-line skaters, BMX'ers and skateboarders, her choreographic works have included commissioned theatre events for the Nott Dance Festival (1997) and Chisenhale Dance/Dance4/Now'97, as part of their Trash season (1997). Sandra has also choreographed for alternative performances such as club events, dance music videos, warehouse parties and fashion shows. Choreographed club events have included sets at the ICA, Oval House and The End London.

Kate Flatt, Senior Dance Lecturer, Middlesex University, Bedford, England

Kate Flatt trained at The Royal Ballet School and the London School of Contemporary Dance, and studied choreography with Nina Fonaroff and Leonide Massine, for whom she worked as an assistant. In 1978 she travelled to study traditional dance in its social and ritual context in Eastern Europe. Early choreographic work was as a British Independent, and broadened in to the fields of national and international opera, theatre and film. Her work includes *Turandot* for the Royal Opera and musical staging for the RSC's *Les Miserables*. In 1994 she created *The Dancing Room*, with Sally Jacobs, filmed for BBC2. She is now a senior lecturer at Middlesex University, a member of the Arts Council Advisory panel and Chair of the British Association of Choreographers (BAC).

Antonia Franceschi, Freelance Dancer and Producer, London, England

Antonia Franceschi was invited by George Balanchine to join the New York City Ballet. There, works were created for her by Balanchine, Robbins, Martins, Lubovitch and La Fosse. Her career in the US has also included working with Makarova & Co., Kevin O'Day Dances, and roles in the films *Fame* and *Grease*. In the UK she has worked with Mark Baldwin, Wayne McGregor, Michael Clark, Arlene Phillips and Matthew Hart. This year she produced and danced in The New York Ballet Stars at Queen Elizabeth Hall.

Vivien Freakley, Co-ordinator, The Black Choreographic Initiative, Burbage, England

Vivien Freakley M. Phil., is a freelance arts education and training consultant working largely in the area of professional development for artists and arts organisations. Until June 1996 she was Head of Performing Arts at Coventry University (formerly Coventry Centre for the Performing Arts). Vivien is also RSA's chief verifier for the Arts & Entertainment Sector NVQs. Current Professional Development Projects include: co-ordination of the Black Choreographic Initiative - a two year programme of artistic development for eight black British choreographers and the Coventry Theatre Network - a three year programme of development for the Belgrade Theatre and seven regionally-based small-scale theatre companies.

Estrella Casero Garcia, Director, Dance Division, University of Alcalá, Madrid, Spain

Professor of Spanish Dance and Dance Director at the University of Alcalá· (Madrid, Spain). Having obtained her degree at the Higher Royal School of Dramatic Dance and Drama of Madrid (1981), she fulfilled a brilliant career as a dancer (National Spanish Dance Company, Anthology of the Zarzuela) and choreographer (Spanish Dance Theater, Boston, USA; her own company and University Dance Group of Alcalá·). Since 1989 she dedicates her time to the organisation and direction of the three main activities carried out at the Dance Division of the University of Alcalá: dance classes for students, a University Dance Group, and the design of the project for the creation of the first university level in dance in Spain.

Rachel Gibson, Freelance Arts Manager, London, England

Rachel Gibson has recently completed the *Independent Dance Review* for the Arts Council in partnership with Gill Clarke. She is currently working in the Development Department at Laban Centre London and is editing a new version of *A Booker's Guide to British Dance* for Dance UK. Her career started at the The Place where she worked in the Theatre Office from 1984 - 1986. This led to programming posts at The Belgrade Theatre in Coventry and Northampton Arts Centre. She was Dance and Mime Officer at East Midlands Arts from 1990 - 1991 and Principal Dance Officer at London Arts Board from 1992 - 1997.

Emma Gladstone, Associate Director, The Place, London, England

Equity card at 17 thanks to Arlene Phillips. History degree, Manchester University. Laban. Mantis. Co-founded and co-directed own company - Adventures in Motion Pictures. Joined the Cholmondeleys (Lea Anderson), core member for eight years. Film work with Wendy Houstoun and Annie Griffin among others. Has lectured and taught in schools, colleges (Surrey University, LCDS), companies (The Cholmondeleys and Featherstoneaughs, DV8, Rosas) and open classes. Produced Rhythm Method with Fin Walker at the South Bank Centre for three years, commissioning and programming independent work.

Leonie Gombrich, General Manager, DV8 Physical Theatre, London, England

Leonie Gombrich has managed DV8 Physical Theatre since 1994, prior to which she was Company Administrator for the Michael Clark Company for one year. Previously she worked at a literary agency and in the music industry, both in New York, and as a researcher for director Mike Leigh.

Ain Gordon, Associate Director, David Gordon Pick-Up Performance Company, New York, NY, USA

Ain Gordon has had his work produced in New York City by Dance Theater Workshop, Performance Space 122, Dancing in the Streets, The Poetry Project at St. Markís, Soho Rep, and New York Dance Theater Workshop. His work has been presented by Dance Place (Washington, DC), the Baltimore Museum of Art, Spirit Square (NC), and the Jacob's Pillow Dance Festival (MA), where he was Artist-in-Residence. He has collaborated with David Gordon (as co-writer, co-director and performer) on *The Family Business*, which received an Obie Award and culminated in a run at the Mark Taper Forum, and on the text for *Punch and Judy Get Divorced*, a musical commissioned by the American Music Theater Festival, and *Art*, which premiered in 1996. They are currently collaborating on *The First Picture Show*, which has been commissioned by the Mark Taper Forum and will premiere in 1999. Gordon's play, *Wallys Ghost*, premiered at Soho Rep and went on to receive an Obie Award in playwriting. His new play, *Birdseed Bundles*, has been workshopped at Soho Rep and presented at the Public Theater's New Works Now series. He is a 1992 and 1998 New York Foundation for the Arts Playwriting Fellow and the recipient of a 1998 John Simon Guggenheim Memorial Foundation Fellowship.

David Gordon, Director, David Gordon Pick-Up Performance Company, New York, NY, USA

David Gordon danced in the companies of James Waring and Yvonne Rainer in the 1960's and made performance work during that period at the Judson Dance Theater. In the early 1970's he worked regularly with the improvisational performance ensemble, The Grand Union. In addition to being Artistic Director of the Pick-Up Performance Co., he has made work for dance companies in the United States and Europe, including American Ballet Theater, Dance Theatre of Harlem, Baryshnikov's Whiteoak company, Groupe de Recherche Choreographique de l'Opera de Paris, Werkcentrum Dans of Rotterdam, Holland and Extemporary Dance Theatre in London. He has also collaborated with Philip Glass on the Brooklyn Academy of Music's production of *The Photographer*. He has worked extensively in film/video and in 1987, three of his video works were screened on the PBS series, Alive and Off Center. That same year, *David Gordon's Made in the USA*, featuring Mikhail Baryshnikov in three of his works, was aired nationally. David Gordon is a Guggenheim Fellow (1981 & 1987) and has served as chairman of the Dance Program panel of the National Endowment for the Arts and as a panellist for the New York State Council on the Arts Dance Program. In September 1984, he received a New York Dance and Art Performance Award (a 'Bessie'), for Sustained Choreographic Achievement. He is profiled in Sally Banes's book *Terpischore in Sneakers*, and by Arlene Croce in the New Yorker. His teaching activities have included residencies at Harvard University, the American Dance Festival, New York University, and the American Center in Paris. The Pick-Up Company featured in a number of Dance Umbrella Festivals both at Riverside Studios and at Sadler's Wells. Most recently, David has found new fame as a theatre director, writing and directing plays with his gifted son Ain Gordon. He has also directed Max Frisch's *The Firebugs* for the Guthrie Theatre in Minneapolis, and both choreographed and directed I B Singer's *Shlemiel the First* for American Repertory Theatre. In a recent interview in Dance Theatre Journal, Roger Copeland writes about David Gordon: 'he isn't the first choreographer to make a contribution to the theatre. (One thinks above all of Jerome Robbins). But Gordon is the first dance person who's as much a playwright as a choreographer' - and it's those special qualities and his experience which he would bring to the 'The Outside Eye'.

Jane Greenfield, Director, Dance 4, Nottingham, England

Jane Greenfield is Director of Dance 4, the National Dance Agency based at PreSet Studios in Nottingham. Dance 4 supports the creativity, experimentation and presentation of innovative dance work through a programme of residencies, commissions and promotions, and presents work through its NOTT Dance Festival and Body Space Image season. The company also runs outreach programmes throughout Nottinghamshire and provides resources, information and advice for dance practitioners in the East Midlands. Previously Jane worked as a programmer for Nottinghamshire 'Next Stage' Adult Education and for Nottingham Playhouse and she was Dance Animateur for Derbyshire and Norwich.

Karen Greenhough, Co-ordinator of Choreographic Studies, London Contemporary Dance School, London, England

Karen's training in Canada was in theatre and dance. She went on to choreograph and perform there and also to teach contemporary technique and choreography, principally at Simon Fraser University. In 1985 she moved to London. After finishing her studies she taught at a variety of dance schools and colleges throughout Britain. As an independent choreographer Karen has often collaborated with other artists to create multi-faceted works which bring together dance and theatre, music and visual design. Presently, Karen works as an independent choreographer and teaches full-time at LCDS where she is Co-ordinator of Choreographic Studies.

Paula Hampson, Dance Performer, Teacher and Choreographer, London, England

Paula has been working as an independent dancer, teacher and choreographer since 1989. She has worked nationally and internationally with renowned companies and artists such as the Gregory Nash Group, Maclennan Dance and Company, Julyen Hamilton, Gaby Agis and Small Bones Dance Company. Her own work has received support from Northwest Arts Board, the Arts Council of England, Merseyside Dance Initiative, local authorities, The Prince's Trust, and both Suffolk and Dance Northwest Agency. Paula is a recipient of a Bonnie Bird Choreographic Award, a Wingate Scholarship and is an Associate Artist with Suffolk Dance Agency. Paula has studied in Europe and North America with Nancy Stark-Smith, Julyen Hamilton, Joan Skinner and Ruth Zapora, developing many skills in improvisation, voice work and Action Theatre. Paula has taught in further education colleges, schools, arts centres and dance agencies and organisations throughout the United Kingdom.

Ismo-Pekka Heikinheimo, Lecturer and Choreographer, Theatre Academy of Finland, Dance Department, Helsinki, Finland

Born in Lapland, Finland, Ismo graduated from London Contemporary Dance School in 1989. He has choreographed 14 major works. The latest creations were *ToF* for the Helsinki Festival, (premiered 8/98), *Bubble Speaks* for Bagnolet Recontres Choreographiques Internationales, *Violet* for Helsinki Dance Arena and *Home Alone*, a dance monologue for the Finnish National Gallery. Has danced for many Finnish dance companies and theatres including The Helsinki City Theatre, Dance Theatre Hurjaruuth, Dance Theatre Raatikko and Aurinkobaletti Dance Company. He has performed in choreographies by Carolyn Carlson, Kilina Kremona, Didier Dechamps, Andrew Degroat and a number of independent Finnish choreographers. In 1996 he joined the faculty of the Department of Dance, Theatre Academy of Finland as a lecturer of Contemporary Dance and as a Choreographer. He is a member of the artistic board of Zodiak - Center for New Dance in Finland.

Nigel Hinds, Artistic Producer, Sadler's Wells Theatre, London

Since 1993 Nigel has refocussed Sadler's Wells' artistic policy, and built artistically and financially successful programmes for Sadler's Wells Theatre (1500 seats) and the Peacock Theatre (1000 seats). He also oversees the programming of the Lilian Baylis Theatre (180 seats) and the managing of the theatre's Community and Education programme. Before working at Sadler's Wells, he was founding Director of Phoenix Arts in Leicester. He has served as a member of the Dance Panel of the Arts Council of England and is a director of the London Dance Network.

Stuart Hopps, Choreographer, London, England

Stuart was Associate Director of Scottish Ballet (1971 - 76). His work includes *Animal, Candid* (Edinburgh); *Pal Joey, Rocky Horror Show* (West End); *The Oresteia, Animal Farm* (RNT); *Julius Caesar, Henry VIII, As You Like It* (RSC). Stuart has also choreographed two pantomimes, *Cinderella* and *Aladdin*. He has created the choreography and musical staging for *The Betrayal of Nora Blade* (Jermyn Street Theatre); *Border Wars* (Channel 4 TV); Verdi's *Macbeth* (The Met); *HMS Pinafore, Merry Widow* (Sadler's Wells); *Orfeo & Euridice* (Glynebourne); *Die Fledermaus* (Scottish Opera); *Yeoman of the Guard* (D'Oyly Carte); *Christmas Eve, Cunning Little Vixen* (ENO); *HMS Pinafore* (New York); *Medea* (Barcelona); *Carmen Jones* (Old Vic); *Carmen* (ROH, Los Angeles, Sevile, Barcelona); *Carmen Idomeneo* (WNO); *Cunning Little Vixen*

(Kennedy Centre, ROH); and his film work includes *Much Ado About Nothing, Frankenstein, Carrington, Othello, Wings of a Dove, Hamlet* and *Amy Foster*. He is currently working on *The Passion*. Stuarts directorial work includes a revival of *Carmen* (ROH) and his own productions of *Die Fledermaus* and *Merry Widow* (Clonter Opera Farm), *II Maestro Di Cappella, Susanna's Secret* and *The Telephone* (Buxton Opera Festival).

Rui Horta, Choreographer, Munich, Germany

Born in Lisbon, Rui Horta studied Physical Education and Architecture. He began at the Gulbenkian Ballet, later living in New York for several years, where he danced in different projects and taught contemporary dance. Back in Lisbon in 1984 he directed the Lisbon Dance Company and later his own project 'Rui Horta and friends' with which he started to tour internationally. In 1991 he moved to Frankfurt where he directed S.O.A.P. for which he created full evening performances that have toured in the most important festivals and venues all over the world. He moved to Munich in the summer of 1998, and works as an independent choreographer in residence at the Muffathalle. He has created pieces for companies such as Nye Carte Blanche, Cullberg Ballet, Grand Theatre de Geneve, and Icelandic Ballet. He has also directed opera, works regularly as lighting designer, and his visual works have been featured in different exhibitions. In 1991 he was awarded the 'grand prix des recontres de Bagnolet' and last year he received the German Producers Prize.

Sue Hoyle, General Manager, The Place, London, England

Sue joined The Place as General Manager in April 1998. Sue was previously Education and Community Officer for London Festival Ballet (now English National Ballet) from 1980-83; Manager of Extemporary Dance Theatre 1983-86; Dance and Mime Officer (1986-89) and Director of Dance (1989-94) for the Arts Council ofGreat Britain; Deputy Secretary General of the Arts Council of England from 1994-97; and until joining The Place was Head of Arts for the British Council in France.

Vilmore James, Freelance Community Choreographer, Leeds, England

Vilmore James was a founding member of the original Phoenix Dance Company. He was a pupil at Harehills and Intake schools in Leeds. Vilmore has worked as rehearsal director for the Dundee Rep Dance Company and is now establishing himself as a community choreographer/teacher in the Leeds area. He is based at the Northern School of Contemporary Dance where he is director of Community Dance. He is passionate about the role of dance to build and heal communities - a passion reinforced by a visit to Ethiopia to work alongside Royston Muldoon on a dance project with street kids in Addis Ababa.

Evelyn Jamieson, Head of Dance, Liverpool Institute for the Performing Arts (LIPA), Liverpool, England

Evelyn Jamieson joined LIPA after working for almost a decade at University College Bretton Hall. She is currently Choreographic Director of Idée Fixe Experimental Sound and Movement Theatre. Before this she danced for many choreographers and companies including Wayne McGregor's Random Dance Company. In the early eighties, she was a member of Antics Community Dance and then Dance Animateur for Peterborough. During this period she still maintained her performance career including guest appearances with Dundee Repertory Dance Company (now Scottish Dance Theatre). She has continually taught and choreographed throughout her career for numerous youth and professional organisations in this country and abroad.

Shobana Jeyasingh, Artistic Director, Shobana Jeyasingh Dance Company, London, England

Shobana Jeyasingh has directed her own company since 1989. The Company has been awarded three Digital Dance Awards and the prestigious Prudential Award for the Arts. Shobana's work for the theatre included *Cyrano* (Royal National Theatre) and for television, *Duets with Automobiles* for BBC2 which was short-listed for the IMZ Dance Screen Award, and *Inbetween*, a BBC2 documentary featuring her company. In 1996 *Palimpsest* was awarded the Time Out dance award for best choreography. In 1995 Shobana was awarded an MBE, an Honorary Doctorate from De Montfort University and an Honorary Masters degree from the University of Surrey.

Rosemary Lee, Choreographer, London, England

Rosemary Lee has built a reputation for creating work in a wide variety of contexts. This has included large-scale site-specific works for mixed age casts (*Ascending Fields* at Fort Dunlop Depot; *Stranded* for the Royal Festival Hall Ballroom) as well as more intimate solos for herself (*Tenderhooks, Heart Home* and *Exhale*). More recently she has focused on solos for others (*The Galliard* for Gill Clarke and *Silver* for Simon Whitehead) which were toured with the Balanescu Quartet in 1997. She has also created new works for Ricochet and Transitions. Currently, Rosemary is working on her third dance film, following the success of her two short films (*boy* and *greenman* originally created for the BBC2 Dance On Camera series).

Veronica Lewis, Director, London Contemporary Dance School, London, England

Veronica Lewis took up the position of Director of London Contemporary Dance School recently after 22 years working in Cheshire. During this time she established Cheshire Dance Workshop, now part of Dance Northwest National Dance Agency as well as leading Cheshire LEA's advisory service for dance. Veronica has been closely and passionately involved with the development of vocational dance training for many years and has a wealth of experience in dealing with the various funding systems. She also chairs the education committees of the Royal Ballet Company and English National Ballet and was awarded an MBE for services to dance in 1994.

Aimé de Lignière, Head of Dance Department, Hogeschool Antwerpen, Lier, Belgium

Aimé is a Belgian choreographer and teacher of classical and modern dance, as well as Artistic Director of the Higher Institute for Dance from the Department of Dramatic Art, Music and Dance of the Hogeschool Antwerpen. He is also Artistic Director and Choreographer for the Compagnie Aimé de Lignière for which he has created almost 50 dance pieces. Aimé de Lignière is chair of the ELIA - European League of Institutes of the Arts 'Dance Section' and Director of 'Projects and Promotion' of World Dance Alliance Europe. Between 1977 and 1994 he was the winner of several prizes for best choreography at the International Ballet competitions of Cologne, Houlgate, Lausanne and Geneva. He won 'The Tech-Art Award' for the most original Belgian artistic creation in 1990. The same year he was awarded the 'Art Compagnon '90', for the best art promotion for *Significant Moments*. He is a 'Laureate' of the 'Sabam Award' of the Belgian Royalty Association for 1992, and a guest teacher for international schools, dance events, workshops, and seminars. He is also advisor and choreographer for various theatre, opera and dance productions as well at TV, film and video production.

Professor Ana Macara, Faculty of Human Movement, University of Lisbon, Portugal

Ana Macara is full time Professor in the Dance Department of FMH-Universidade Tecnica de Lisboa, with an MA in Dance from University of North Carolina at Greenboro. She also has a Doctorate in Dance from FMH-Universidade Tecnica de Lisboa. As a researcher she is interested in choreography and the study of the dancer's experience, attitudes and self-perception and its relation to dance teaching and performance. As a dancer choreographer since 1979, she has created dance pieces for theatre, TV and multimedia performances. She has been guest choreographer in Grupo de Danca de Almada Contemporary Dance Company since 1991.

Russell Maliphant, Choreographer, London, England

Russell Maliphant has worked with Sadler's Wells Royal Ballet, DV8 Physical Theatre, Michael Clark & Company, Laurie Booth, Rosemary Butcher and Kirsty Simson. He has explored a diverse range of techniques and began creating and performing his own choreography in 1991, working with collaborator, lighting designer Michael Hulls. He teaches regularly and maintains a private practice in Rolfing Method of Structural Integration. His company works, *Unspoken* and *Decoy Landscape* toured in the UK and Europe during 1996 and 1997. *Critical Mass*, a duet with DV8 performer Robert Tannion toured in Spring 1998. A new solo, commissioned by Dance Umbrella Festival, premieres on 20 October 1998.

Maria Manzaneque, Assistant to the Director, University of Alcalá, Madrid, Spain

Maria Manzaneque gained a degree in English Language and Literature at the University of Alcalá (Madrid, Spain) 1995. Since 1995 she has been working as assistant to Estrella Casero Garcia, Dance Division Director, collaborating in all national and international projects related to dance carried out at and from this Division.

Victoria Marangopoulou, Kalamata International Dance Festival, Kalamata, Greece

Born in Athens in 1951. Victoria Marangopoulou studied dance at the Yannis Metsis Dance School where she got a Diploma, and the Royal Ballet School in London (1969 - 1973). She was a member of 'Piramatiko Balleto Athinon as a dancer (soloist). In 1978, she opened her own school where she taught until 1995, and began to teach Ballet, Theory and Methodology at the Athens State School of Dance where she still teaches. She has produced 40 Special Broadcasts on Dance (Greek Radio 3), writes articles on dance and participates on committees for dance. From 1987 until now she is the Director of the Kalamata International Dance Centre and International Dance Festival.

Ron McAllister, Artistic Director, Lawrence Batley Theatre, Huddersfield, England

Ron worked with touring theatre companies in Central Scotland before moving south to become Head of Music and Festivals at South Hill Park Arts Centre in Bracknell where he worked for six years. During this time Ron commissioned many new works for major composers such as Michael Nyman and Jonathan Lloyd, producing the World premiere of *The Lost Domain* - a community opera by Gary Carpenter. Ron moved to the Borders in 1998 to open the Maltings in Berwick-Upon-Tweed, hosting a major dance residency lasting two years with David Massingham Dance. Since 1991 Ron has lived and worked in Yorkshire, opening and establishing the Lawrence Batley Theatre in 1994 where he has remained as Artistic Director. In February the theatre launched the *Egon Schiele* tour with the Featherstonehaughs and has now embarked upon an audience development programme for Contemporary Dance, supported by the Arts Council of England.

Dick McCaw, Artistic Director, International Workshop Festival, London, England

In 1979 Dick McCaw created the Actors Touring Company with Director John Retallack, and toured extensively throughout the UK and abroad. By 1981, Dick had formed the Medieval Players with Carp Heap. As producer, actor and musician, they produced over 30 plays from the Medieval and Renaissance repertoire, including adaptations from Chaucer, Gimmelshausen and Rabelais. In 1993, he was appointed Artistic Director of the International Workshop Festival, presenting over 200 workshops, talks, demonstrations and presentations with invited teachers from 36 countries to nearly 4000 participants. For over fifteen years, since the mid-1980's, he has given lectures and seminars throughout Britain, Europe and Australia. Dick is currently writing a PhD at Royal Holloway College on 'Bakhtin's Other Theatre', and he has recently been commissioned by Silviu Purcareteto to write a play.

Wayne McGregor, Artistic Director, Random Dance Company, London, England

Wayne created Random Dance Company in 1992, touring nationally and internationally to critical acclaim. Outside of his work for Random, Wayne has choreographed for English National Opera, Shobana Jeyasingh Dance Company and Ricochet Dance company. In 1996, he was nominated for an Olivier Award in the category of Best Choreographer for the Royal National Theatre's production of *A Little Night Music*. He is presently working at the National on Sean Matthias' new production of *Anthony and Cleopatra*. McGregor was recipient of the prestigious Arts Foundation Fellowship in Choreography in 1994. McGregor and Random have represented Britain throughout the world in Bancs d'Essai Internationaux; SKITE project in Lisbon and the European Choreographic Forum. He is a 1997 recipient of a Lisa Ullmann Travel Scholarship for research and development in dance and new technology in Japan and a recipient of a 1998 Prix d'Auteur du Conseil Général de Seine-Saint-Denis.

Jane Mooney, Artistic Director, Suffolk Dance (National Dance Agency), Ipswich, England

Jane's career in dance has included experience as a performer, teacher, choreographer, manager and director. Originally trained at the Laban Centre and Goldsmith's College, she has worked with companies and organisations such as Ludus Dance Company, Phoenix and Contemporary Dance Trust. In directing the NDA, she has developed innovative collaborations between professional and community dance activities locally, nationally and internationally, established a dance house network of theatres and an Associate Artist Scheme for professional choreographic development. Suffolk Dance has been awarded a major EU Kaleidoscope Award and one of the largest A4E Awards for dance.

Gregory Nash, Drama & Dance Officer, The British Council, London, England

Gregory was an independent dancer, choreographer and teacher for seventeen years working internationally in the fields of theatre, dance and opera. In 1995 he made a career transition, gaining an MA in Arts Management from City University and joining Val Bourne at Dance Umbrella as Programme Manager. He is currently Drama and Dance Officer at the British Council in London where he has responsibility for projects in Western Europe, Scandinavia and Africa.

Gail Parmel, Artistic Director, African Cultural Exchange, Birmingham, England

Gail and Ian Parmel are the Directors of African Cultural Exchange based in Birmingham. Gail trained at the Northern School and has performed with Peter Dabejo and with Kokuma. African Cultural Exchange was set up in 1996 to 'develop an African and Caribbean dance technique for the future whilst taking with them the traditions of the past'. The company is developing a reputation for its education work with programmes such as *A taste of Ace*.

Valerie Preston-Dunlop, Adviser for Postgraduate Study & Research, Laban Centre London, England

Valerie Preston-Dunlop, M.A., Ph.D., is an independent practical dance scholar and currently consultant for postgraduate studies and research at the Laban Centre London. She pioneered the development of Choreological Studies, the practical theory for dance as a performing art. She is a teacher, lecturer and mentor to young dance artists and teachers, working internationally. Her current books are *Looking at Dances: A Choreological Perspective of Choreography*, (Verve Publishing, 1998) and *Rudolph Laban: An Extraordinary Life* (Dance Books, 1998), the long awaited biography of this leader of the 20th Century European dance revolution.

Steve P Purcell, Co-Director of Kaizen Arts,
Programme Leader for Performing & Media Arts, University of Derby, England
Steve Purcell is currently Programme Leader for performing and Media Arts at the University of Derby. He has made text based and visual performance work for The Green Room, the ICA, The Riverside Studios and The National Review of Live Arts and has recently worked alongside Victoria Marks on *The Changing Room*. His research has focused on the work of Javier de Frutos.

Jerril Rechter, Dance Fund Member, Australia Council and
Artistic Director, Stompin Youth Dance Company, Tasmania, Australia
Jerril Rechter is well known and respected in the Australian arts and is considered to be at the forefront of Youth Dance practice in the country. She is the Founder, Choreographer and Artistic Director of Stompin Youth Dance Co., Australia's premier Youth Dance Company. The Company has received critical acclaim for its ethos of providing a context for young artists to create and present work, underpinned by a philosophy that youth are valid creators of dance performance. Jerril is the ex-deputy chair and current member of the Australia Council Dance Fund, the Australian Government funding and advisory body, and is presently in the United Kingdom undertaking a Churchill Fellowship investing youth dance activity.

Allen Robertson, Dance Editor, Time Out, London, England
Allen Robertson has been the dance editor at Time Out since 1984 and is a regular contributor to both The Times and Dance Now, plus other publications both here and in America. He teaches an annual dance writing course during the South Bank's Ballroom Blitz season. With Donald Hutera, he co-authored The Dance Handbook which is set to be published in a new edition by Dance Books next year.

Gun Román, Danshögskolan, Stockholm, Sweden
Gun Roman is Vice-Principal and Senior Lecturer at the University College of Dance in Stockholm. She is also head of the Modern and Contemporary Dance section, and has responsibility for international liaison. She worked as a dancer from 1968 to 1989, and has taught at the Danshögskolan since 1975, specialising in dance methods, dance technique, composition, dance theory and dance history. For some years she was chair of the Swedish Dance Committee, and board member of the Theatre Union, and is now a committee member of the National Swedish Council for Cultural Affairs. She was a member of the ELIA Dance Section Executive Committee from 1990 to 1997.

Sanjoy Roy, Co-Editor, Dance Now, London, England
Sanjoy Roy studied dance at the Laban Centre London, and received an MA in cultural studies from Goldsmith's College, University of London. He is co-editor and designer of Dance Now, and designs and edits publications for Dance Books Ltd. He has contributed to Dance Now, Dance Theatre Journal, Animated and the International Dictionary of Modern Dance, and is the author of *Dirt, Noise, Traffic: Contemporary Indian Dance in the Western City* in the Dance in the City, ed. ll. Thomas (Macmillan, 1997).

Rivca Rubin, Co-Director of Kaizen Arts, Research Fellow in Performance
at Manchester Metropolitan University, England
Rivca has been involved with the design and development of performance training projects since the late 70's. She has worked as a choreographer, producer and performer for/with various professional companies including Le Grand Jeu, Alison Andrews Theatre Company, Insomniac Production, The Green Room (Manchester), Physical State International.

Jason Salvin
Jason has now over ten years experience in lighting design and production management in the entertainment industry. During this time he has worked with some of our most prestigious companies such as Opera North and Northern Ballet Theatre. Jason is currently Production Manager at Powerhouse 1 Showcase Theatre for Bretton Hall, Wakefield. This has provided the chance to pass on practical skills to students and become involved in creating new productions.

Abdelaziz Sarrokh, Artistic Director, HUSH HUSH HUSH, Ghent, Belgium
Abdelaziz marked the beginning of his dance career by taking part in the 'Best Belgian Dance Solo' competition. He has been a teacher in hip-hop for the Al Fath group in Ghent with whom he created many small-scale performances. He currently works with Les Ballets C De La B with whom he appeared in *Bonjour Madame* and *Tristeza Complicite*. *Carte Blanche* was his first piece as a choreographer for his dance company HUSH HUSH HUSH. In *Carte Blanche* he achieved his aim of combining the techniques and acrobatics of hip-hop and street-dance with the artistic accomplishment of modern dance.

Janet Smith, Artistic Director, Scottish Dance Theatre, Dundee, Scotland

Janet Smith trained in Dance and Drama at Dartington College of Arts, and spent two years studying contemporary dance and choreography in New York and St. Louis. Janet Smith and Dancers was formed in 1976 following two solo programmes and the company toured nationally and internationally, as clients of the Arts Council and British Council. Janet has also choreographed internationally and for opera, TV and theatre. Her work with dance education includes directing the performance company 4D at the London School of Contemporary Dance. From 1993-97 she was a lecturer in dance at University College Bretton Hall before becoming Artistic Director of Scottish Dance Theatre in June 1997.

Sophie Smith

Sophie has been working as a freelance composer and musician and co-director of Assault Event company since 1995. Composition work has included soundtrack commissions for advertisements and TV documentaries, live club sets alongside musicians such as 4 Hero, Autechre, Mr. C and inclusion on a forthcoming CD release showcasing the best in European female experimental 'dance' music.

Alistair Spalding, Head of Dance and Performance
Royal Festival Hall, London, England

After completing a degree in Linguistics and Philosophy Alistair Spalding taught in primary schools in Liverpool and London for six years specialising in music and language development. In 1987 he then joined the team which opened the Hawth Theatre, a 850 seat main auditorium and 120 seat studio complex in Crawley. As well as developing a thriving dance and theatre programme he initiated the Beyond Words festival of Mime and Physical Theatre and the Outside In Jazz Festival with Serious Productions. He moved to the Royal Festival Hall in 1994 where he is now Head of Dance and Performance. He is responsible for the programming of all dance, mime, physical theatre, and live art events across the three halls and foyer spaces including the Ballroom Floor. He is currently a member of the Arts Council of England dance panel and a board member of the Birmingham DanceXchange. He is also an advisor to London Arts Board and West Midlands Arts Board.

Gwen Van Spijk, Freelance Arts Manager, Leamington Spa, England

Gwen began working in arts management in 1998 having previously worked in the commercial sector. After three years as Business Manager at Peterborough Arts Centre (1988 - 1991) she took on the Arts Council/East Midlands Arts Dance Administration Scheme, following this with five years as Administrative Director for Motionhouse Dance Theatre. In Spring 1997 she embarked upon a freelance career offering Administrative, Management and Consultancy services to the performing arts. She works on an ongoing basis with a core of artists/companies, including Wendy Houston, Small Bones and the Claire Russ Ensemble. Alongside this Gwen undertakes short-term projects and recent consultancy projects have included: a Marketing Audit for Foursight Theatre, an Organisational Review for Kokuma Dance Theatre, and West Midlands Arts' Management Initiative.

Ann Stannard, Administrative Director, Central School of Ballet, London, England

Ann trained at the Rambert School of Ballet, taught Classical Ballet classes to young people, then devoted herself to her family for fourteen years before returning to the Rambert School to work closely with the Director of Administration. As a co-founder and Director of Central School, Ann is responsible for administration and financial stability, together with the care and concern for the development of each individual student. Ann believes strongly that the artistic talent should be encouraged and that it is essential to provide students with the most careful guidance towards their personal and individual development as dancers and as mature, responsible adults.

Clare Stewart, Touring Officer, Arts Council of England, London, England

Previous to taking up her current position, Clare worked as a freelance dance manager with a range of clients such as Mark Baldwin Dance Company and Javier de Frutos, and undertook development projects for South East Dance Agency and Dorset Dance Forum. She also worked for Dance 4 as Project Manager during the year of Dance and was Administrative Director of the Scottish Youth Dance Festival.

Mairead Turner, Projects Officer & Festival Director, Yorkshire Dance, Leeds, England

After completing a dance degree, Mairead worked as a freelance contemporary dance administrator, for choreographers including Bunty Mathias and Aletta Collins, before working for the Siobhan Davies Dance Company full-time. Last year Mairead moved to Yorkshire Dance as Projects Officer where she has worked on a variety of projects including British Dance: edition 1998, and The Greenhouse Effect. She has recently been made Festival Director for work on the upcoming alt. dance:98.

Charlotte Vincent, Choreographer, Vincent Dance Theatre, Sheffield, England

Vincent Dance Theatre produces work which disrupts received ideas of what dance can be and challenges traditional values in dance and gender politics. Work is made in collaboration with other artists, is text informed, reflects the personal politics of the collaborators involved and demands that dance, as an art form, can reflect issues of social and political importance. The company have produced four live works since 1994, and this year have made *Glasshouse*, a ten minute dance film. Charlotte is currently collaborating with a writer and photographer to produce *Body: Ink*, a publication commissioned by Photo '98, UK Year of Photography. She teaches, lectures and choreographs in a wide variety of educational and community contexts, including prisons, universities, colleges, dance agencies, and art galleries, with people of all ages.

Suzanne Walker, General Manager, V-TOL Dance Company, London, England

Suzanne is originally from Peterborough and trained in music, drama and dance at Birmingham University. From 1988-91 she worked in Peterborough as a freelance performing Arts Worker, Assistant Dance Animateur and Youth Theatre Director. She has also lectured in theatre studies at Further Education level. In 1991 she received an Arts Council bursary to train in contemporary dance administration on placement with London Contemporary Dance Theatre, Siobhan Davies Dance Company and The Kosh. Suzanne became General Manger of V-Tol Dance Company in 1992. V-Tols' artistic work explores the integration of dance and film in live performance. The company is a fixed term client of the Arts Council of England and tours internationally to middle scale venues. For the last five years Suzanne has also been a member of the London Arts Board Dance Advisory Committee.

Katherine Watson, Associate Director, Lab de Danse, Ottawa, Canada

Katherine Watson has been Associate Director for Le Groupe Dance Lab in Ottawa, Canada, for nine years. The Lab is an international centre for choreographic development, offering research and development opportunities to choreographers at all stages in their careers. Her work in the Lab included facilitating collaborations between choreographers and new technologies and the development of international new-technology projects. Katherine was also president of the Canadian Association of Professional Dance Organisations and the dance representative for several years for the Canadian Conference of the Arts. She is currently contracted by the British Council in Canada as the director of Ukaccents, a yearlong showcase of contemporary Britain in Ottawa.